WHERE THE WORDS ARE VALID

Recent Titles in
Contributions in Drama and Theatre Studies

For Wendy Simonds
with love

Where the Words Are Valid

T.S. ELIOT'S COMMUNITIES OF DRAMA

Randy Malamud

Contributions in Drama and Theatre Studies, Number 58

GREENWOOD PRESS
Westport, Connecticut • London

Library of Congress Cataloging-in-Publication Data

Malamud, Randy
    Where the words are valid : T.S. Eliot's communities of drama /
Randy Malamud.
      p.   cm. — (Contributions in drama and theatre studies, ISSN
0163–3821 ; no. 58)
    Includes bibliographical references and index.
    ISBN 0–313–27818–0 (alk. paper)
    1. Eliot, T. S. (Thomas Stearns), 1888–1965—Dramatic works.
2. Verse drama—History and criticism. I. Title. II. Series.
PS3509.L43Z717   1994
822'.912—dc20   94–22018

British Library Cataloguing in Publication Data is available.

Library of Congress Catalog Card Number: 94–22018
ISBN: 0–313–27818–0
ISSN: 0163–3821

First published in 1994

Greenwood Press, 88 Post Road West, Westport, CT 06881
An imprint of Greenwood Publishing Group, Inc.

Printed in the United States of America

The paper used in this book complies with the
Permanent Paper Standard issued by the National
Information Standards Organization (Z39.48-1984).

10 9 8 7 6 5 4 3 2 1

Contents

Acknowledgments

I thank all my colleagues at Georgia State University for innumerable forms of support while I was writing this book. My present chair, Robert Sattelmeyer, and my past one, Virginia Spencer Carr, have been tireless in their enthusiastic devotion to the department's scholarly enterprise. I am grateful to Dean Ahmed T. Abdelal and Associate Dean Robert Arrington for released time and for their commitment to upholding the highest academic standards throughout GSU's College of Arts and Sciences. Grants from Cleon Arrington in the university's Research Office funded two years of graduate assistantship and enabled me to examine the T. S. Eliot Collection at King's College, Cambridge; I thank that library's modern archivist, Jacqueline Cox, for her assistance. The librarians at Georgia State University's Pullen Library and Emory University's Woodruff Library have also been of immense assistance at every stage of this project.

Deborah Browning's research and editorial assistance have been an immeasurable contribution: her efforts have helped make this book a better one than it would otherwise have been. In the homestretch, Noelle Baker's contributions were invaluable; she has been an incisive and perceptive reader. I thank David Galef for commenting upon my work constructively, and Dabney Hart for being a never ending source of advice on matters large and small. The English department support staff has been just that—I thank, especially, Patricia Bryan for keeping the funds flowing and James Poulakos for his computer wizardry.

All the editors I have dealt with at Greenwood Press have made my work, on this book and a previous one, rewarding and efficient.

I am, as always, indebted to Daniel, Judith, and Lisa Malamud, Wendy Simonds, and Jacob Simonds-Malamud, for their encouragement, tolerance, and inspiration. A man named Dale has irrefutably affirmed for me the enduring virtues of community support.

Introduction

My interest in T. S. Eliot's plays began ten years ago in graduate school, in a masterful seminar on Eliot taught by Jeffrey Perl. Under his direction, in a master's thesis entitled "The Importance of Eliot's Later Work: Society and Transformation in *The Cocktail Party,*" I argued that Julia Shuttlethwaite represents a crucial development in Eliot's career, emblematic of a new outlook in terms of his treatment of women, human beneficence, and social interaction. That work sparked my interest in how Eliot's drama embodies a social agenda and how his movement in this direction relates to the overall trajectory of his literary career. A decade later, my rudimentary work seems surprisingly compatible with what has developed since then. I quote from the final paragraph of my master's thesis, both to indulge myself and because I think it is important to recognize and identify one's formative critical experiences.

Eliot has arrived, by 1949, at a visionary plateau that allows him to forgive the lady settling a pillow or throwing off a shawl that Julia might have been in her youth, and to forget the self-centered Aunt Helen that Julia was in Eliot's youth. Eliot has embraced the community that he simultaneously creates in the play, and has learned the need for spiritual guidance in every drawing room. . . . In such an egalitarian community of housekeepers, the one who best embodies the ideals that will protect the community is rewarded simply by being perceived as the guiding force of society. Of course, it would be superfluous and counterproductive for the Guardians or their flock to acknowledge anything more than the nebulous outlines of their community, as Julia does when she calls the Guardians together to proceed to the next cocktail party. It is, rather, only the detached audience, which has observed the machinations of their society, that identifies Julia's importance, the recognition of which fulfills Eliot's desire that we apply to our own lives the values we have learned in making this identification.

As a graduate student, I chose the topic largely out of a sense that new avenues of scholarly approach to Eliot were rare, perhaps nearly exhausted; the plays seemed to offer fresh ground, especially for a young scholar over-whelmed by the PS/3509 shelves. To a certain extent, this sense sustains my interest in Eliot's plays. Besides that, though, I have found that I greatly enjoy reading them. They are *pleasant,* well crafted, piquant, fresh, and at the same time, Eliotic, whatever that means (deep? careful? enchanting? perverse? mas-ochistic?). Reading them, I get a sense of being closer to Eliot than when I marvel and shudder at the poses that fill his poetry. I felt this closeness espe-cially when I studied the dramatic drafts and manuscripts in the T. S. Eliot Collection at King's College, Cambridge. As I examined his careful editorial precision (he sometimes contemplated five barely different variants of some pedestrian phrase) I saw a master craftsman who had, for some reason I hoped to understand fully as I completed my research for this book, chosen to engage in what an earlier Eliot might have lambasted as bourgeois tripe.

When asked what my thesis about the plays was, I joked: that there are some nice bits in them. While riveted by Eliot's poetry, I felt that the plays provide something more *accessible*—something that must be read carefully and examined minutely, precisely (in a way that the plays have not very often been studied, especially in comparison to his poetry), to understand something about his complete oeuvre. The plays are one way of getting at the core of Eliot's sensibility, which presents scholars with fundamental insights into the modern age and its aesthetic. I state this perception despite a deepening critical and political antipathy to Eliot, with which I am sympathetic. To understand Eliot's weighty contribution to the pantheon of modernism, I argue, one must take serious account of his dramatic career. Ultimately, if this book succeeds, its most important function will be to bring to modernist scholars' serious attention a large body of work that has often been glibly patronized and relegated to near obscurity.

Though the plays are often dismissed as lightweight or popularized tangents to Eliot's more profound earlier aesthetic, this study attempts to unearth in them a sensibility that in many ways extends, undiminished, his famous poetic from the 1910s and 1920s. I believe that Eliot's plays embody more significant connections than disruptions with the rest of his work and that they are inte-grally related to it. Further, I have discovered in them a deep and richly sugges-tive autobiographical vein that illuminates the persona and psyche of Eliot the playwright (and, as well, throwbacks to Eliot as a younger poet and critic). Since Lyndall Gordon's stellar biographical scholarship, the Eliot industry has gradually come to accept the primacy of understanding and uncovering the man behind Eliot's texts. His chronicle of the intellectual, aesthetic, and emotional history of the first half of the twentieth century is conducted from a profoundly idiosyncratic and autobiographically interiorized point of view. To appreciate this perspective fully, it is necessary to know the man and his mind more intimately. The plays enable this endeavor. They consistently direct the audience and the scholar toward the roots—autobiographical, psychological, and otherwise—of Eliot's elaborate poetic of traumatic alienation; and, in tandem, toward the counterforce to this alienation, the succor of community beneficence that an older Eliot came to embrace in his texts and in his life.

The plays are, of course, substantially different in tenor from the poetry: the poems project a harshly fragmented, incommunicable, solipsistic social vacuum, while the plays embody a quest for social unity and coherence. The plays present a *revision* of the poetic and ethos for which Eliot the poet is better known, but they are not, as many assume, a wholesale refutation of it. Eliot's drama continues and completes the mission he set for himself as a young man: communicating the modern condition, in a language he had to craft as he went along because no extant voice could encapsulate its scope. The poems show the desperation and near futility of the communicative enterprise, while the plays demonstrate its success. But Eliot's poetry and drama are ultimately part of a unified and consistent undertaking and are conducted in remarkably congruous terms, despite obvious generic and stylistic dissimilarities. One cannot appreciate the full effect of the poetry without attention to the resolution inherent in the plays, just as Dante's *Inferno* cannot be wholly understood without the *Paradiso*.

Eliot's interest in drama was longstanding: as early as 1919, critical essays he wrote about such dramatists as Edmond Rostand, Christopher Marlowe, William Shakespeare, and Ben Jonson show an incisive attention to craft and form that presages his own incipient theatrical aspirations. In a variety of ways, Eliot was consistently involved in and attentive to drama and dramatic issues throughout his career—this involvement is perhaps the closest thing he had to a constant focal point. (At the same time, I must concede that none of Eliot's plays was an unqualified success; if Eliot had left only the legacy of his dramatic canon, it would have been an unsatisfying one.) Eliot's drama points (or, perhaps, yearns) toward a community sensibility—admitting the possible nature of modernism as conducive to community, rather than incontrovertibly isolationist—that forms a fundamental component of his total vision. It seems that Eliot knew something was missing from his writing in the 1910s and 1920s: some cohering force, some more secure and credible stance of control, some substantial essence or completion or moral or hope. I believe he felt, even as he looked back from decades later, that this deficiency was acceptable, even imperative, in his earlier work. As he saw it, the world was not ready for this force, or didn't deserve it, at the time; and neither was Eliot himself receptive to such a poetic wholeness.

In 1927, Eliot came to a recognition and remediation of this deficiency in his personal life. His conversion to Anglo-Catholicism betokened a precise location, a confident fixing, of a self that previously had been drifting untethered. His professional life featured the publication of *Sweeney Agonistes* that same year.[1] Even in retrospect, the correlation between these momentous occasions in Eliot's private and public lives is oblique. Eliot's religious experience and

Sweeney's "Hoo-ha's" hardly seem related to each other, let alone part of an enterprise that would lead to the literary manifestation of a dramatically expressed community imperative. Eliot's career has a keenly complex pattern in the carpet, as one would, of course, expect. But this pattern, this sense of direction in Eliot's canon, increasingly asserts itself in fits and starts and in experiments—successful and otherwise—involving primordial social rituals, religious drama, music hall, jazz rhythms, verse drama, historical drama, choral performance, classical transpositions, conversationally bantering light comedies; his efforts span the gamut. They were at times erratic, as he was himself aware, but I find them bravely and honestly so for the writer who had so carefully guarded his work in the past, releasing tiny snippets of highly worked poetry after years of gestation and only when they were perfectly intractable and impenetrable poses, as harshly chiseled in stone as the sculptures of Jacques Lipchitz or Henri Gaudier-Brzeska.

The connection between Eliot's early and late texts is language, words. In *The Language of Modernism,* I examined how Eliot (like Virginia Woolf and James Joyce) wrenches his poetic language, reworks it, smashes and reassociates it, so it can convey something that it could not previously have done: it describes a landscape that had seemed unspeakable in the language of the past. In the present book, as I study a later phase of Eliot's career, I find that he retains his obsession with words. He shows a conviction that the nature of language is a threshhold concern in any confrontation with the nature of the surrounding world. But now, linguistic exploration and expression come much more easily than they had before. The speakers *will* this new fluency (as, of course, does the writer). Eliot has come to recognize that even in the modern age one can choose to make things difficult or to make things easy.

In the first half of his career, Eliot reveled in making things difficult and then brilliantly "getting out" of that difficulty (to the extent that a successfully completed poem is always a triumph over muteness, which for Eliot signifies the difficulty of language). By the late 1920s, and even more so by the late 1930s and after, he tries to make things easier with respect to language. In a nutshell, he does so through community: creating communities, upholding them, celebrating them. Drama is itself inherently communal, and the communities in Eliot's plays are consummately self-conscious of their debt to drama and the extent to which they grow out of drama (both the drama at hand and the larger surrounding traditions of drama). The crux of Eliot's dramatic community is that it is, by nature, composed of people who interact, who communicate, who use language, commonly, successfully, with each other. People understand what other people mean; language works.

In and through drama, Eliot found a place "where the words are valid"; I take this expression from act 2 of *The Cocktail Party.*[2] The Guardians offhandedly use the phrase to indicate that when Peter Quilpe has become settled into a stable personal and community equilibrium, it is language that will validate his success. Valid words (obviously appropriate to the social enterprise of drama, where people must hear and be heard by other characters as well as the audience) represent the antidote to what Eliot bemoaned in his earlier poetry: in "Prufrock," for example, where "It is impossible to say just what I mean." I have latched onto the identification and affirmation of valid language in *The Cocktail Party* as the defining moment of Eliot's dramatic career. I define "communities of drama" in the last section of chapter 2, admittedly a good way into the book for what I present as such a crucial concept in Eliot's dramatic practice and ideals. I reach it only after a protracted discussion of his work up to that point, because Eliot himself reached it only after a long and laborious process: slogging through the wastelandish terrain of Sweeney's agon and the right-hearted but aesthetically unpromising endeavor of a pageant for a church fund-raising drive.

Though I hope this book serves as a fairly comprehensive treatment of Eliot's drama, it is not a start-to-finish trot; some topics, such as Eliot's Greek dramatic analogies, the context of mid-century verse drama, and performance aspects of the plays, are treated relatively minimally. Each chapter has a kind of logic and pacing of its own (or, perhaps, of *my* own, which I hope the reader eventually discerns). I offer a kind of meditation on each play, reflecting what I have found most provocative; my aim is to identify an ingress to the core of each work and to highlight its significance in Eliot's dramatic development. Dissimilarities in my treatment of different plays perhaps result in a cubist approach that presents seven different views of Eliot's communities of drama, from seven different vantage points. There are also, however, fairly important continuities in each play and each chapter, reflecting my conviction that Eliot had an overall program in mind for the dramatic enterprise that he undertook: a search for communities of drama, established in a realm where the words are valid.

1

Sweeney Agonistes: "I Gotta Use Words"

Sweeney Agonistes is often dismissed as unperformable "closet drama." But in this "Aristophanic Melodrama," as in his various incarnations throughout Eliot's poetry of the early 1920s, the title character is consummately a public figure and one who demands to flourish on stage. Indeed, the manifestation of Sweeney's persona constitutes Eliot's turn from an inward poetic to an extroverted, communal drama.

Eliot's earliest poetry is at root dramatic: peopled with compelling characters in highly charged settings, richly atmospheric, laden with intrigue that awaits resolution. "It may be . . . that there is a dramatic element in much of my early work," he writes in *The Three Voices of Poetry*; "It may be that from the beginning I aspired unconsciously to the theatre" (98). But in this poetry the dramatic fruition of performance is perverted into solipsistic stasis as Prufrock, Gerontion, the Rhapsodist on a Windy Night, and the Portraitist of a Lady retreat into one-man shows sans audience. Prufrock, for example, frustrates dramatic development and climax as he refuses to pose his overwhelming question. He defuses dramatic denouement: he has *already known* all the evenings, mornings, afternoons. He teasingly announces the boundaries of playspace and its promise of character interaction in the drawing room where the women talk of Michelangelo, waiting for the protagonist to enter and bring the dialogue to the audience. But he misses (or ignores) his cue and retreats. Prufrock flirts with inscribing himself in traditional dramatic figures only to disappoint by declining the roles. He is not ultimately Prince Hamlet or even fully—only *almost*—the Fool.

In "Portrait of a Lady," once again, the poem's venue and its tableaux are poised for drama: the Lady, a would-be stage-manager/director, has arranged a scene—or, somehow, her scene has arranged itself, suggesting a kind of underlying dramatic immanence or compulsion. The reader-as-audience awaits the first line (the scene is "[p]repared for all the things to be said"), or even a preamble to dialogue, perhaps a foreshadowing gesture ("or left unsaid" [8]). But again, the male lead declines the performance; he answers the Lady's scripted and carefully rehearsed lines with only an inhospitably cynical interior monologue. Three times in three aborted scenes he flees, as Prufrock did. Gerontion attempts a soliloquy but generates only fragmentary paranoid musings and a surreal montage of depraved drunken whispers, darkly vacant drafts of wind—imagistically rich but dramatically barren and incommunicative, as he admits in the poem's final line: "Thoughts of a dry brain in a dry season" (31). Eliot's early poetic characters are richly endowed with the potential for dramatic performance because they have had masterful poses bestowed upon them (by their creator, himself a master of poses): of the dandy, the *gentilhomme,* the philosopher, the aesthete. But these poses are each in turn deflated as the poet refuses to raise the curtain because the audience might not appreciate the play. The playwright-manqué's greatest fear is a bad review: " 'That is not it at all, / That is not what I meant, at all' " (7).

SWEENEY AND POETIC PROTODRAMA

Sweeney's emergence in *Poems* (1920) promises to free Eliot from the confines of F. H. Bradley's "finite centre," which by definition closes off shared expression: "My experience falls within my own circle, a circle closed on the outside; and, with all its elements alike, every sphere is opaque to the others which surround it. . . . In brief, regarded as an existence which appears in a soul, the whole world for each is peculiar and private to that soul." Eliot quoted this passage in an endnote to *The Waste Land*; clearly, such solipsism absolutely forestalls drama.

But Sweeney punctures the introverted bubble of solipsism, the opaque sphere: he does not retentively hoard his experiences but, rather, *acts* out of primordial instinct. Sweeney acts without thinking, without posing, without withholding or constraining any emotion. His pure compulsion to act marks the inception of Eliot's inclination toward drama. Like Frankenstein's monster, Eliot's Sweeney is a force that, once created, cannot be controlled but will rampage through the text at will, unrestrained. Sweeney's primally cathartic force enables the poet to escape from the tedious banalities of the genteel drawing room poseurs. This dramatic power, which will culminate in *Sweeney Agonistes,* begins to surface in the poems that offer Sweeney starring roles ("Sweeney Erect" and "Sweeney Among the Nightingales") and cameo appearances ("Mr. Eliot's Sunday Morning Service" and *The Waste Land*).

One verb in "Sweeney Erect" highlights Eliot's need for this new character: Sweeney "jackknifes."

> This withered root of knots of hair
>   Slitted below and gashed with eyes,
> This oval O cropped out with teeth:
>   The sickle motion from the thighs
>
> Jackknifes upward at the knees
>   Then straightens out from heel to hip
> Pushing the framework of the bed
>   And clawing at the pillow slip. (34)

The first of these stanzas builds with stark descriptive anticipation to the verb that powerfully "jackknifes" the next stanza into action: a sexual assault that Eliot likely finds distasteful less for its violence than for its sexuality. The image, like the character, is offensive—an unlikely impetus to move Eliot out of his wasteland and, decades later, into the kinder, gentler world of soothing, tolerant, dramatic beneficence. But the key dramatic event here is an action, action of a scale, an immediacy, and a reflexive energy previously absent in Eliot's poetry. (The twist of the knife at the end of "Rhapsody on a Windy Night" might seem like a comparable moment of action, but that image is divorced from the implicit action of the stab itself; it is metaphorical, cerebral, unlike Sweeney's undeniably literal jackknifing.)

Sweeney represents a test Eliot sets for himself: if he can transform Sweeney—the emblem of a worst-case scenario for the condition of humanity in the modern age—into a theatrical medium, then his dramatic enterprise will have proven its strengths and can encompass (only more easily) any subsequent dramaturgical sensibility. In the same vein, *The Waste Land* shows Eliot's determination to locate the modern grail quest in as difficult a terrain—as inhospitable an intellectual landscape—as possibly imaginable within the bleakest aesthetic standards. Only if the task can be accomplished in the face of the most imposing obstacles will Eliot accept its strength and value. (Ralph Waldo Emerson's philosophy, Eliot suggests in "Sweeney Erect," is inadequate because Emerson had not taken into account the facet of humanity represented by a character such as Sweeney; intellectual reflections that fail to acknowledge the depths of human depravity are irrelevant to Eliot's modern world.) Eliot's task is to coopt and develop the promise inherent in the swift shooting open of the blade-like Sweeney character. If Sweeney were to "escape" Eliot's control, the results would be as disastrous as the escape of Frankenstein's monster.

Among the nightingales ("prostitutes"), Sweeney is similarly volatile: he veers closer to ignorant animalism than to humanity—ape-necked, zebra-striped and swelling like a defiled giraffe. An oppressively opaque and awkward protoplayspace is inhospitable to Sweeney's presence or to the coherence of smooth, comprehensible dramatic action:

> The person in the Spanish cape
> Tries to sit on Sweeney's knees
>
> Slips and pulls the table cloth
> Overturns a coffee-cup. (49)

Surreal and dangerous, Sweeney metamorphoses into uncontrollable (and nearly imperceptible) chaotic manifestations; he is a "silent man in mocha brown," then a "silent vertebrate in brown," next a "man with heavy eyes," and finally only a Carrollesque "golden grin" staring invasively into a room from outside a window (49–50). The ominously protean character tends toward primitive evil. As in "Sweeney Erect," the poem suggests violently murderous assault, most pointedly in the epigraph, which recounts Agamemnon's death cry. The strange metamorphoses testify to Sweeney's irrepressibility. It is as if the audience (and poet) nurture the dense darkness of "Sweeney Among the Nightingales" because they find the title character so repellent, and yet in one reincarnation after another he is determined to reappear and force himself, as it were, in our face. Unlike the earlier failed actors in Eliot's poetry, Sweeney is consummately public—he cannot be hidden or tamed. In his aggressive boorishness, he demands to be seen by the outside world, and he unhesitantly plunges into that world as he will do again in *Sweeney Agonistes,* as the rowdy, drunken life of the party. Eliot embraces this persona, nurturing it in his poetry and drama, I believe, in the conviction that only someone with as much seething, literal power as Sweeney could lead him out of his reclusive, interiorized, and emotionally tormented (anti)social condition.

In *The Waste Land,* Sweeney is miscast: that poem is too overwhelmingly antidramatic, in the mode of Eliot's poetry of the 1910s, and Sweeney cannot carry off the burden of achieving drama. Elisabeth Schneider sees *The Waste Land* as incipient drama, noting that Eliot's working title for the poem, "He Do the Police in Different Voices," might have indicated a kind of dramatic chorus, a social panorama of voices; but she finds that "in the end the only passages conspicuously answering to that intention were the scenes involving Madame Sosostris and Lil" (94). That poem is burdened with too many poseurs and inept actors for there to be vital drama—Mr. Eugenides, the young man carbuncular, Stetson, and so forth. Further, like "Portrait of a Lady," *The Waste Land* tends toward mute retreat (epitomized, for example, by the scene with the hyacinth girl) rather than clear dramatic declamation. Even with a few other supporting actors who are genuinely dramatic, such as the fortune-teller and Lil, Sweeney cannot infuse the poem with dramatic life.

But Sweeney's other cameo appearance, in "Mr. Eliot's Sunday Morning Service," points to the dramatic power that Eliot sees lurking in the character. His role is barely even a walk-on: Sweeney merely shifts his hams in a bath, as if indifferently (or more likely, uncomprehendingly) deliberating the Rev. Mr. Eliot's wrenched ontology of Logos, art, original matter, and the polymathic intellect. Yet his striking effect in this bit part—shattering the service's fragile poetic of civilization—announces the star quality Eliot will nurture in an upcoming production, *Sweeney Agonistes: Fragments of an Aristophanic Melodrama.*

Certainly the hostile and erratic action that typifies Sweeney appears wholly devoid of communal promise, not in any obvious way redeeming. But in fact it is this character, this action, that jackknifes Eliot into drama. The difficulty of "rescuing" this image, which seems firmly ensconced in Eliot's early solipsistic poetic of petulant misogyny, barren infertility, points to the difficulty of the dramatic enterprise that lies ahead for Eliot (as he must make the transition from sinister characters such as Rachel née Rabinovitch to altruistic ones such as Julia Shuttlethwaite). Sweeney acts, and Eliot's task is now to take that germ or essence of action and determine how to nurture it, reshape it, and ultimately redeem it as a foundation for drama. Eliot's drama, I believe, *is* firmly rooted in his poetry, however disjunctive his writing in the two genres may appear. Many critics assume that Eliot simply rejected or disavowed his earlier wastelands after his 1927 conversion to Anglo-Catholicism (as the contrast between the crisply detached, brittle tenor of *The Waste Land* or "The Hollow Men" and the smoothly lulling music of *Ash-Wednesday* or *Four Quartets* would seem to indicate). Actually, though, he set for himself the difficult task of wrenching his drama out of his earlier poetry—a task far more intricate than simply wiping the slate clean by beginning anew in a different genre. Even near the end of his poetic career, Eliot emphasizes his commitment to his past poetry in part 2 of "The Dry Salvages." He writes of "not forgetting . . . the backward half-look / Over the shoulder, towards the primitive terror," that is, toward *The Waste Land*; and "[n]ow, we come to discover that the moments of agony"—evoking "the agony in stony places" from "What the Thunder Said"— "are likewise permanent," and thus accepted (194–95).

POETRY AND DRAMA: TRANSITIONS AND CONNECTIONS

Eliot mentioned to Virginia Woolf his intention to write a verse play inhabited by four characters of Sweeney as early as 1920 (noted in her diary entry for 20 September), and discussed with Arnold Bennett in 1924 his plan "to write a drama of modern life (furnished flat sort of people)," as Bennett recorded in his diary (quoted in Ackroyd, 145). Eliot published the two "fragments" that make up this work in *Criterion,* "Fragment of a Prologue" in 1926 and "Fragment of an Agon" in 1927, and Faber & Faber published the play (with the title *Sweeney Agonistes* given for the first time) in 1932. Eliot corresponded with Hallie Flanagan, director of the 1933 Vassar premiere of the play, offering advice about presentation, production, staging, and atmosphere, and writing an additional twenty-five lines to add at the end of that performance.[1]

In 1934 and 1935, the play was staged at London's avant-garde Group Theatre (which Eliot had recently joined, taking a serious interest in its operations for a few years), where W. B. Yeats and Bertolt Brecht attended a performance. It may seem incongruous that Eliot gave such extensive attention to a work as harsh and risqué as *Sweeney Agonistes* during the period when he was undergoing a spiritual conversion and reawakening and was publishing devout poetry, drama, and prose (such as *Ash-Wednesday,* the "Ariel Poems," *The Rock, Murder in the Cathedral, Thoughts After Lambeth,* and *After Strange Gods*). Perhaps Eliot saw this play as a sort of penance for his earlier period of futile desperation; perhaps, too, he realized the importance of exploring Sweeney's troubling incarnations even in the context of the more serenely confident poetic that was coming to characterize his verse and would later infuse his verse drama.

Sweeney Agonistes connects Eliot's poetry and drama. Its affinities with Eliot's poetry are clear and have been well documented by scholars. Eliot included the work under the heading "Unfinished Poems" in his editions of collected poems from 1936 on. The character of Sweeney seems to be a creature of the poems. Sears Jayne, for example, reads *Sweeney Agonistes* as a poem, citing stylistic and structural affinities to Eliot's poetic oeuvre; and Elisabeth Schneider writes that it only "nominally marks the beginning of Eliot's career as a dramatist" because "among his plays it has no sequel" (95). Its links to the dramatic career that occupied Eliot through the 1950s are subtle but crucially important if one is to understand the genesis of Eliot's dramaturgy and its relation to his poetry.

The main distinctions between the text of this play and of Eliot's next six would seem to be its lack of Christian touchstones and its stark, jarring language. In terms of performance, too, there is a disjunction. Eliot's other six plays are all conventional dramatic productions, drawing upon various traditional conceptions of performance and audience (in the genres of verse drama, pageant, religious drama, and commercial popular entertainment). *Sweeney Agonistes,* though, demands an esoteric theatrical coterie of those hospitable to experimental drama.[2]

In fact, an elusive Christian presence may be detected in *Sweeney Agonistes,* although it is not as pronounced as in the later plays—more in the mode of Phlebas the Phoenician's marginal evocation of redemption in the pseudobaptismal waters of *The Waste Land.* An epigraph from St. John of the Cross suggests that Sweeney's life beyond the ending of this play may offer more than the obvious dissolution: "Hence the soul cannot be possessed of the divine union until it has divested itself of the love of created beings." "St. John found God," writes Kinley E. Roby. "Perhaps the man in Sweeney's story will be equally successful in his quest" (25). (*Sweeney Agonistes* does indeed become more promisingly uplifting as one becomes more attuned to Eliot's implications of what happens beyond its ending; I will return to this point later.) The murdered girl in the bathtub may evoke a "macabre baptism, with Lysol rather than

God's grace serving as the preserving agent" (13), Roby suggests. Carol H. Smith, too, sees Sweeney as "natural man experiencing the agony of human depravity and guilt" and thus embodying the Christian path toward spiritual suffering and salvation ("Jazz," 92). Sweeney's equation of life and death has led some critics to view him as at least a parody of a Christ-figure.

THE VORTEX OF DRAMA

But the main focus for establishing the coherence between this play and Eliot's later drama rests with its language and Eliot's use of language to form a socially viable (and dramatically viable) community: this play, like all Eliot's others, is a quest for a condition, established through a deft fusion of language, tradition, and drama, "where the words are valid." There are copious reasons why *Sweeney Agonistes* would not seem to provide this condition: why this sketch (which might seem more of a sardonically wry "skit" than a bona fide dramatic offering) would seem to forestall communication or—in the mode of Eliot's more desperate poetry—allow a limited communication only to taunt the audience with the impossibility of using this discourse to foster anything more fecund or interactive or dramatic.

Yet I hypothesize that Eliot embeds in this play the germ of a dramatically oriented language of social intercourse. If this hypothesis seems unrealistically overdetermined, a proleptic consideration of his entire dramatic oeuvre indicates that Eliot will consistently attempt to create drama that seems to overreach or exceed the terms it has defined for itself. Finally, though, Eliot always manages to reconcile expectation and fulfillment, conceit and closure, in some way—not always ideally, but at least with a brave attempt that advances his long-term quest toward communities of drama.

Consider, for example, that murders should not happen in cathedrals and that a murder in a cathedral would not seem to portend the strength of an established Christian community. *The Family Reunion* will present an unlikely scenario for the dysfunctional reunion of an antagonistic family, several members of which are absent. The literal consummation of the eponymous communal celebration in *The Cocktail Party* happens only offstage, only years after it is originally scheduled, and among people who do not very much relish each other's party chat in the first place. The shared "confidences" in *The Confidential Clerk* are actually pervaded with deceit, miscommunication, and confusion throughout much of the play. In *The Elder Statesman,* the protagonist's lack of merit in his role as a trusted public figure is exceeded only by his greater incompetence overseeing his own family. Throughout his career, in fact, Eliot's dramaturgy is predicated upon the unlikely transformation of an inhospitable assocation of individuals into something that, through the dialogue enabled by the language of the play, becomes the viable foundation for a community—if not gloriously and resoundingly viable, then at least a pragmatically workable common ground or middle way. This happens as the characters teach one an-

other to speak and listen to this newly interactive variant of Eliot's language
that had offered only dramatic frustration in his earlier poetry. As the characters
acquire these language skills, drama skills, and social skills, so does Eliot's
audience.

Sweeney Agonistes seems to offer minimal promise of succor; there is little
communal interaction that would lead to a community whose coherence is
achieved through the crafting and sharing of language. (This is the paradigm—
communities of language, where the words are valid—that I posit as the essence of Eliot's dramatic enterprise.) The play's working title, *Wanna Go
Home, Baby?*, seems tauntingly cruel. There is not much that resembles a home
in this play, and Loot Sam Wauchope's coterie is jockeying to lure Dusty and
Doris not to any place resembling a home of safety or beneficence but rather
to a temporary "home," for a portion of the late evening, where their intentions
no more closely approximate the ideal of a nurturing domicile than quick commercial sex implies love.

But in fact, Sweeney presents a performance, from start to finish, without
any of Prufrock's hesitations, the Portraitist's stagefright, or Gerontion's obfuscatory pseudoprofundities. This performance may be the play's only unmitigated "success"; still, it betokens Eliot's first step on the path to more fulfilling
drama ahead. Sweeney brings Eliot wholeheartedly into the realm of drama. He
steps in front of the audience, ensuring that his presence has some *impact* upon
them, contradicting Eliot's earlier solipsistic sensibility. And Sweeney performs
and presents his story, a fairly coherent narrative, which represents a turnabout
from the pervasively oblique antinarratives of Eliot's poetry. The story
Sweeney tells is, incidentally, in some ways Eliot's own story as well: certainly
Eliot "needs to . . . do a girl in"—his wife, Vivien, whom he blamed for much
of his personal misery; and Humphrey Carpenter notes that Eliot used to sign
his name F. X. Sweeney (508). *Sweeney Agonistes* initiates Eliot's habit of self-
inscription in his dramatic narratives. As his playwriting career advances, Eliot
will increasingly use the theater as a forum for autobiographical exposition,
examination, and atonement.

Sweeney Agonistes, still, may seem minimally satisfying as a token of commitment to a dramatic expression of community; indeed, Eliot himself admits
as much in the play. *Sweeney Agonistes* hovers between life and death, a dialectical opposition seen in all Eliot's work of the 1920s (as, in *The Waste Land,*
barrenness and fertility, dryness and rain, are the pervasive metaphors for the
tenuous dialectic between life and death). Perhaps Eliot's 1921 breakdown
brought him psychologically, emotionally, intellectually, and even literally to
this pass of life and death. Eliot *must* have been hovering—between negation
and affirmation; between a clipped, harsh, stinted sensibility and the possibility
of a more accessibly shared vision—in the mid-1920s, as he composed the last
work he would write before his conversion. In *Sweeney Agonistes,* "Death is
life and life is death" (123), as, in *The Waste Land,* "I was neither / Living nor
dead, and I knew nothing" (54). The play in its resolution seems even more

bleak than *The Waste Land*. While the poem ends with the glimmer of transcendental peace embodied in "Shantih," the play's closing words forestall even an ambiguous optimism: "perhaps you're alive / And perhaps you're dead" (124). "Shantih" promises imaginative mystical and spiritual possibilities; Sweeney, finally, offers only plain hard facts.

Yet *Sweeney Agonistes* is fundamental to Eliot's dramatic enterprise because it positions itself so vitally close to this fulcrum mediating the space (or, in modernist parlance, the vortex) between life and death, drama and solipsism. *Sweeney Agonistes* is a high-stakes, drastically committed fight for expression.

THE PROBLEMS OF LANGUAGE

In the same way that *Sweeney Agonistes* hovers between dialectical antitheses of life and death, success and failure, its language may be seen alternately to facilitate or hinder community expression. Four aspects of the play's language argue against its success in generating or fostering a resultant community:

First, the language is full of exuberant hostility that is unconducive to any kind of concord, dramatic or otherwise: "You can't trust him!" (111). "Pereira won't do" (112). "[C]an't you stop that horrible noise?" (112). "A quarrel. An estrangement. Separation of friends" (114). "THE COFFIN!!" (114). "Yes I'd eat you!" (118). "Birth, and copulation, and death. / That's all, that's all, that's all, that's all" (119). "Any man has to, needs to, wants to / Once in a lifetime, do a girl in" (122).

Second, a good deal of the play's content is banal, with little apparent dramatic resonance: a prolonged and minimally successful attempt to read the future in a deck of cards and extract some meaning or guidance; the veterans' small talk preparatory to anticipated copulation for cash; Sweeney's incontinent and distasteful sexuality.

Third, the dialogue seems to be merely simplistic patter—linguistically and poetically inane, repetitive and static rather than developmental. It is, at various times, numbing, puerile, and offensive.

Fourth, to the extent that the play embodies a philosophy or poetic of dramatic language, Eliot cloaks this philosophy in an unheroic, unadventuresome, unpromising, unempowering linguistic expression: simply and resignedly,"I gotta use words when I talk to you" (123).

Without denying the validity of each point, there are nonetheless grounds for rebuttal. Paradoxically, the play simultaneously embodies, in a delicate balance, both the hostile and the countervailing benevolent natures of language; only Eliot's later plays indicate which way the balance finally tips. To redeem *Sweeney Agonistes* as successful, meaningful theater with the potential for community expression, the play's problematic issues of language may be resolved as follows:

First, as in *The Waste Land*, the worst must be faced for the quest's fulfillment, however mitigated by the landscape's torpor, to be valuable. In a Freudian sense, the manifestation and expression of fear, hostility, and torpor are necessary steps toward resolving them. In Bergsonian terms, breakdown is a necessary precondition for a more durable eventual synthesis. In a Christian schema, one must be lost to be saved. The telephone's horrible noise is an example of the modernist sensibility of overwhelming, encroaching technology that threatens to dehumanize the individual. The "Ting a ling ling" seems to embody (its own and Pereira's) hostility; but, as will be explained later, this hostility is ultimately displaced and transformed. Similarly, all of the play's personal animosities seem to be, if not quite defused by the end of the play, then at least trivialized, subsumed into a larger scope.

Second, the most popular plays of the 1920s were fairly vacuous. When Eliot began writing plays, the London stage was dominated by such offerings as Noël Coward's comedies, derivative of Oscar Wilde's plays. The attraction was the sharp, perky style in which actors bantered, rather than what they might have been talking about. Somerset Maugham's plays were also in vogue, about which Harry Blamires writes, "Their dialogue rings hollowly now. Flippant slickness masquerades as wit. . . . The supercilious cynicism is obsessive" (127). Coward's and Maugham's attention was to style and form rather than content, as was the case with the ubiquitous "well-made play," which gave audiences little concern about exactly *what* was well made. In *The Rise and Fall of the Well-Made Play,* John Russell Taylor notes that the French inventor of the form, Eugène Scribe, set out "to devise a mould into which any sort of material . . . could be poured" (11–12). Of chief importance was keeping the audience attentive and spacing and preparing effects to this end; for the English theater, William Archer adds the dictum of a "clear, neat, balanced overall construction" (15). Additionally, Stephen Staunton lists as characteristics of the well-made play "a pattern of increasingly intense actions and suspense prepared by exposition" and "the *scène à faire,* or obligatory scene, in which a fraudulent character is unmasked and fortune restored to the hero" (xii-xiii). This is not to argue that *Sweeney Agonistes* is a well-made play. Rather it is to suggest that, for one thing, it *does* have some elements in common with that genre—the prominence of style, form, dramatic effect, and a pattern of dynamic acceleration, all perhaps at the expense of attention paid to content;[3] and for another, that when Eliot's first play is examined in the context of other contemporary offerings, its apparent lack of compelling, momentous subject matter is not striking.

Third, Gareth Lloyd Evans, in *The Language of Modern Drama,* points to the cunningly crafted effect Eliot intends in his dialogue: it eventually "becomes completely hypnotic in its effect because of the interplay between the beat and (firstly) verbal repetitions and (secondly) the sound of words. 'Pereira' is like a rattle of kettledrums: 'How about Pereira?', 'What about Pereira?', 'You can have Pereira,' 'He's no gentleman, Pereira.' Throughout *Sweeney,* this interplay between sound and rhythm . . . is both strong and effective. It goes deeper than the creation of a generalized emotional reaction in the listener; it helps to create character. Notice how in Dusty's speeches the repetitions and the empha-ses on 'I think' and 'I hope' and 'she says' and 'she hopes,' and 'mustard and water' not only give a remarkable impersonation of real speech, but help to identify the flapdoodle mind of the speaker. Her lengthened pronunciation of 'Goooood bye' clinches the over-gushing personality who is speaking" (146).

Ronald Bush argues that Eliot "had since 1922 considered the creation of ritually stylized drama his most important project"; it was his "strongly held view that 'the drama was originally ritual' and that it was born in 'the beating of a drum' " (96–97; Bush quotes Eliot's essay "The Beating of a Drum"). In the same vein, Andrew K. Kennedy cites the intricacy with which *Sweeney Agonistes* presents sound as rhythm and thus evokes, via "the beating of a drum," the roots of shared communal performance. Kennedy finds the play "most successful as an experiment in speech, or more precisely, in turning speech into rhythmic sound effects. We know that Eliot intended the whole work to be accompanied by 'light drum taps to accentuate the beats (esp. the chorus which ought to have a noise like a street drill)' "—as he wrote to the play's first director, Hallie Flanagan—"and that emphatic modern rhythm was associated by him with the internal combustion engine. We are meant to experi-ence the play upon our pulses. . . . we should recall how many elements of the play are language-as-sound: the constant repetition of names, questions and greetings, for phonic play . . . the telephone bell's 'Ting a ling' and the 'knock knock' woven into the texture of the dialogue (spelt out as fourteen lines); Sweeney's speech, about *his* unutterable experience, merging into crooning . . . the six visitors, with the unnecessary names, forming a broken chorus even before they burst into jazz song and into the final nightmare chorus" (101). Sound is the origin of language, communication, drama (in a rudimen-tary sense, but Eliot's drama in the 1920s is rudimentary as well). Morris Freedman's essay "Jazz Rhythms and T. S. Eliot" extensively anatomizes the play's tempo and its various jazzy signatures that point toward a poetic intri-cacy which may not be fully apparent in reading this text—though perfor-mances of the play have drawn strongly upon its syncopated structure.[4]

In Eliot's program for modern verse drama, such rhythmic sound was a prominent concern; he wrote copious essays on the importance of crafting a poetic form and style precisely appropriate to the intricate demands of verse drama. In "The Need for Poetic Drama," Eliot explains that good poetic drama involves a play wholly conceived and composed in terms of poetry, embodying a pattern like that of music. "The Future of Poetic Drama" criticizes actors improperly trained in the delicate musical nuances of prosody. In *The Music of Poetry,* Eliot criticizes nineteenth-century verse plays such as Shelley's *The Cenci* because of their artificial speech rhythms. In *Poetry and Drama,* Eliot explains how the rhythms, stresses, and caesuras in his plays are meant to approximate normal speech and argues that ideally poetic drama imposes a pattern or order on life; action and language combine to evoke, simultaneously, dramatic and musical order.

These essays show a careful focus on the nature of the prosody of dialogue generally throughout the plays. The importance of drama (and especially dramatic rhythm) as ritual is perhaps the main connective focus of Eliot's theorizing on verse drama. In the event, the actual effect and prominence of a rhythmically resonant prosody eluded many of his audiences for his later plays. John McClain's review of the 1954 New York premiere of *The Confidential Clerk,* for example, states that "Much of Mr. Eliot's poetry is lost," and Richard Watts, reviewing the same production, writes that "There is little sign here of the poetic touch." In retrospect, *Sweeney Agonistes* is clearly the most intently metrical of all Eliot's plays; readers and audiences who may find the rhythmic sensibilities of his later plays too subtly elusive can discover more clearly in his first dramatic effort the original basis of his ideals for verse drama: the early importance he placed on rhythmic language.

Fourth, Sweeney's linguistic encomium—"I gotta use words"—hardly approaches, say, the Shakespearean bravado of the sonnets:

> But thy eternal summer shall not fade . . .
> When in eternal lines to time thou grow'st.
> So long as men can breathe or eyes can see,
> So long lives this, and this gives life to thee. (Sonnet 18)

Sweeney's complaint about language more closely evokes Hamlet's "Words, words, words," which is a memorable line for Shakespeare's title character in the same way that "I gotta use words" is for Eliot's. Each protests too much about the inadequacy and limitations of language. Hamlet's complaint reflects a pose he takes for Polonius' benefit (as Sweeney's complaint is a pose for Eliot) intended to keep the hero's lurking intention covert: both Hamlet and Sweeney are poised to blow us away with words. Hamlet will do so by deconstructing a static playscript into a cunningly subversive and accusatory "mirror held up to life"; and Sweeney will undergo an unexpected apotheosis from a jackknifing phallus into the germ of pious, tender, human drama.

The problematically elusive logic or redemption in the language of this play points toward Samuel Beckett. William V. Spanos reads *Sweeney Agonistes* as an anticipation of Beckettian absurdist minimalism: "Just as Beckett's characters, whether Gogo and Didi or Hamm and Clov, rely on each other to act out meaningful, or, at least, amusing and thus distancing dramatic illusions in their obsessive efforts to evade the meaninglessness of life . . . so Eliot's ladies see Sam and his friends as a means of escaping consciousness of their predicament in the erosive circularity of life in the wasteland" ("Absurd," 10).

Like all Eliot's poetry (but mostly unlike the plays that would follow), the language of *Sweeney Agonistes* is at various times dense, hard, eerie, stylized, macabre, haunting, cold, surreal. It shows influences as diverse as imagism, jazz, post-Impressionism (Gauguin's touch colors Sweeney's crocodile isle), and the quick pace of the music hall. Its structural composition is quintessentially modernist: it shows the paratactical clipped technique, approximating contemporary film editing, that Ezra Pound had taught Eliot. Modernists associated the style and technique that infuse *Sweeney Agonistes* with the imposition of formal order upon chaotic lunacy (as Eliot demonstrated when his breakdown generated the incontinent manuscript of *The Waste Land,* which became worked into the tightly and elaborately organized final version of the poem).[5] The unpromising linguistic potential that Sweeney seems to embody is a conventional modernist conceit amid the chaos perceived to pervade the 1920s. The writer pleads nolo contendere and deflates literary expectations but then goes on—against all odds, as he himself has portrayed it—to voice his seemingly ineffable age with a poetic uniquely attuned to its condition.

COMMUNITY VISIONS: 1

Sweeney Agonistes features numerous aspects of communities ranging from the intimately personal to the global. The first community shown in Eliot's first play is Pereira's seraglio. Details are scarce: Are there more women in it, or just Dusty and Doris? What is Pereira's power over them? What do the women do? How do they survive? The audience knows little about the constitution, the community relationship, of the group of women under Pereira's control. In default of specific information, their language and demeanor lead the audience to reach for vaguely defining social stereotypes: perhaps the women are tarts or prostitutes or even more ambiguously, flappers.[6] In their apparent state of oppression and constraint, Dusty and Doris indicate the need for some alternative vision of community, one that will serve them better. They do provide support for each other, though; there is strength in numbers, and even if there are only two of them, they are better able to withstand Pereira's threats or a roomful of rowdy party guests than if they were alone. Their community, albeit tenuous, is at least vaguely discernible. In their case, as in *Sweeney Agonistes* itself, Eliot invites his audiences simply to notice the existence of various kinds of communities, however dubious or mitigated. Subsequently, he will attend to the task of improving the nature of these communities.

The second community is Sweeney's own version of Pereira's seraglio, with softer scenery and props—bamboo trees and breadfruit. Essentially, this community is identical to Pereira's: Dusty and Doris would find little advantage if they were to switch from Pereira's to Sweeney's community. Recognizing this fact, they refuse to take Sweeney's bait: Doris informs him, simply, "I dont like life on your crocodile isle" (120). Dismal though this community would be, since Sweeney's demeanor is equally as oppressive as Pereira's, there is nevertheless a point to it. Sweeney's island presents, at least nominally, a second community option for Doris and Dusty. Although the choice is substantially negligible, it raises at least the possibility of other choices, better choices, that might exist elsewhere. Just as Pereira's community, though it was a bad one, raised the issue of a community's potential, this choice, though itself unappealing, reminds Dusty and Doris that they have options. Though Sweeney's tropical "scenery" looks gaudy and false, it indicates, at least, that one community *can* have a different look from another. The next step is to envision and create a community that not only looks different but is different. That does not happen for Dusty and Doris in this play, but the possibility of it is at least implanted.

The veterans' carnivalesque party evokes a third community, the postwar image of the "demobbed" and somehow shattered soldier, trying to reestablish himself within the home-front community that had itself become transformed by its experience of war. Klipstein, especially, wants to talk about his war experiences as the four men come together for their reunion; Krumpacker, though, cuts him off—perhaps needing to repress the reality of the Great War—and instead turns the conversation back to a topic (a memorable poker game in Bordeaux) more appropriate for a casual party. From the first, the party has minimal potential to fulfill traditional festive expectations: it is flat, drab, mechanical, desperate. In fact, as Christopher Ames explains, the gathering is typical of parties described in literature of *l'entre deux guerres:* "The tropes of imprisonment and immobility are crucial to the party scenes of this time," reflecting "the sense of futility perceived beneath Europe's temporary peace. . . . The typical party of this era—at least in its literary manifestation—is characterized by a frenetic and decadent avoidance of control that generates a sort of mock transgression" (127). In *Sweeney Agonistes,* Sweeney's braggadocio about murder and cannibalism serves this function of mock transgression. The party of this period, Ames continues, "is characterized by an artificial straining for spontaneity and excess that ultimately leaves the partygoers unsatisfied" (127). This unsatisfaction is apparent as the veterans finally fail to resolve their war experiences, to reestablish any communal companionship with one another, or to enjoy consummating a fling with Dusty and Doris. The party, then, facilitates a community that is once again a failed community but, also again, an instructive failure. The partygoers' ineffectual attempt to come together and satisfy their interpersonal and community needs indicates the fragile condition of European society in the 1920s. In *Sweeney Agonistes,* Eliot sounds a warning about the difficulties people have in unifying, forming communities, in the wake of the Great War.

The veterans, at least some of whom are Canadian, suggest a fourth community, the trans-Atlantic cosmopolitan community of *l'entre deux guerres. Abroad,* Paul Fussell's book about British literary travel between the wars and its consequent popular perception, explores the fellowship of travelers that the North Americans would have belonged to an ocean away from home. During the Great War, travel had been largely restricted; in the 1920s, people going on journeys partook of what Claude Lévi-Strauss calls "magic caskets full of dreamlike promises" (in Fussell, 226). International travelers formed an enchanted community of exotic nomads. The veterans, though deprived of a meaningful postwar soldiers' community, are functioning members of this world community. While Klipstein, for example, is unable to find the fellowship he needs to confront his wartime experiences, he effusively revels in this alternate community: "London's a slick place, London's a swell place, / London's a fine place to come on a visit" (117).

Swarts and Snow's masque evokes a fifth community, the cultural community of the jazzy music hall and, through it, the rich semiotic of the jazz age itself. Morris Freedman discusses the play's infusion with a period tempo in "Jazz Rhythms and T. S. Eliot," noting that "Fragment of an Agon" "opens with a duet between Sweeney and Doris suggestive of a leering couple doing a tap dance in a vaudeville or burlesque house, stopping every so often, after the manner of principals in a minstrel show, for an exchange of a few inanities. . . . The jazz rhythms marvelously enhance the spiraling quality of increasing stupor and confusion as the crowd gets more and more drunk" (429). Barbara Everett, in "The New Style of Sweeney Agonistes," further notes a wisecracking American prohibition-age tenor: echoes, for example, of the Chicago gangster in Sweeney's speech, of the speakeasy camaraderie in the veterans' speech, and of the dumb blonde in Dusty's speech. Eliot evokes prominent touchstones and sensibilities of the jazz age: spicy nights on the town, roving parties, leering repartee, vaudeville routines, best-selling gramaphone records, newspaper stories of glamour, adventure, and horror—all of which defined and reified the popular culture. In the 1960s the musical *Hair* drew upon a stylized version of popular culture and dramatically encapsulated what often seemed the incoherence of the world beyond the theater. In the same way, *Sweeney Agonistes* offers a relatively orderly theatrical experience of the chaotic, freewheeling jazz age outside. The play's audience thus interacts, at least by proxy, with that sleek, lightning-fast-paced glamorized and dangerous community[7]—in a safer and more palatable way than, say, going to a real speakeasy. The audience is less likely to end up in a drunken brawl and more likely to perceive the experience as conducive to a shared cultural community.

COMMUNITY VISIONS: 2

All these visions or suggestions of community are grounded in the status quo: drawing correlations between *Sweeney Agonistes* and extant paradigms of potential communal connection. *Sweeney Agonistes* also aspires beyond this point, toward a community that offers something wholly subversive of its bleak status quo: escape from the predatory clutches of Pereira, the deadening confines of Sweeney's world, the jazzy decadence of the 1920s, and the delayed trauma of the postwar period. To discover this aspiration requires a meticulous attention to the play's texture, its structure, its rhythms, its sounds.

At the beginning of *Sweeney Agonistes,* Pereira is equated with "Ting a ling ling," the noise that brings him into Dusty and Doris's flat and represents his presence there. (He never appears on stage in person, but every time the bell rings, Doris and Dusty respond, "That's Pereira.") He is calling to check up on his investment or perhaps to set up an assignation. The noise is a jarring and increasingly omnipresent sound of modern culture; it is a loaded signifier. The bell empowers Pereira, loudly announcing his capability to intrude into the women's lives and home at will. Via this bell, Pereira embodies the modern image of all-reaching technology. The degraded "music" of the telephone bell (in contrast to the vital and energized music of the jazz rhythms) becomes a tool for oppressively setting up cash liaisons. David E. Jones describes "the slightly artificial rhythm of a telephone conversation, which arises from the fact that the speakers cannot see each other" as Eliot reproduces it in Dusty's anxious one-sided patter; he also characterizes "that ridiculous modern affectation, the telephone voice, and . . . the excessive politeness of prevarication" (28). In *A Sinking Island,* Hugh Kenner writes of the discomfort and dislocation generated by the culture of telephones: " 'Are you there?' was what people instinctively said into a phone; some were still saying it as late as mid-century. 'Are you there?' was a sensible question, since where *was* that voice? It was in one's head, nowhere else; 'voice' no longer denoted 'presence.' The attention Eliot had paid to the telephone derived from . . . a Harvard training in phenomenology" (150–51). "Ting a ling ling," then, connotes the aura, or zeitgeist, of technological urban modernism: seemingly quotidian and innocuous, yet insidious in its potential confusion, deceit, manipulative control, and invasion of privacy.

Sweeney Agonistes ends with a complementary set of noises, similarly elemental, striking, overdetermined: "Hoo ha ha" and "KNOCK KNOCK KNOCK." Like "Ting a ling ling," each forms a three-stressed foot; the rhythmic structures of this play are extensive and intricate. The beginning and ending sounds establish a continuum; at the beginning of it is community failure—the bell is a signifier of Pereira's constraining voice and of a technological device that ultimately offers only falsely invalid communication. At the other end of the continuum is a condition that is not a complete failure and warrants a closer look if only because it is antithetical to "Ting a ling ling." The sounds at the play's end replace, or drown out, the "Ting a ling ling." At the beginning of "Fragment of an Agon" as Sweeney presents an interim stage in the quest for a new community to supplant Pereira's—his crocodile isle—the bell has already been disconnected: he pointedly reminds Doris that there are no telephones on this island.

The ending sounds (eschatological? apocalyptic?) are portentous, perhaps horrible, like the heart of darkness, but worth exploring for the same reasons Joseph Conrad thought "the horror" merited Marlow's quest: because there is greater horror in the banality left behind. Marlow's Europe is gloomy, exhausted, mendacious; the truth rests at the heart of darkness, where he faces the reality of modernity, the horror.

The more active assault on horror—Marlow's quest, and Eliot's—offers the possibility of a purgatorial refinement by fire or an expansion of consciousness that could allow escape from the banality and anticommunity of the status quo. In a B-movie chase scene, when the bad guys are chasing the good guy, the hero simply runs down whatever street or through whatever door happens to be available, even if there are funny noises coming from behind the door; anywhere else is preferable to instant capture. This, I suggest, is the situation of *Sweeney Agonistes:* a desperate attempt to move, to flee—*somewhere,* no matter where—away from the modernist bogey of introverted isolation and toward something that might, somehow, point the way toward a community.

The end noises represent hysterical madness and death (i.e., the knock of the hangman, as the final chorus explains). Dramatically, though, as well as emotionally, this chorus of madness expresses a cathartically primal scream; its cleansing and freshening force allows Eliot to go on to write such sedate works as *Ash-Wednesday* and *The Rock.* The knocks may be transformed and redeemed as an echo of Christ's Sermon on the Mount: "Ask, and it shall be given to you; seek, and ye shall find; knock, and it shall be opened to you: For every one that asketh receiveth; and he that seeketh findeth; and to him that knocketh it shall be opened" (Matthew 7:7–8). The unsettling knocking at the end of *Sweeney Agonistes* is subliminally (and more palatably) a sign of asking and seeking: Sweeney seeks the nature and bounds of life and death; Dusty and Doris seek the meaning of the cards and of their futures; the veterans seek a party, home, love. The play's most potent aspect, perhaps, lies beyond the ending: the audience must wonder *what* will be opened to him that knocketh here? In *Sweeney Agonistes* there is no manifest answer, as the knocks conclude the play; but each of Eliot's later plays answers a version of this question more explicitly.

The knocks offer, more simply, an imagistic counterpoint to the telephone's "Ting a ling ling." If the telephone bell signifies an intrusive and disembodied modernist attempt (likely futile) to communicate vitally, then the knock on the door is a more promising way of trying to connect with a person. Knocking, Eliot might reason, signifies how a member of the medieval era (which he found immensely more coherent than his own time) would have gone about visiting someone else in the community. (When some unknown intrusive caller reaches me on the phone, my modernist reflexes are so well honed that I hang up before the depersonalized stranger has even finished mispronouncing my last name. When someone knocks on my door, though, I see the person, make eye contact, establishing some deeper interpersonal relationship than I do with the phone caller; I have to deal with someone whose knocking indicates that he or she has physically traveled to see me.)

Eliot offers a further provocative connection between knocks and bells. In his letter to Hallie Flanagan (quoted in Carol H. Smith's *T. S. Eliot's Dramatic Theory and Practice,* 62) about her Vassar production, he notes that an additional ending fragment he wrote should appear just after "Fragment of an Agon" ends with "18 knocks like the angelus." Though an early draft of *Sweeney Agonistes* (T. S. Eliot Collection, item V7) has eighteen knocks at the end, the play's published text shows only nine knocks at the end of "Fragment of an Agon." There is no apparent reason why Eliot would refer to the draft written at least seven years previous to his letter to Flanagan, as opposed to the published text of *Sweeney Agonistes* that had appeared only months earlier. There are nine knocks in "Fragment of a Prologue" that Eliot might be conflating with the nine at the end of "Fragment of an Agon"; or Eliot might be counting the nine syllables of the "Hoo ha ha" passage that precedes the knocks at the end of "Fragment of an Agon" as "knocks" of some sort, perversions of the first nine beats of the Angelus. Perhaps Eliot could be misremembering the number of knocks at the end of the play's published text and still accurately connecting the knocks with his intention to evoke part of the pattern of the Angelus service, which consists of three Ave Marias and a collect for the Incarnation of Christ: a bell is rung three times for each Ave and nine times for the collect (so Eliot's knocks could allude only to the bells ringing for the Incarnation[8]). In any case, there is a neat and intricate dynamic of symbolism in all these knocks and bells: the unsettling bells of the opening "Ting a ling ling" are transformed as more resonant and dramatically potent knocks at the end. These knocks retain their own unsettling aspect (evoking the hangman and the madman), but at the same time, on some level, Eliot hears the knocks transformed back into bells that are much more promising than the opening bells, as they now symbolize Christ's spiritual unification of divinity and mortality. This symbolism illuminates the complex pattern that unifies the disparate levels within (and outside) *Sweeney Agonistes.*

BEYOND HORROR AND ENDINGS: TOWARD COMMUNITY

The "Hoo-ha's," like the knocks, manifestly promise terror, but it is a kind of terror that can be confronted and transcended through an intricate revaluation and refocusing, transformed into something informative and thus somehow redemptive. The play's first epigraph quotes the final words of Orestes in the *Choephoroi,* the middle play of Aeschylus' *Oresteia* trilogy. Orestes is tormented by demons, dripping blood from their eyes, who are forcefully present to him though unperceived by the Chorus. The Chorus suggests that Orestes cleanse himself with the help of the seer Loxias, but Orestes insists, in a paranoid fear as he flees the stage and the play, that these spirits are hunting him down and so he must move on. Aeschylus' entire play, like Eliot's, is infused with an atmosphere of horror. The *Choephoroi* begins in front of the tomb of Agamemnon, horribly killed upon his victorious return home from the Trojan war by his wife, Clytaemestra [*sic*], who had killed Agamemnon in retaliation for his sacrifice of their daughter Iphigeneia, and who became the victim of Orestes' matricide, and so on. The Chorus creates an aural sense of fear that serves much the same function as Eliot's stylized "Hoo-ha's": "Terror, the dream diviner of this house, belled clear, shuddered the skin, blew wrath from sleep, a cry in night's obscure watches, a voice of fear deep in the house,

dropping deadweight in women's inner chambers. And they who read the
dream meanings and spoke under guarantee of God told how under earth dead
men held a grudge still and smoldered at their murderers" (Lattimore 94). The
origin of this fear in Aeschylus, "in women's inner chambers," is paralleled by
the opening of *Sweeney Agonistes* in Dusty and Doris's flat. Aeschylus' smol-
dering grudges of dead men—who are, thus, not really quite safely dead—
evoke the terror just before the "Hoo-ha's" in Eliot's play, where life is death,
and where Swarts and Snow disagree about whether these murderers always
get pinched in the end.[9]

Orestes, in fact, does not get pinched in the end. In the final play of the
Oresteia, The Eumenides, he is called for trial at Athena's temple on the Acrop-
olis and receives equal votes for his guilt and innocence; Athena had announced
previously that a hung jury would mean acquittal for Orestes, so he returns
home. His final words are a benison for the grace and well-being of Athena's
city (not his own): "I shall go home now, but before I go I swear to this your
country and to this your multitude of people into all the bigness of time to be,
that never man who holds the helm of my state shall come against your country
in the ordered strength of spears . . . while they keep the upright way, and
hold in high regard the city of Pallas, and align their spears to fight beside her,
I shall be their gracious spirit. And so farewell, you and your city's populace.
May you outwrestle and overthrow all those who come against you" (162–63).

This is a far cry (pun intended) from the anguished terror that characterized
Orestes at the end of the previous play. As with the knocks, the "Hoo-ha's"
encourage reading beyond the ending. Eliot announces through the epigraphs
(the first Greek, the second Christian) that the audience must bring to this play
two larger systems of moral and cultural reference; we must apply these systems to, or superimpose them upon, whatever the play offers on the literal
level.[10] This can be done only by extrapolating beyond the play's literal boundaries[11] and its carnivalesque, jazzy, dissipated veneer.

In the case of the knocks, one must read beyond the literal "ending" of life
and (following the tenor of the Christian epigraph) toward a promised afterlife,
wherein the door shall be opened, the last shall be first, and so forth. In the
case of the "Hoo-ha's" (guided by the Greek epigraph), one must read beyond
the second play in the *Oresteia* and into the third, with its restoration of social
order: the murders are atoned for, and the personal terror that had pursued
Orestes in the vision of the Furies is finally diminished through the catharsis
Athena provides in an orderly legal ceremony. Athena's ceremony represents
society's passing judgment on Orestes. Temporarily alienated from his society
because of the murders and the ensuing horror that forms his own version of
the "Hoo-ha's," Orestes had thus been deprived of the succor that results from
being part of a calm social order. Having undergone the trial and received
society's acceptance and forgiveness—even if only barely, the jury still grants
Orestes this—he is once again allowed access to society's support.

Since Orestes has been so traumatized by his society—his house cursed by a legacy of brutality, Agamemnon and Clytaemestra having proven themselves unstable leaders for the Atreidae—it is unsurprising that Orestes ends by lauding the orderliness and power of a *different* society from his own. He displaces the requisite resolution for a tragedy, affection for the blessings of community, onto Athens. Similarly, in *Sweeney Agonistes,* one would not expect a redemptive vision of community merely to perpetuate the status quo of Sweeney's depraved society. Loot Sam, Swarts and Snow, the man with a girl in his bathtub, Pereira—*these* are not going to be the basis for a recreated community. The best outcome for Sweeney, as for Orestes, as for Moses, is to indicate the way toward a "promised land" and then vacate the stage, leaving it for other characters who are more qualified (and less implicated in habits antithetical to community) to continue and complete the quest toward community. Eliot's next dramatic work, *The Rock,* reinforces this point: it depicts the laborious endeavor to create a spiritual community over several centuries.

The "Hoo-ha's" at the end of *Sweeney Agonistes* do not take Eliot's audience quite as far as Aeschylus took his, but they do point in the same direction: vaguely promising an ultimate redemption, a creation of community that will eventually supplant the deranged madness. The promise is, certainly, tenuous and marginal. Similarly, in Eliot's Aeschylean model, the hero achieved only a tie vote: the gods' intervention determined that a tie would go to the hero. In *Sweeney Agonistes,* this intervention is paralleled by Eliot's own incipient conversion to a greater "godliness" (that is, the belief in the possibility of externally imposed order for a community that accompanies his Christian faith but that was absent from his earlier poetry, which featured such fragmented and isolated anticommunity panoramas as the cityscapes of "Preludes" and "Rhapsody on a Windy Night"). Aeschylus informs us that the paranoid, personally tormenting madness inherent in Sweeney's final "Hoo-ha's" is only a temporary state, the darkness before the dawn. Such erratic, lunatic volatility is endemic to mortals, but it is ultimately anathema to the forces that oversee larger assemblies of mortals over larger chunks of time. The madness must eventually dissipate as the gods eventually restore the communities in their charge to order.

In both *Sweeney Agonistes* and the *Oresteia,* a hero is tormented by the screeches of mad voices that are, ambiguously, both external and internal. He flees from that society and undergoes judgment. (Sweeney's long final speech about life and death and "what we gotta do" serves as his summative statement in defense of his behavior; the final full chorus represents the jury of his peers.) This process inculcates a renewed awareness of community virtues. Even if the hero is too troubled to enact these virtues himself, he still performs a useful community function if his drama has led the audience (which is itself, of course, a community), to appreciate the value of some other orderly community (for Aeschylus, Athens) than the hero's own.

The drama is triumphant if the audience reaffirms the value of being an orderly member of an orderly community. In a tragedy, this often—perhaps always—involves some kind of displacement of the immediate drama at hand.

In the *Oresteia,* ultimate closure, restoration, redemption, catharsis, all occur only after Orestes is dispatched from the scene (and after the playspace is "cleansed" of his presence). Then, Athena demonstrates her consummate beneficence; the community gently and comfortingly achieves healing unity under her protective guidance. Most important, the chorus of Furies is tamed, defused, stripped of its power to chase and torment anyone; it is deftly reintegrated into a social communion, as Athena offers the Eumenides a constructive rather than destructive role in a reformed community. ("No household shall be prosperous without your will," Athena promises; "my hate is going," the Furies respond [166–67].) Similarly, *Sweeney Agonistes*—Eliot's tragedy of modern banality— is poised to offer restorative elements after Sweeney is dispatched.

COMING ATTRACTIONS: ANTICIPATING SUBSEQUENT DRAMATIC COMMUNITIES

Eliot is engaged in a quest for a realm of community "where the words are valid," and yet, paradoxically, the dramatic scenarios described above are *not* defined through words. They are, rather, characterized by primordial rhythms or noises (bells, knocks, raves) and by silences (the succor promised after Christ and Orestes have left the stage and ceased speaking). Eliot's stage is far from ready for dialogue coaches like Alexander MacColgie Gibbs (from *The Cocktail Party*) to spout the glib, easy lines that can establish a community for Peter Quilpe and thus save him. But these incipient tinkles, grunts, ejaculations in *Sweeney Agonistes* are the germ of such a language. David E. Jones writes that "clearly, one of Eliot's chief concerns in *Sweeney Agonistes* was to come to terms with the speech of the time" (29).[12]

This speech of the time is not (yet) the speech of the sleek, suave dramatic ensembles that will infuse Eliot's West End plays with the spirit of beneficent community. Nevertheless, Jones's observation confirms that *Sweeney Agonistes* succeeds in confronting and integrating the demeanor of a community that surrounded Eliot. Though Eliot did not find Sweeney's world very promising, he may be admired for having taken it on, given its wastelandish torpor (which Eliot was, in 1926, trying hard to leave behind him). I have made the point earlier that the character of Sweeney, from his earliest appearance in Eliot's poetry, represents Eliot's worst-case scenario: if Eliot can deal with him, he can deal with anybody. Similarly, in *Sweeney Agonistes,* Eliot's mission is to confront the worst imaginable dramatic manifestation—here, an unremittingly sordid community. Having done that, he will simply modify the community temperament in his later plays until he arrives at the communities of drama that are palatable, tenable, and durable. Eliot's plays evolve from the vulgar and dangerous primitivism of *Sweeney Agonistes* into the immensely more tempered, placid, controlled dramaturgy of his later work. The awkward and hysterical dramatic insecurity, or uncertainty, of his first play will become transformed into a gnostic calmness as Eliot tests the waters of this social enterprise

of drama and becomes increasingly comfortable with the creation of various
"valid" communities. Sweeney simply plunges, heedlessly and violently, into
the world. It is for Eliot to establish a smoother communal interaction, to find
workable paths to love, compassion, and social intercourse.

A LIFE-AND-DEATH STRUGGLE

Toward the end of *Sweeney Agonistes* occurs the story of the murderer who
killed a girl and kept her body in a bathtub of Lysol. Murder is, of course, the
ultimate assault upon community. At the same time, though, as with the first
murder in Genesis, such an outrage generates a reaction—after the death, the
community must determine how to withstand it and survive. Murder can compel a community to bond together, to examine and reform itself, in the hopes
of avoiding future murders. Sweeney says that the murderer, though mostly a
loner, "used to come and see me sometimes / I'd give him a drink and cheer
him up" (122). In *The Cocktail Party,* the ritual of offering and sharing drinks
embodies a mystical communion denoting the Guardians' portentous guidance
and protection. Could Sweeney's drinking here anticipate that ritual? In any
event, it evokes a quintessential communal bond; a metaphorical phoenix is
rising out of the ashes of the murder. The communion is at least the smallest
bit uplifting; despite the preponderant sarcasm, it is heartening to see the killer
kicking up his feet and sharing a drink.

Whatever minimal movements or inclinations toward community may be detected in *Sweeney Agonistes* are, in keeping with Eliot's poetic, fragments
shored against the ruins. Amid the nightmarish noises of pervasively encroaching death, madness, despair, and sordidness, even a faint and sarcastic
glimpse of community is potentially valuable. It is an ember that may generate
an eventual flame, as this ember of a play eventually generates Eliot's full-
fledged career of more conventional attempts to create a sense of community
via performance—both the dramatic performance on stage and the social performance that it metaphorically represents.

Hovering between the worlds of life and death, Eliot's murderer evokes both
the Greek and Miltonic embodiment of the agonist. (As in any classical or
biblical narrative, the hero is empowered by this knowledge of both worlds. An
ultimate embrace of life is all the more meaningful, because it embodies an
actual knowledge of its opposite.) For both murderer and victim in *Sweeney
Agonistes,* death evokes the blurry, horrible confusion of the shades who inhabit
Dante's *Inferno* and *The Waste Land.* The eerily close and interrelated worlds
of life and death are vaguely defined, perceived, bounded; and in that vagueness
lies tremendous danger, for it implies that the (nominally) living characters
might be doomed to stumble around in near dead wastelands as long as their
sensibilites remain clouded. Eliot connotes the vague boundaries between life
and death in *Sweeney Agonistes:*

If he was alive then the milkman wasn't and the rent-collector wasn't
And if they were alive then he was dead.
There wasn't any joint
There wasn't any joint
For when you're alone
When you're alone like he was alone
You're either or neither (123)

The life and death confusion separates the individual from a possible community (the milkman and rent-collector); the murderer is inescapably "alone," as damningly as Eliot's earlier poetic characters were ensconsed in their Bradleyan "finite centres."

The battle for life or death, for madness or sanity, for solipsism or community, is not, finally, resolved in this play. Eliot's dramatic success is simply that the terms of the agon are defined; the importance of the quest for drama, for community, is made manifest. *Sweeney Agonistes* forthrightly announces that it is not going to reveal everything, that some questions about the agon between the forces of alienation and community are beyond the scope of this play: "Well here again that dont apply . . . I tell you again it dont apply"—because this play is not yet poised to offer substantial dramatic community; and again, "if you understand or if you dont / That's nothing to me and nothing to you" (123). These statements must suffice for now. They close off larger questions Eliot is not prepared to resolve in *Sweeney Agonistes* but will in *Four Quartets* and in his later plays.

2

The Rock: "There Is No Life That Is Not in Community"

Critical consensus finds *The Rock: A Pageant Play* an embarrassing failure, both as dramatic performance and on its literary merits. Eliot's script lacks "that precipitation of the spirit without which stage dialogue is tedious and flat," writes Michael Sayers in his 1934 *New English Weekly* review of both text and performance; the verse

"stays on the ground"; it walks, with irregular steps, in a circle. It does not stir us by a bold advance, though it may disappoint us by a feeble recession. . . . Its emotional gamut is restricted, dropping from satiric levity down to hopeless despondency, but reaching neither really comic impetuousity on the one hand, nor tragic contemplativeness on the other hand. . . . the content is equally as uninspiring as the form.

The reviewer for *Tablet* writes, "The scanty action and copious talk are expressed partly in not very successful *vers libre* and partly in a cockney dialect with the omitted aspirates so laboriously indicated as to make the long speeches of the bricklayers exceedingly tiresome to read. Unhappily, there is little freshness and beauty of thought to mollify the exacerbating diction." The *Everyman* review complains that "The trappings of a doctrinal humility do not at all become a poet of Mr. Eliot's standard."

Literary critics escalate the attack: Grover Smith calls Eliot's efforts in *The Rock* "so unfortunate . . . that scarcely anyone could have predicted for him a successful future in theatrical writing" (171). David Ward calls the pageant "a failure, an uneasy association of modes in which a crude expressionism alternates with rather flaccid experiments in the choric mode. Eliot's ear for the

rhythms and intonations of British working class speech which had served him
well in *The Waste Land* II fails him" (180).

In 1934, Conrad Aiken writes in *Poetry* that he is "more than ever uncom-
fortable about [Eliot's] present predicament, his present position and direction."
Eliot's work of this period indicates a "contraction of both interest and power
. . . a diminution of vigor and variousness: the circle has narrowed, and it has
gone on narrowing" (161–63). Aiken typifies the uneasiness with which Eliot's
adulating audience received this work. His followers are hesitant to state definitively that he has lost his touch—Aiken conjectures at the end of his essay that
perhaps Eliot's "experiment with dramatic form" will "release him . . . in ways
which neither he nor ourselves can foresee" (165). Aiken seems to hope *The
Rock* represents merely a passing phase; Eliot's 1934 readers are wary and feel
abandoned or betrayed by the standard-bearer of modernist malaise who has
apparently found such an easy respite in conventional Christian thought.

In *The Three Voices of Poetry,* discussing the significance of *The Rock* in his
career as a verse dramatist, Eliot himself offers what amounts to an apology:
"The invitation to write the words for this spectacle . . . came at a moment
when I seemed to myself to have exhausted my meagre poetic gifts, and to
have nothing more to say. To be, at such a moment, commissioned to write
something which, good or bad, must be delivered by a certain date, may have
the effect that vigorous cranking sometimes has upon a motor car when the
battery is run down" (98). He goes on to explain how the play, especially the
Chorus, fails to attain "the third voice," the apotheosis of dramatic address to
the audience.

As Aiken perceives, there is certainly a sizable component of *The Rock* that
is not of very significant literary quality or interest and that will not be discussed here at any length: the play offers embarrassing straw men, predictable
flat churchliness, rote prayer and spirituality; it literally preaches to the converted, with a profusion of facile and sometimes chauvanistic propaganda.

Yet despite these unpromising details, beyond which most critics have been
unable to penetrate, there are some more interesting facets of this pageant play.
There is a genuine (and in many ways successful) attempt to find a simple
serenity in language, as if Eliot is performing a finger exercise for *Four Quartets,* where he will force himself to prove or validate his dogma more systemati-
cally. The language of *The Rock* is in many ways an outgrowth of the acclaimed voice of modernism that rose from *The Waste Land,* but it is also,
importantly, matured and refined. It is less self-obsessive, more communicable:
often as vital as in Eliot's poetry of the 1910s and 1920s but stripped of gratuitous and counterproductive harshness. Eliot has adapted himself consciously
and successfully to the cutting edge of good new poetry, in the mode of W. H.
Auden's, Stephen Spender's, and Louis MacNeice's acclaimed fresh styles—
the themes, the tenor, the sensibility, and the spirit that were winning them
acclaim.

In 1942, in "Little Gidding," Eliot seems dejected that "next year's words await another voice" (204), that his poetry is no longer au courant; *Four Quartets* is pervaded by such belatedness. *The Rock,* from 1934, represents the last project in which Eliot was not anxious about being outdated; it is a work in which Eliot indeed breaks new ground, crafts and presents a poetic uniquely attuned to the tenor of the moment, needing no apology for a lack of newness. By the late 1930s, his writing no longer offered such fresh novelty; *Four Quartets* is a resigned acceptance of the power of the tautology, the self-enclosed system of meaning, made valid by repetition and reenactment of the same thing, which is presupposed to be valid. In "East Coker" 3: "You say I am repeating / Something I have said before. I shall say it again. / Shall I say it again?" (187). Eliot's final five plays basically repeat a safe and comfortable form. (The sincere comfort Eliot found in decades of playwriting does not contradict his dejection about the displacement of his voice in "Little Gidding": the poet who had forged his career on the cutting edge of the modernist avant-garde laments the loss of currency in his poetry; but regarding his drama, as subsequent chapters will disclose, Eliot equally accepts the static conventionality of form and sensibility.) In *The Rock*—which is certainly drama, but which Eliot preserved in publication disembodied (only its Choruses), apparently as poetry—he balances the two genres' opposing natures. As drama, its orthodoxy reflects his perception of a stable dramatic tradition that pervades his own plays and essays on historical and contemporary drama; as poetry, it retains the fresh, original strains of modernism for which Eliot was renowned.

Four Quartets is a swan song, a graceful farewell from center stage before the poet loses his potency. But in *The Rock,* Eliot's avant-garde experimentalism, his daring forging of the modern voice, is still going full force, and it generates some tremendously interesting (if not critically appreciated) poetry and drama. Ambitiously and importantly, this work shows a determination to combine, or interlock, the idea of modernism with the idea of community. This intention is successful, at least within the tautological Christian discourse that is "the rock," the foundation, of this pageant, and to some extent even beyond those boundaries. This subtle enterprise, underlying the entire play, is more intricate and interesting than the pageant's manifest function of convincing churchgoers that churches are important.

SINGING, DANCING, COMEDY, AND A LIVE ANGLICAN BISHOP!

At least some of reviewers' and critics' antipathy to *The Rock* stems from a misperception of its genre or an unwillingness to accept Eliot's intentions for the play. Audiences seem to have liked the pageant: in its May 1934 run at London's Sadler's Wells Theatre—the only performances ever given, so far as I have been able to determine[1]—audiences numbered as many as 1,500 per night, vastly more than saw Eliot's first play, *Sweeney Agonistes.* Though Eliot had feared a dull, lethargic audience of churchgoers, Bonamy Dobrée writes,

"He need not have feared. The audience . . . seemed far from lethargic" (in Browne, *Making,* 17). In *An Assessment of Twentieth-Century Literature,* J. Isaacs reminisces: "I remember very vividly the audience of *The Rock* at Sadler's Wells in 1934. It was the first time poetic drama had really come to the people. It was a simple and devout audience, a rapt and uncomprehending audience. . . . It was an audience of church workers, of mothers' outings, of shepherds and their flocks, and a few 'highbrows' like myself" (152–53).

At least one reviewer, J. E. Sewell in the *London Daily Telegraph,* appreciated Eliot's dramatic sensibility: he lauds the pageant's "imaginative brilliance" and, most presciently, "its satirical force." (Sayers, too, as quoted in his review at the opening of this chapter, had noted the play's satire but only to berate it.) Perhaps *The Rock* is so widely criticized simply because it is taken too seriously. The conceit—that scores of historical incarnations are interacting with each other, as mediated by three Cockney workmen—is purely comical. This comedy is drily (and sometimes, as in the Cockneys' more slapstick scenes, not so drily) in the mode of the music-hall spectacle that Eliot found so vital.

In his obituary essay for the star music-hall performer Marie Lloyd, Eliot writes effusively of her widespread popularity and her gift of expressing the life of her audience; she understood her admirers, sympathized with them, and publicly embodied their private virtues. The medium of music-hall performance served a crucial role in establishing a dramatic communality, and Lloyd was strikingly successful at this. "The working man who went to the music-hall and saw Marie Lloyd and joined in the chorus was himself performing part of the act; he was engaged in that collaboration of the audience with the artist which is necessary in all art and most obviously in dramatic art" (407). Because the middle classes have no parallel "expressive figure," he writes, they lack the cohesion of the "lower classes" (whom he identifies as Lloyd's primary audience and whose cohesion is a result of the community fostered in the music hall). In the same vein Raymond Williams confirms, "The urban working class created in the Industrial Revolution found in [music-hall] performers their most authentic voices" (*Revolution,* 265). Eliot writes that when the music hall passes out of vogue (because of the encroachment of cinemas and gramophones), its audience, too, may lose their sense of social definition and "will tend to drop into the same state of protoplasm as the bourgeoisie" (407).

In *The Rock,* even such gratingly obvious propaganda as the portrait of the Agitator becomes less offensive if one accepts the scene's predominantly burlesque effect. This "villain" resembles those in another of Eliot's satires, *Old Possum's Book of Practical Cats.* That cat community certainly has its "roughs" comparable to the Agitator, such as the notorious Mungojerrie and Rumpleteazer, but these gruff characters ultimately turn out to be harmless, even a bit endearing. The Agitator perhaps approximates the Pekes and Pollicles even more closely: *dogs,* barking away ominously in a land of cats (as the Agitator barks among the churchgoers). The canines are finally dispersed comically and harmlessly at the appearance of the GREATRUMPUSCAT, who stalks into the midst of their conflagration, gives a great yawn, and takes a great leap, at which "every last [dog] scattered like sheep" (35). A durable community of cats is restored easily and is not very seriously threatened by the barking of intrusive agitators, who are full of sound and fury but signify nothing.

Indeed, the Agitator scene in *The Rock* could be quite pleasantly comic in the mode of the cat poems, played up for guffaws, especially given the antipathy to an atheistic Agitator that would be a foregone conclusion from a devout churchgoing audience. A stock villainous character needs no rigorous dramatic deflation but can be played for immediate dismissive humor and farce—exactly as cat fanciers would be sure to see dogs' characters. The Agitator's blusters provide vintage buffoonery:

And what's a church, you asks. It's a place where they practices a degradin' and out-worn superstition, an abomination what ought to be swept off the face o' the earth, in what they call these enlightened times. Did you ever 'ear o' Darwin? Well, 'e was a scientific bloke what lived more 'n a hundred years ago, mind you, and 'e showed up the 'ole blightin' swindle as I can prove 'ere by this book which is published by the Rationalist Press Association for the price of one shillin'. (31–32)

Eliot fills the scene (like most of those involving the Cockneys) with the ornate rhetorical "eloquence" and colorful jousting in rich dialect that generate engaging caricatures and form the staple of English music-hall dialogue. Though not profound, the banter is pleasantly bouncy and diverting, engagingly lively. "All I 'ave to say to you, mate, is: You're a ruddy Nosey Parker. You 'op it" (33); " 'Arf a mo', leave 'im to me, Fred. 'Ave a fag? Got a match? Thanks. I know 'ow to talk to 'im" (33); "Well, that's an idea, that is. That takes a bit o' thinkin' out, that do, and no mistake" (33); "Why, it's plain as the nose on your face" (34). Typical of the pageant's comic touches is the Agitator's appeal to the workmen on the basis of his common bond with them as a "manooal labourer." Alfred shoots back: "It's a shame to allow you to show your igno-rance, old son. Us manual labourers? We're bricklayers, as you'd see for your-self if you wasn't stone-blind." And Edwin chimes in: "We're *brain* workers, we are. As for you, you're nothin' but a *lung* worker" (34).

The most pronounced music-hall aspect of *The Rock* is its general sense of spectacle: 300 actors representing characters of widely disparate periods and stations—biblical, historical, famous, pedestrian, individualized, stereotyped, prophetic, histrionic, caricatured—involved in dozens of scenes, changes, tab-leaux, elaborate costumes. The play features scenes specifically in the mode of a music-hall program, such as Bert and Mrs. Bert's ballad, "At Trinity Church I met my doom" ("a ditty" Eliot wrote as "an attractive variation on an old song" in the music-hall style, Browne writes [12]), and the ballet of Dick Whit-tington and his cat. The general tenor of the Cockneys' patter, which structur-ally unifies the pageant, identifies the genre as vintage music hall: their stage presence is marked by broadly comic dialect, humor, exaggerated earnestness, heavy-handed setups for each other. The Cockneys function as masters of ceremony for the rest of the wide-ranging variety acts that interrupt their story, which plods determinedly onward despite the intrusions of monks and crusaders.

The clearest evidence that *The Rock* is a spectacle in the style of music hall comes from two lines that do not actually appear in Eliot's text but are reported in the *Blackfriars* review of July 1934 as having been spoken by Dick Whittington's cat, introducing that ballet interlude:

> A pageant's rather like a pantomime,
> Where anything may come, at any time!

(Pantomime skits were staples of a music-hall ensemble's repertory.) These lines may have been ad-libbed; they are not in the published text; such a spontaneous ejaculation is all the more fitting as an emblem of this pageant's roots in the music hall. The *Blackfriars* reviewer incisively perceives that these lines accurately reflect the pageant's nature: the reviewer goes on to write that " 'Anything' included not only ballet, mime, history, tragedy, comic relief, but a live Anglican Bishop who, in full canonicals, as part of the final tableau, blessed the audience." Eliot's Christian music hall (complete with "live Anglican Bishop," as it might be billed) is a creative new genre representing an innovative fusion of performance styles and formats.

BETWEEN MUSIC HALL AND PAGEANT

In detailing the correlation between *The Rock* and the genre of music hall, I am overlooking a more obvious dramatic model: the vintage English form of the religious pageant, which the subtitle itself points to. Director E. Martin Browne, who was working on a more conventional church pageant when he first began to discuss *The Rock* with Eliot, describes that form:

The open-air pageant was in its heyday before the First World War, though it continued to flourish until the Second. Its purpose is to celebrate the history either of a place or of an institution, and it does so by showing a chronological series of scenes, each led up to by a processional entry. It gives a great multitude of amateurs, concerned with the subject of the pageant, an opportunity of taking part without any severe strain on their ability (the leading actors are usually chosen rather for their lineage or other connection with the affair in hand than for skill in acting) except, for some of them, that of riding a horse. The total effect can hardly be called dramatic; it is a display of panoply, a more relaxed and less disciplined version of a great parade. (4)

A conventional pageant is more formulaic and predictable than the eclectic fusion of performance offered by *The Rock*. Browne himself writes that when he learned the event was to be performed at a large central London theatre, "This, to my mind, invalidated the idea of a pageant, since processions on any considerable scale became impossible, and the effect would rather be that of a series of tableaux. It would certainly need the addition of a speech commentary, through which in fact the ideas behind the show would have to be conveyed" (4–5). Pageants are not generally performed indoors, and certainly not in London theaters; it was clear to Browne from the beginning that *The Rock* was not a run-of-the-mill pageant. An initial scenario that Browne wrote, involving tableaux and historical sermons—much closer to a conventional pageant—was rejected because "it would not give us what we wanted. It was unexciting in itself; and it gave no opportunity of confronting the situation of 1934. . . . We needed a framework of dramatic action in a contemporary setting. And to lift the imagination of the audience . . . we needed a poet. Spectacle there should be, but as an imaginative stimulus to action" (5–6).

If a stimulus to action was the response Eliot hoped for, he was wise to draw upon the energetic music-hall style more than staid religious pageantry. Structurally, with its brief dramatic sketches interspersed with performances in different genres—ballet, ballad, chorus, spiritual incantation, responsive prayer, benediction, and so forth—*The Rock* closely resembles a music-hall program. Because music halls were licensed for music and dancing only, they "were not officially allowed to perform dialogue in play form" (149), write Raymond Mander and Joe Mitchenson in *British Music Hall*. In 1904, the Theatrical Managers' Association published a statement with respect to the "Sketch Question":

In course of time there has arisen a practice of presenting at music halls, in addition to the variety entertainments consisting of songs, dances, and other performances, slight sketches, with two or three performers, and lasting about a quarter of an hour. Attempts have been made from time to time in past years by the music halls to extend such performances, but these encroachments have frequently been met by proceedings under the . . . Stage Play Act. During recent years, these sketches have gradually grown into plays; but so long as they did not form the principal part of the evening's entertainment, and did not constitute too serious a breach of the law, no action was taken by the managers. (150)

Music halls surreptitiously expanded the dramatic component of their programs until eventually they would "present complete dramatic pieces, with unlimited characters, numerous scenes, and occupying as much time as the particular proprietor thinks desirable" (150).

The legitimate theater managers who published the 1904 broadside resented the encroachment by music halls into what they considered their well-delineated domain. *The Rock,* with its dramatic sketches broken up by what would have been known as "variety" or "revue" acts in music halls, closely resembles the offerings decried by these theater managers, falling somewhere in between legitimate drama and a more wide-ranging entertainment format. *The Rock,* then, presents an entity that is in some ways conventionally theatrical but (like *Sweeney Agonistes*) is in other ways an assault, even subversive—as the theater managers felt music halls were—of the status quo and of established dramatic institutions. *Sweeney Agonistes* bears a relation to *The Rock,* too, in a more direct way: Eliot's first play, like his second, resonates with the tempo and style of music-hall, or vaudeville, patter. The stichomythia in *Sweeney Agonistes* evokes the same sort of music-hall banter as the Cockneys' clownish blather. Carol H. Smith perceives Eliot's indebtedness to music halls in *Sweeney Agonistes,* where the slick patter and jazzy crooning show Eliot's interest in the genre: "His conviction of the 'social usefulness' of dramatic poetry made him seek his models in the music hall which might be transformed into a vehicle as valuable to the modern playwright as the Elizabethan theater was for Shakespeare. A theater with 'something for everybody' " (*Dramatic Theory,* 55). *The Rock,* though, represents the fruition of the communality Eliot idealized in the music-hall experience (as described in "Marie Lloyd"), which in *Sweeney Agonistes* is latent at best.

The music hall's atmosphere was strikingly unlike the theater's: D. F. Cheshire calls "drinking in the auditorium . . . the main attraction (or disadvantage) of the music halls. In fact many considered that the main purpose of the halls was the encouragement of drinking" (82); he quotes an 1864 author, Richard Doyle, describing the music hall in *Bird's Eye View of Society:*

A great want must surely have been met when promoters and managers of the People's amusements first conceived the happy thought of combining singing and tumbling, and eating and drinking, and smoking . . . to be able to sit, with a little table before one, with, for instance, a bottle of beer upon it, to have one eye turned upon an acrobat, the other gazing affectionately at the drink, a cigar hanging lazily from the mouth . . . considering each song, dance, or other performance with an impartial look of languid contentment, a hazy, sleepy, stolid, stupid, sense of smoke, and drink, and general enjoyment. (In Cheshire, 82)

This description of the music hall as carnivalesque spectacle does not, of course, literally equate with the experience Eliot offers in *The Rock,* but he sought to use and coopt some part of this sensation for his Christian music hall. In view of what is now regarded as the stale dramatic fare offered by the legitimate theaters of the day—playwrights such as Arthur Wing Pinero and William Archer have not stood the test of time—Eliot seems to have seen that there was more life, more excitement, more freshness in the music halls. Drama, Eliot felt, should be replete with exactly these characteristics and should offer them back to the audience.

The music halls seem to have been especially interesting to Eliot (again, based on his observations in "Marie Lloyd") because of their prominent audience engagement and participation. Spectators honestly and immediately let the performers know if they liked them or not. And if not, Cheshire writes, then "people begin to talk, to flutter with their programmes, and perhaps some one may hum an irrelevant air. . . . it makes one think of the thumb-down attitude in the Roman circus. The curtain drops in the middle of something that is half hum and half silence" (86–88). But one does not talk or flutter for long amid the extravaganza of the music hall. W. L. George observes in his 1921 *London Mosaic:* "You can't drowse in a music-hall: from the moment when the conductor, in his elaborately luxurious and irremediably faulty dress suit, addresses his first and infinitely disabused bow to the audience, to the time when he calls upon the band to produce the smallest possible scrap of 'God Save the King,' and hurries out loyalty on the wings of ragtime, there is no flagging" (in Cheshire, 80).

For *The Rock* Eliot hoped to attain this level of audience involvement and response. He knew, from his fascination with the music hall, the enthusiasm (positive or negative) of which audiences were capable, and he wanted to tap into that enthusiasm. Certainly, given Eliot's topic, a religious service is a more obvious model than a music-hall program for this kind of desired social participation. There are, in fact, extended passages of prayer and other religious ceremonies in *The Rock*; they form a part of Eliot's appeal to involve and affect his audience—for a religious pageant play, indeed, a more conventional part. But combined with this element, more unusually and in greater measure than the prayer, is the discourse and technique of the music hall. Eliot would have recognized the image of the music-hall patron as the smoking and partly drunken spectator that Richard Doyle described in 1864: content, luxuriantly surfeited in terms of sensory and intellectual stimulation. Obviously, Eliot did not intend to inundate his audience with this same literal sense of satiation; but rather, he sought a more spiritually elevated variant of this sensation. The *Blackfriars* reviewer, who seemed as thrilled and dazzled by the spectacular manifestation of "a live Anglican Bishop" as he might have been at the apparition of a dancing bear, demonstrates how *The Rock* succeeds at unifying two disparate dramatic styles.

The heyday of music halls had passed when *The Rock* was performed; Mander and Mitchenson cite the 1920s as its period of decline, owing to such factors as the competition of cabarets and the wireless. Still, in the 1930s, West End theaters featured several nostalgic reenactments of music-hall programs, indicating that the genre still held a fond appeal in audience's hearts. In 1933 a show called "Old Time Music Hall" was offered at the Garrick Theatre, and in 1935 a nostalgic old-timers show featuring music-hall stars of years past was titled "Cavalcade of Variety." The wireless, which had usurped the music halls' audience, itself offered programs such as the long-running series "Palace of Varieties," evoking the period of music-hall glamor. (171, 195). Audiences would have clearly recognized *The Rock* as a variant of these resuscitations of the once popular genre.

Objections to *The Rock* on the grounds that it is bad drama, badly written, involve unfair standards; the large pageant staged by an immense cast of volunteers was not meant to be conventional commercial drama. Its performance at the elegant Sadler's Wells Theatre reflects no presumptuous claim for its aesthetic force but simply the choice of a convenient location for an event intended to attract as large an audience as possible to garner support for the Forty-Five Churches Fund and its church-building program. In fact, the notion of Sadler's Wells as one of London's most prestigious theatrical venues is a recent one: in the late 1920s the theater underwent a revival and renovation, and since 1931 it has been renowned for its opera and ballet companies as well as legitimate dramatic programs. But as Dennis Arundell chronicles in *The Story of Sadler's Wells: 1683–1964,* the house's history dates back to eighteenth-century origins as a "musick-house," and as late as the 1900s and 1910s it was offering programs including pantomimes, murder-thrillers, comedians, boxing contests, large bears, cinematographic singing pictures, and other novelties. In fact, the balletic presentation of the legend of Dick Whittington and his cat in *The Rock* was not the first time that story was performed in that vein at Sadler's Wells; Arundell notes that a show running at the end of 1910 featured "a twice-nightly pantomime *Dick Whittington* at this 'Popular Theatre for London Toilers' " (180). In 1934, given the grab bag of contemporary offerings at Sadler's Wells, the spectacle of Eliot's pageant drawing upon a rambling profusion of dramatic genres, including the music hall, would not have seemed as much out of place as it might today.

Much of what recent critics perceive as glib writing, sloppy structure, and a haphazard dramatic spectacular, then, would have appeared differently to a 1934 audience, which would have appreciated how *The Rock* fit with integrity into a genre. Eliot caught his audience's attention by enveloping them in the familiar, harmless music-hall performance and putting a different kind of twist on it. This tactic may seem like religious brainwashing: indeed, some passages from Eliot's essays reinforce the idea that he may have considered a bit of brainwashing proper for the dramatist. In the famous passage from *The Use of Poetry and the Use of Criticism* where he characterizes the theater as the most socially useful venue for poetry because of its myriad levels of significance, he discusses how "the sensitiveness of every auditor is acted upon by all these elements [plot, character, style, rhythm, and so forth, in a manifold layering] at once, though in different degrees of consciousness. At none of these levels is the audience bothered by the presence of that which he does not understand" (146–47). Although what we do not understand, or liminally perceive, does not *bother* us, as Eliot writes, it is still there: and this fact, combined with Eliot's reference to the different degrees of consciousness, implies that there can be (or should be) material in a play that some members of the audience do not notice but that nonetheless permeates some subliminal level of their consciousness.

Eliot is more explicit about these dynamics in a short essay called "Five Points on Dramatic Writing," where he advises the playwright how to present a play: "If you can keep the bloody audience's attention engaged, then you can perform any monkey tricks you like when they ain't looking." Further, Eliot suggests, this is a desirable thing to do: "[I]t's what you do behind the audience's back so to speak that makes your play IMMORTAL for a while" (10).

I do not suggest that Eliot turned to a dramatic career with the express purpose of brainwashing the masses of England; only in a few unguarded moments does he go so far as to characterize drama as something approaching psychological manipulation. Rather, I would say, he attempts to use a safe, easy, comfortable, light dramatic genre to get across something deeper, something more important that he did not feel like doing within more standard dramatic forms. And he will continue to perform such "monkey tricks . . . behind the audience's back" when he finds a niche more versatile than imitation music hall—verse drama with a light surface but a richer, resonant substance—for his later plays.

Although *The Rock* is full of a haphazard range of dramaturgy running from the ridiculous to the sublime, it did in fact give Eliot a basic background, an apprenticeship in conventional theatrical matters. It offered him the valuable experience—more intensely than with the Group Theatre's slight productions of *Sweeney Agonistes*—of working in a theater, with producers and technical crews, and with as difficult a troupe of actors (amateurs and at least a few primadonnas) as he would ever encounter. Browne asserts that Eliot had been interested in working on *The Rock* partly "to see at first hand at least the final throes of making a production" (11). Further, "I do know that one of his main reasons for accepting the Forty-Five Churches Fund commission was that it had a guaranteed audience for its two weeks' run in a large theatre. He would thus be assured of witnessing the response of audiences" (17). The enterprise involved in presenting *The Rock* was both communal and meta-communal—that is, a community was putting on this parable of community. Perhaps most important for Eliot's subsequent dramatic career, this pageant play initiated his close professional and personal relationship with Browne, who would direct all his subsequent plays (and would, as well, have a strong influence on their plots, composition, drafts, and revisions).

BETWEEN *THE ROCK* AND A HARD PLACE

At the core of the dramatic texture that permeates *The Rock* is the Chorus. Eliot crafts a community of drama concurrently with a language through which this community communicates, establishes itself, asserts its identity as a social entity. Eliot's language is specifically tailored to this enterprise and flourishes mainly in the Choruses, which form a substantial proportion of the entire pageant and unify an otherwise free-form production. (The Cockney interludes, too, unify the pageant, though not as satisfyingly in aesthetic terms; probably Eliot intended them to be parallel to the Chorus, on a more plebian plane.) The choral language is extremely precise, controlled, and incisive, as contrasted with the looseness of some of the pageant's other patter and dialogue. This treatment reflects Eliot's contention that a community's equally shared voice can unify anything, even the unpromising scenario that was given him to flesh out into *The Rock*. This voice (or language, or poetic), constantly aspiring toward social unity, is exactly antithetical to the choral community failure in "The Hollow Men," where "[o]ur dried voices, when / We whisper together / Are quiet and meaningless" (79). In *The Rock*, nothing is dry; on the contrary, it is all richly fecund, presenting an embarrassment of riches in terms of community portrayals throughout Western culture.

The Choruses embody a poetic tone and mood of a quality for which Eliot is not often credited.[2] It is generally conceded that his poetry contributed only an initial germ of style to the poetry of the period after conventional "high modernism" (which ends, essentially, with "Shantih" in 1922). This movement in English poetry is seen as being taken out of Eliot's hands and developed by poets such as Spender with his pylons and Auden with his tramlines, chain stores, and power houses, into the voice of (what Auden called) the "low dishonest decade," the 1930s beset by depression, the doomed attempt to recover from the destruction of the Great War, the cloud of impending fascism and holocaust. Yet like these other poets Eliot, too, in the Choruses, crafts a finely honed variant of his early 1920s wasteland modernism precisely fitting the poetic tenor that characterizes the best verse of the 1930s. The sensibility embodies guarded perceptions—cautious awareness—of complex local and international realities; deflation of cultural grandeur (with an acceptance of this deflation, unlike in *The Waste Land*); and a more resigned, workable, practical, and tolerant adaptation to the modern world. The tone tends to be partly sardonic but not unilaterally dismissive: when Eliot discounts "devising the perfect refrigerator" (31) he feels this (parodic) consumerism is a less desirable activity than the search for spiritual goodness, but he realizes that the two in fact coexist with each other as characteristics of the modern world.

Eliot never seemed especially pleased with *The Rock*. The text bears an author's disclaimer as a Prefatory Note: he states that he does not view himself as the author of the work but only of the words printed, since he wrote and rewrote the dialogue and choruses under the guidance of his director, Browne, with suggestions incorporated from the Rev. R. Webb-Odell, the director of the Forty-Five Churches Fund; they had given Eliot the scenario upon which he was told to base the pageant.[3] In a gibe at the actor who played Bert, Eliot writes that the Rev. Vincent Howson has so wholly rewritten and revised the Cockney's dialogue that he should be cited as joint author. Eliot takes credit for having literally authored only one scene, which Browne identifies as the totalitarian ideological satire at the end of part I.[4]

Perhaps some of Eliot's displeasure with the play (the full text of which was never reprinted after its first edition) derives from dissatisfaction with its actual production. Its messiness, imperfections, and inadequacies may have overshadowed his earlier enthusiasm for the first large public performance of any of his work. (Remember the strength of Eliot's private and antidramatic sensibility in his earlier poetry, and his reticence to public exposure.) A few days before its opening, Eliot wrote to the director of his first play, Rupert Doone, that it "seems to me to be in a limp and chaotic state. . . . most of the players seem to me dismally lacking in vitality" (in Browne, 10–11). Browne adds, "Eliot no doubt got a shock when he witnessed the trials of putting together so huge a show with an untrained cast; and at that stage it looked a superhuman task to make an entertainment out of it" (11). The business of revising and developing the scenarios given to him seems to have been more difficult and less satisfying than he had thought it would be. Additionally, Eliot's marriage had recently become increasingly traumatic: Lyndall Gordon writes, "At the end of 1933 Vivienne refused to sign the Deed of Separation, and it became obvious that she would never consent to her husband's freedom." His work did not come easily, according to Gordon: "As he began to compose *The Rock* it was like cranking a machine" (*New Life,* 25).

Most critics assert that the Choruses are relatively well written and the rest of the pageant is dross. One reason why the Choruses may stand out from the rest of the play is that in these passages character and plot are subordinated to pure communal speech/voice. Eliot may have found this convention less constraining than the scenario, which had been plotted by others. Critics' isolated approval of the Choruses conveniently eliminates the rest of the play; one does not really get a sense of the play's plot or focus, except in an abstract sense, if one reads only the Choruses as reprinted in the *Collected Poems.*[5] They seem, in that context, more like the disembodied spiritual meditations from *Ash-Wednesday* and *Four Quartets*—which is what critics want them to be, to fit more coherently with the way Eliot's work of this period is traditionally appraised and categorized. But the Choruses are more than just dry runs for *Four Quartets:* it is wrong to ignore the context that originally surrounds them. They were written as drama, not textual poetry, although (as with *Sweeney Agonistes*) the fact that they are reprinted only in *Collected Poems* tends to obscure this point for most readers.

ELIOT'S 1930s STYLE

The fresh vein of poetry that emerged from Eliot's experience of writing *The Rock* should mitigate the critics' determination to condemn the play as facile propaganda. The play contains a great deal of what I call the "1930s style" (a handier term for what David Perkins calls "The Period Style of the 1930s in England" in *A History of Modern Poetry,* where he examines it elaborately). The tenor is immediate, highly contemporary; it eschews mainstream modernism, Perkins asserts: "The esotericism, phrasal density, formal complexity, and avant-garde experimentalism of high Modernism had less appeal, for they made poetry difficult and thus relegated it to a small number of readers. . . . Poets wished to address issues in a language appropriate to intellectual discussion, and hence they used discursive or generalizing language" (111). Introducing *New Signatures,* the 1932 anthology of poets who would come to epitomize this 1930s style, Michael Roberts writes that they "shared an effort to overcome artistic isolation and detachment . . . 'say something to an audience,' and 'find solidarity with others' " (in Perkins, 113).

The key point of reference for these writers was, simply, the reality of the outside world, and it was a reality about which there was striking agreement: they "inhabited more or less the same imaginative world," Perkins writes, substantially informed by "the newspapers. By 'newspapers' I mean what was news in the 1930s—unemployment, depression, Communism, Fascism, spies, street mobs, dictators, treaties, arms races, wars—and also the fears, hopes, and strivings with which English intellectuals responded to these events" (115).

The 1930s reaction against the earlier modernist aesthetic involved "a feeling of reaching out to an audience from isolation and to subject matter and life from form and art," Perkins writes, "a demystifying of poetry. The poetic state of mind was no longer to be conceived as especially privileged—more complex and integrated, or more uplifted toward the beautiful, eternal, and true. And a poem was not, like *The Waste Land* or *The Cantos,* a grand web of myths. A poem was now to be a piece of ordinary consciousness and talk" (123). The tenor "was conversational. More exactly, it was a poetic imitation of conversation, more heightened, metaphoric, and formally patterned than ordinary conversation, but more like talk than was common in English poetry" (127).

It is not often noted that the Choruses—besides being good poetry according to the keen general standards of craft and tone that Eliot maintained throughout his life—are good in a way that is different from the rest of Eliot's good poetry. They are bleak, understated, stripped of the harsh petty elitism of Eliot's earlier poetic. Nor are the Choruses exactly in the mode of the later mature style that typifies Eliot's postconversion poetry, which is a transformation of the early poetic into a smoother and more genteel but similarly elite, vatic, and spectacular (rather than earthy) voice. There are just a few other occurrences of this sort of poetic from the Choruses in the rest of Eliot's canon. Parts of the "Ariel Poems" embody a voice that is close to the tenor (or "the quantity of the sounds," as Eliot's essay "In Memoriam" quotes Tennyson's description of his poetry) of *The Rock.* "Journey of the Magi" describes the trip through the desert:

> . . . the camel men cursing and grumbling
> And running away, and wanting their liquor and women,
> And the night-fires going out, and the lack of shelters,
> And the cities hostile and the towns unfriendly
> And the villages dirty and charging high prices:
> A hard time we had of it. (99)

This style effectively transposes, or adapts, a scene from biblical Israel to one of unpretentious modern immediacy, wonderfully unhampered in this transposition by the incongruity of "camel men." Eliot infuses the passage with a straightforward naturalism; it is unmomentous, yet sufficient in detail and thus convincing. The lines are not technically or syntactically elaborate, but they are effectively workmanlike, solid, in their basic elemental concatenation.[6] In "Animula":

> The pain of living and the drug of dreams
> Curl up the small soul in the window seat
> Behind the *Encyclopaedia Britannica.* (103)

In "The Cultivation of Christmas Trees":

> There are several attitudes towards Christmas,
> Some of which we may disregard:
> The social, the torpid, the patently commercial,
> The rowdy (the pubs being open till midnight). (107)

The power of the images in passages like these—their idiosyncratic tenor, their air of genuine quotidian experience untainted by the pretention of false humility—derives from the integration into Eliot's poetry of the simple, average, ubiquitous life of the masses: not with the sociopolitical implications of the Orwellian or Soviet proletariat but simply reflecting an appreciation and acceptance of the common life, the common experience, of the European in the depressed and muted 1930s.

Such passages are relatively latent throughout Eliot's poetry, and they appear most prominently in such "minor works" as the Choruses from *The Rock* and these "Ariel Poems." But those that do appear elsewhere are powerful—for example, the underground scenes of *Four Quartets:* the "place of disaffection" (178) in "Burnt Norton" 3 and the train passengers with their "fruit, periodicals and business letters" (196) as they depart from the platform in "The Dry Salvages" 3; and the darkly banal venues of bleak modernism in *Four Quartets* such as the hollow theater in "East Coker" 3.

In these passages from Eliot's poetry—as, more pervasively, in *The Rock*—the language, the tenor, the topos, the location of this verse stake out new ground. Its subject matter extends the radically "improper" and jarring coffee spoons and butt-ends from two decades earlier in "The Love Song of J. Alfred Prufrock." Unlike *Prufrock and Other Observations,* though, this poetry projects no irony—or very little—at the juxtaposition of "high culture" (which Eliot had thought, then, was the poet's inherent domain) and "low." Eliot's assertion in *Ash-Wednesday,* "I rejoice that things are as they are" (85), could serve as a motto to his poetry of this period and to his entire dramatic career: it reflects the acceptance of social realities that pervades all his works influenced by the 1930s style.

Such an acceptance signifies a fundamental stage in Eliot's transition from poetic solipsism to dramatic community. Eliot is crafting and presenting a new language, one of wider potential range than anything he had written earlier. He is writing beyond introversion, beyond the "finite centre," and toward some more widely comprehensible and meaningful social drama. The words are becoming valid: we are watching the moment of transition (and its mechanics, its nuts and bolts) from "April is the cruellest month" to

> *JULIA*
>
> . . . Edward, give me another of those delicious olives.
> What's that? Potato crisps? No, I can't endure them.
> Well, I started to tell you about Lady Klootz.
> It was at the Vincewell wedding. Oh, so many years ago!
>
> *[To the UNIDENTIFIED GUEST]*
>
> Did *you* know the Vincewells? (*The Cocktail Party,* 15)

Eliot's ventures into the 1930s style in the "Ariel Poems" and *The Rock* are at the same time technical, poetic finger exercises and a monumental aesthetic metamorphosis. The reader is privy to Eliot's development as it unfolds. In his earlier poetry, he tried to wrench his readers to see the world through *his* idiosyncratic point of view, his detached, cynical, elitist sensibility (and he felt he was doing his readers a service, teaching them to see the world and the modern aesthetic the right way: *his* way). Thus, for example, in his 1915 poem "Mr. Apollinax," a memory of a conventional Harvard luncheon party with Bertrand Russell becomes grotesquely and bizarrely transformed, horribly and perversely caricatured:

> His laughter tinkled among the teacups. . . .
> He laughed like an irresponsible foetus.
> His laughter was submarine and profound
> Like the old man of the sea's
> Hidden under coral islands
> Where worried bodies of drowned men drift down in the green silence,
> Dropping from fingers of surf. (23)

But under the sway of this newly emerging 1930s aesthetic, instead of imposing his perspective upon his audience, Eliot tries to see things as the rest of the (saner, calmer) world does.

In *The Rock,* this aesthetic is somewhat indebted to Eliot's vintage modernism, the tenor of *The Waste Land*; there are some incidences of this poetic in the pageant, and to a certain extent, Eliot's 1930s style grows out of this. Examples of the wastelandishness (or, at least, passages that, when isolated, convey a fairly close approximation of that poem's sensibility) in *The Rock* follow:

• The chorus of voices of the Unemployed: "We stand about in open places / And shiver in unlit rooms. / Only the wind moves / Over empty fields, untilled" (10). This passage evokes the imagery of the title characters from "The Hollow Men," which is essentially an extension of *The Waste Land.*

- The vision of urban malaise and torpor, beset with a dehumanizing mechanical intricacy: "O miserable cities of designing men, / O wretched generation of enlightened men, / Betrayed in the mazes of your ingenuities, / Sold by the proceeds of your proper inventions" (29). Compare the cities described here with the "Unreal City" in *The Waste Land,* populated by a Dantean procession of the damned, and with such earlier cityscapes as the base streets of "Preludes" and "Rhapsody on a Windy Night" and the deviously "insidious" streets of "The Love Song of J. Alfred Prufrock."

- The stagnancy of a tepidly bourgeois populace with their comatose intellect and spirituality: "I journeyed to the suburbs, and there I was told: / We toil for six days, on the seventh we must motor / To Hindhead, or Maidenhead. / If the weather is foul we stay at home and read the papers" (8).

When, toward the end of the pageant, Alfred remains somewhat mystified as to how the church building has come along as smoothly as it has against the odds, Ethelbert, frustrated that his colleague has not accepted what he sees as the obvious spiritual force that has aided their labors, rebukes him: "Fred, I'm afraid you've got that disease they call the modern mind" (65). This disease reached epidemic proportions in *The Waste Land,* which is an etiology and case study of the sickness of modernism; Eliot's task in *The Rock* is to provide an innoculation against this disease. Although Ethelbert perceives that a trace of it lingers in Alfred, it is clearly in the process of being treated: isolated within, and ultimately eradicated from, Eliot's aesthetic. The traces of Eliot's wasteland tenor that appear in this poem are like weakened strains of a virus posing little threat on their own, used only as a vaccine to make the "organism" (the community) aware of possible threats, against which it can produce antibodies.

ELIOT'S NEW LANGUAGE: THREE CLOSE READINGS

But *The Rock* does not rest here in its aesthetic vision of modernity. The play goes beyond *The Waste Land,* a poem that is infused with a paramount sneer, and attempts to integrate the modern world. *The Rock* accepts the predominant social reality as a "valid" and legitimate referent and, more technically, as fodder for poetry. We have, then, vintage Eliotic modernism adapted to a world as it is really inhabited by the fishermen, madwomen, and typists who were no more than flat types of modern torpor in *The Waste Land.* This tenor of Eliot's 1930s style, as in parts of the "Ariel Poems" and *Four Quartets,* is firmly and honestly rooted in an acceptance of the quotidian on its own terms. In *The Rock,* Eliot profusely offers passages in this style as prototypes: they are a training ground for a language that he would use, sparingly but with strong effect, in the last decade of his poetic career and then, more easily and unstintingly, throughout his drama. This language is, thus, at the heart of whatever it is that connects Eliot's drama to his poetry.

Eliot's work of this period suggests links to the younger poets in the 1930s—much closer affinities than are often acknowledged. Steve Ellis incisively refutes "a tendency among critics writing on the 1930s to displace Eliot from that decade, to ignore or obscure the connections between his work and that of the rising poetic generation" (141). That rising generation had something new to say, and in a new way, contrasted with the poetry of high modernism that appeared in the wake of World War I. Examining Eliot's writing in the context of these poets illuminates a significant new strand in his work, one that will be similarly prominent in his other plays of the 1930s and will endure throughout his dramatic oeuvre. The following pages will closely examine three instances (among many) of this voice and explore how Eliot retools his language to make it a viable medium for a poetic that demands the creation and sustenance of community images (and, of course, of community itself).

In the first instance, The Rock chastises the modern citizen, at his first appearance, for his ignorance of spiritual realities:

> . . . you neglect and belittle the desert.
> The desert is not remote in southern tropics,
> The desert is not only around the corner,
> The desert is squeezed in the tube-train next to you,
> Squeezed like tooth-paste in the tube-train next to you,
> The desert is in the heart of your brother. (9; Chorus 1, 149, in *Collected Poems*)

This is a neatly encapsulated example of Eliot's poetic in the process of transformation: the passage starts out resembling something that could fit in almost anywhere in *The Waste Land*—evoking Marie's similar willful repression of geographical reality in the mountains; the poem's literal desert of clutching roots, stony rubbish, dead trees; the profusely repeated images of a barren landscape and its pervasive power (which, The Rock reminds us, as Eliot did in *The Waste Land,* cannot be neglected or belittled). Yet The Rock's lines are subtly but definitely reformulated to reflect Eliot's 1930s style. This voice is achieved through the easy juxtaposition of the global ("southern tropics") and the local ("around the corner"), indicating a parallel between these two realms despite what would first seem a striking imbalance. The parallelism suggests the possibility of confronting what had appeared in *The Waste Land* to be unbearably implacable global forces of barrenness. A local manifestation of that force is more manageable—it can be processed and confronted. The casual juxtaposition indicates how individuals can define and delineate their focus so as to interact meaningfully with the world around them. If the image of a remote tropical desert is daunting and unapproachable, the "tooth-paste" simile poetically signifies a more casual and local, almost comic, accessibility. (This line from the English first edition was cut from the American edition, and from Eliot's later reprintings of the Choruses in *Collected Poems*; perhaps Eliot considered it *too* drastic a shift in tone, too casual and local, too facile. But the movement from global to local that he intended remains in this passage, even without that line; it merely becomes a more subtle shift.)

This image's resonance derives from the weird turn, or twist, in which the desert is "squeezed"—a word chosen to humanize its force without negating it—into a tube train (anticipating other underground scenes in *Four Quartets*). Part of the effect of this humanizing image is to belittle the force of the desert, a neat trick, which had been impossible in *The Waste Land*. (The weird twist is even weirder, and the force of the desert even more greatly belittled, with the unexpected "tooth-paste" squeeze; I would argue for the textual restoration of that line, which, I believe, serves Eliot's intentions effectively.) The diminution is only imagistic: a desert seems less quantitatively oppressive if it is in a tube train. Yet it was the very imagery of *The Waste Land*, almost regardless of the spiritual and intellectual portents behind it, that announced the near impossibility of rejecting or mediating the poem's terrain. This cosmetic "reform," then, makes the poetic less daunting and thus potentially more communal and communicable. Qualitatively, though, we must realize that a localized desert remains as threatening as one in the southern tropics. True, the metaphorical "desert" takes up a much smaller space, specifically the space defined by the mass of a fellow commuter in the tube; but this space the size of a person (evoking, of course, a person himself or herself) can be as dry, as deadening, as a literal desert. Just as a desert, geographically, frustrates community with its sandy waste, so can a force squeezed into a tube train portend ominous barrenness.

Eliot's anaphora carries the choral poetry smoothly from vintage wastelandish imagery into the 1930s style. The first two terms governed by the anaphora are negative ("the desert *is not* . . . "), while the last two are affirmative; obviously, Eliot sees his more recent style as capable of affirmation in a way that his earlier poetic was not. Even though the latter lines paradoxically *affirm* a *negative* (barren) condition, they still do so by active, forthright definition (which Eliot sees as braver, just as Dante found active sinners more significant than the neutrals in Hell), rather than passive, pessimistic definition by negation.

Eliot has segued into his 1930s style by the end of this short passage—the toothpaste and the tube train are the obvious indications of this transition. In terms of mechanics and craft, this style is perfectly harmonious with the wastelandish poetic in the ominous barren opening of this passage: the verse progresses evenly and naturally; the anaphora functions effectively as a connective force. Yet at the same time, the two voices are antithetical, just as solipsism is antithetical to community. And just as the wastelandish desert becomes transformed into a less oppressive localized image, the second-person address, when it first occurs, embodies what one would expect (from preconceptions about Eliot's wastelandish tenor) to be a voice of angry prophetic blandishment. It recurs, however, in a softened context, becoming the voice of the companion, the helpmeet: the social equal and community colleague who speaks of "your brother."

In a second instance of Eliot's new voice, the Chorus, lamenting the life that
is unmindful of a community imperative, says:

> And now you live dispersed on ribbon roads,
> And no man knows or cares who is his neighbour
> Unless his neighbour makes too much disturbance,
> But all dash to and fro in motor cars,
> Familiar with the roads and settled nowhere.
> Nor does the family even move about together,
> But every son would have his motor cycle,
> And daughters ride away on casual pillions. (21; Chorus 2, 154 in
>   *Collected Poems*)

The vague suburban roadscape evokes many of Auden's inadequately communal villages: his, like Eliot's here, are unsettled and unsettling, populated
predominantly by spies and sullen strangers. One example from Auden's poetry
is the land, "cut off," which

>   will not communicate,
> Be no accessory content to one
> Aimless for faces rather there than here.
> Beams from your car may cross a bedroom wall,
> They wake no sleeper (1)

in "Who stands, the crux left of the watershed." Another is the "insufficient
units . . . Supplied with feelings by an efficient band," (14) i.e., a radio—
representing the sterile commercial culture that usurps a humanized community
sensibility— in "Consider this and in our time." Still another is the appallingly
bleak domestic life in which

> The glacier knocks in the cupboard,
>   The desert sighs in the bed,
> And the crack in the tea-cup opens
>   A lane to the land of the dead (62)

in "As I walked out one evening." (Note how similar Auden's technique of
localizing the desert is to Eliot's: sighing in beds the desert is just as intimately
close as Eliot's squeezed into the next seat in the tube.) In *British Writers of
the Thirties,* Valentine Cunningham describes the source of antipathy to these
suburban villages: "The life of suburbs and garden cities grated because it was
neither fish nor frankfurter, neither completely town nor country. It served a
delusion, a 'widespread day-dream,' as Orwell called it in his long '40s essay
'The English People,' of being a 'feudal landowner,' a 'country gentleman.'
. . . the pretending was widespread, and attacked from all sides" (257). In *The
Idea of a Christian Society,* Eliot blames urbanization and suburbanization for
the decay of community (23).

Eliot's passage echoes writing by other members of the Auden Group, indicating the coherence and integrity of this 1930s style across a range of poets. In section 32 of *The Magnetic Mountain,* C. Day Lewis writes,

> You who go out alone, on tandem or on pillion,
> Down arterial roads in April,
> Or sad beside lakes where hill-slopes are reflected
> Making fire of leaves, your high hopes fallen:
> Cyclists and hikers in company, day excursionists,
> Refugees from cursed towns and devastated areas . . .
> You above all who have come to the far end, victims
> Of a run-down machine, who can bear it no longer. (115–16)

Stephen Spender, in *Forward from Liberalism,* describes "*laissez faire* gone mad, a huge inflation of Tudor villas on arterial roads, wireless sets, tin cars, golf clubs—the paradise of the bourgeoisie" (in Cunningham, 257).

The connotations of the roadway in Eliot's passage anticipate car crashes in his later plays (which are discussed in more detail in chapter 7). This sensibility regarding roads and driving provides just a small example of Eliot's imagistic consistency throughout his playwriting career: the road here, as in *The Family Reunion* and *The Elder Statesman,* symbolizes social discord, confusion, chaos. It is the epitome of modern sterility on the largest of scales. Later in *The Rock,* the Chorus castigates an empty society: "Here were decent godless people: / Their only monument the asphalt road / And a thousand lost golf balls" (30). The road is a place where people crash into each other at high speeds, rather than driving safely, mindful of other drivers with a sense of community responsibility toward any citizens who happen to be on or by the road. In *The Rock* the crashes have not yet occurred, but they are surely just around the insidiously winding bend of this disunified collection of individuals, erratically dashing to and fro. Chaotic automotive devastation is the logical extrapolation of the roads in *The Rock,* which symbolize aimless traveling and dispersion of communities.

Eliot's ribbon roads are the setting for the same kind of poetic transformation as occurred with his image of global and local deserts. "Neighbour" at first connotes the majestic, somber spirit of the Old Testament: "Thou shalt love thy neighbor as thyself" (Leviticus 19:18); in its immediate recurrence it also (and more prominently but without negating the Old Testament connotations) simply denotes that kindly gentleman across the garden wall. As in the previous passage this all happens, stylistically, with casual understated subtlety as the same word repeated immediately (here, "neighbour," repeated twice, four words apart; earlier, "desert," four times in the same position at the beginning of four successive lines) changes—or rather, the *audience* changes as its contexts change.

As when he brings a tropical desert into the tube to confront it more easily, Eliot localizes the universal failure of community amid the ribbon roads in

terms that are precise, uncomplicated, but nonetheless potent or foreboding for
that. A family is the integral, local unit of community (and it will prominently
function as a paradigm for the larger community in Eliot's final four plays);
yet it moves not together as a unit but in isolated spheres and directions. Eliot's
crowning touch in portraying the modern dissolution of family and community
is the image of the daughters—evoking the most patriarchally idealized images
of virginal purity—riding away on casual pillions. (A "pillion" is an extra seat
or pad on a motorbike for a supplemental passenger.) For "casual pillions,"
hear the distraught puritanical implication of "casual sex," as a budding pubes-
cent daughter rides off with her arms wrapped among some casual acquaintance. As in Day Lewis's image of the riders "on tandem or on pillion" from
The Magnetic Mountain, the riders are, despite their companionship, ironically,
alone.

If this scene were in *The Waste Land,* the motorbiker would have been more
precisely identified, probably as a type of the young man carbuncular, and the
horror of the entire scene would have been dragged out in its tedious glory.
Here, Eliot is satisfied that he has encapsulated this horror in an image as
controlled and distilled as that of the desert around the corner (which nevertheless remains a full-fledged desert). The "casual pillions" denote casual poetry
but by no means weak or watery poetry: simply poetry that in its casualness is
that much closer to its audience and to the tempo of modern society and thus
that much better poised to penetrate its audience. Eliot's youthful anxious poetic sensibility generated a sense of cool, detached alienation among his reading
audience; his casual demeanor here, conversely, fosters connective engagement
with his dramatic audience.

In a third instance of Eliot's new voice, the Chorus berates those who turn
from God to prideful self-obsession,

> To schemes of human greatness thoroughly discredited,
> Binding the earth and water to your service,
> Exploiting the seas and developing the mountains,
> Dividing the stars into common and preferred,
> Engaged in devising the perfect refrigerator,
> Engaged in working out a rational morality,
> Engaged in printing as many books as possible,
> Plotting of happiness and flinging empty bottles,
> Turning from your vacancy to fevered enthusiasm
> For nation or race or what you call humanity. (31; Chorus 3, 157, in
>   *Collected Poems*)

To the modern sensibility, there is a canny connotation to exploiting seas, developing mountains, dividing stars on a ledger sheet—Perkins cites the creation
of fresh metaphors from the realms of finance and bureaucracy as typical of
the 1930s style (132).[7] Eliot knows this, and accepts it, while still trying to

point out the underlying spiritual dangers of this condition. His copia is in a distinctly contemporary vein, as announced most explicitly by the image of the search for a perfect refrigerator. This scheme/quest is obviously parodic, but at the same time it epitomizes something that occupied a tremendous amount of attention and symbolized the kind of technological advance that was coming to characterize not just the material life, but also the intellectual life and arguably even the spiritual sensibility, of the twentieth-century citizen. The pedestrian modern sensibility in *The Rock* is no longer viewed from a perspective of detached haughtiness but, rather, as part of a world of which the poet is very consciously aware from his own "immediate experience" and in which he is himself implicated. In his 1930s style, Eliot indicates his own participation in this world: he is intimately familiar with the process by which the quotidian has assumed the stature of the sacred, and his critique of mass culture is tactful rather than vitriolic.

Eliot explicitly indicts himself in this Chorus as he describes modern humanity "[e]ngaged in printing as many books as possible." As editor at Faber & Faber, Eliot was employed to print "as many books as possible" of poetry by contemporaries whom he deemed important and was constantly trying to discover and publish new poetic talent. He had, incidentally, published twenty-five of his own books or bound pamphlets in the previous seventeen years when he wrote that line in *The Rock.*

The passage is manifestly a jeremiad, yet it is still a gentler one than Eliot has produced in the past. As is appropriate from a Chorus, sharing a perspective in common with those in the audience, the speech is addressed across, not down, to the listeners. The images of humanity's perversion of nature and the natural order are tremendously tamer than they would have been in Eliot's earlier poetry: earth and water are merely bound to our service, without any drastically morbid or apocalyptic modifiers. The common modern person plots not treachery or moral turpitude or intellectual manipulative deceit or physical desiccation, as was the case in the Dantean schema of *The Waste Land,* but only the more subdued, innocuous, and understandable "happiness."

This passage, like much of Eliot's 1930s style, is "Audenesque,"[8] or what we have been trained to identify as such, though it may be argued that Eliot is writing in this vein as well as Auden and contemporarily with him. Bernard Bergonzi defines what the Audenesque has come to mean. Among his indicators of the Audenesque voice are a prominent use of the definite article (which "points to the recognisable if not to the already known. It recalls an actually or possibly shared experience, as well as . . . reflecting the preference of modernist poetics for the particular against the general. . . . Auden's use of the definite article arises from his sense of reality as known and charted and intelligible, where all elements are potentially at least capable of classification" [*Thirties,* 41–43]). Another indicator, following Eliot, is the use of "the bizarre or unexpected simile" (43). A third is the "reliance on adjectives and adjectival phrases . . . sometimes scientific or clinical . . . partly descriptive, partly affective, with the exaggerated overtones of a familiar register in English middle-class speech: 'wonderful,' 'marvelous,' 'lovely,' 'horrible,' 'appalling,' 'tremendous,' 'ridiculous,' 'doubtful,' 'enormous,' 'absurd.' When applied to natural objects, or to unlikely human artifacts or institutions, the effect, as with the similes, is reductive, suggesting that there is nothing in reality that cannot be contained within the conceptual and verbal confines of the poet's world of discourse" (44).

Steve Ellis describes Auden's technique as "a common, quasi-standardized poetic diction for presenting the most uncommon, unstandardized things; an outrageous choice of details"—exactly like Eliot's perfect refrigerator—"is presented in a seemingly 'straight,' documentary, impersonal tone, heavily dependent on the definite article" (157). Ellis's characterization of the Audenesque voice perfectly suits Eliot's Audenesque passages.

Bergonzi asserts that the Audenesque was widely imitated—"by the end of the thirties it was disseminated throughout the English-speaking world, and can be called a collective style" (51)—and explains its appeal: "At a time of world economic depression there was something reassuring in Auden's calm demonstration, mediated as much by style as by content, that reality was intelligible, and could be studied like a map or a catalogue, or seen in temporal terms as an inexorable historical process" (51). Perkins concurs: "Auden's work gripped a whole generation. His rhythms, images, and habitual emotions; his comic descents and preachy elevations ('woozy,' he called them); his montage of facts, gestures, or dictions that reveal deep-lying faults in the psyche and in society; his unification of depth psychology with social analysis, pervade the writing of the period" (116).

Eliot was "particularly absorbed by that formal, detached, rather prosy voice [in Auden's poetry] that anticipates the diction and tone of the *Quartets*," writes Ellis. "Its deliberately rather pedestrian, exegetical character is an important influence in Eliot's development" (144). Ellis explains the attraction Auden offered Eliot: "in the later 1920s, Eliot, with his increasing absorption into English contexts—royalism, Anglo-Catholicism—and his growing interest in classical English, would have seen in the public-school and Oxford-educated Auden an authentic English voice, from which he could learn" (144–45). (Parts of *The Rock* are more explicitly indebted to Auden than merely to a general "Audenesque" zeitgeist: the expressionist agon between the Redshirts and Blackshirts, as numerous critics have noted, is fairly clearly an appropriation of Auden's and Isherwood's earlier dramatic style and sensibility.)

While Auden generally gets the credit for the poetic and linguistic sensibilities Bergonzi and Perkins describe, these sensibilities are equally prominent facets of Eliot's work, especially of his 1930s style, and particularly of *The Rock*. Bergonzi identifies the full fruition of "that particular manner of Auden's that became a collective idiom" (39) as beginning "only in his second collection, *Look, Stranger!*" which was published in 1935, a year after *The Rock*. Auden's legitimate claim to having established a compelling and unique voice in the

1930s need not be refuted: but *The Rock,* though often overlooked, offers evidence that Eliot is crafting a similar voice concurrently with Auden.

Not that Eliot would have minded charges of plagiarizing the Auden Group: as he writes in *The Sacred Wood,* "Immature poets imitate; mature poets steal" (125). And Cunningham explains that Auden in his earliest poetry was influenced by Eliot; Auden's "Eliotic tricks have been returned, stamped with the label 'Audenesque,' and Eliot has been happy to use these remoulded, recharged devices" (20–21). Ellis puts it nicely: "These two poets, who certainly watched each other's work very carefully, exercised a mutual influence" (142).

Perkins writes that prominent poets of the 1930s turned away from, or escaped from, the pervasive influence of Eliot: they "absorbed yet also rejected Eliot's characterization of the modern mind. . . . though the young poets might find themselves quite as bereft of tradition, community, faith, and purpose as the figures in *The Waste Land,* and might feel in themselves the same emotional fragmentation, alienation, guilt, futility, and fear, they denied Eliot's pessimism. What he portrayed was not the ineradicable condition of man, they said, but an expression or result of the social isolation of Modernist art" (122). Perkins is absolutely right in this analysis, except that one must carry it a step farther to complete the point. Eliot, too, is rejecting Eliot: that is, Eliot's work in the 1930s, most prominently *The Rock,* refutes his poetry of the 1920s as well as any of the other prominent 1930s poets refute Eliotic high modernism. Perhaps Eliot's refutation is even better than theirs, since he was best poised to react against this poetry. Who knew better exactly what had to be rejected and how it could be most effectively deconstructed?

AS THE WORDS APPROACH VALIDITY

While Eliot's 1930s style is a fixed and coherent entity in his canon on its own terms, it can also be perceived as hovering between the 1920s and the 1940s, written in a space he has carved out that is bounded by the touchstones of his more prominent poetry. What had been disarming flashbacks to *The Waste Land* at the beginning of *The Rock* become, at the end, premonitions of *Four Quartets.*

The Chorus, for example, describes a moment of Christian salvation as occurring at "a moment in time and of time, / A moment not out of time, but in time, in what we call history; bisecting the world of time, a moment in time but not like a moment of time" (50). These temporal and poetic pyrotechnics, a dazzling variation on the theme of how people relate to and place themselves in time, evoke passages that infuse the fabric of *Four Quartets,* especially the first sections of each poem, with their meditations on trying to fix or suspend time and on exploring its nature as both finite and infinite, mortal and spiritual.

In a second anticipation of *Four Quartets,* the Rock admonishes a faint-hearted Chorus to remember that "In every moment you live at a point of intersection, / Remember, living in time, you must live also now in Eternity"

(52). This passage anticipates the still point of the turning world in "Burnt Norton," although that image (which recurs throughout *Four Quartets*) is a richer and more mystically resplendent figure of intersecting sensibilities.

In another instance, the Chorus describes the genesis of language:

> Out of the sea of sound the life of music,
> Out of the slimy mud of words, out of the sleet and hail of verbal imprecisions,
> Approximate thoughts and feelings, words that have taken the place of thoughts and feelings,
> There spring the perfect order of speech, and the beauty of incantation. (75; Chorus 9, 168 in *Collected Poems*)

Slimy words and verbal imprecisions that beset secular and popular language are contrasted with some form of the Logos, arising out of incantatory perfection. In "Burnt Norton" 5, similarly, the fragility of popular words that "Slip, slide, perish, decay with imprecision" is resolved as language ascends toward what Eliot portrays as more valid: the Word. In both these passages, the fundamental strength of language is that it finally asserts itself, its validity and viability as a medium for community, in terms that it has established itself—through a continual process of trial and error, crafting and cleansing, refining and building on its own previously established foundations and strengths. This language represents the end point of a continuum that began in obscurity, solipsism, raving grunts, decadent near incoherence. In both passages Eliot points to the immensely difficult quest for a language he has undertaken up to the 1930s. Concurrently, like Janus looking back and ahead, Eliot sees his language as having an increasingly enduring power to carry him forward into the arena of dramatic community. He scouts out the terrain between what he knows (from his early poetry) as the disturbing emblems of the modernist panorama and what he seeks (for his future poetry and poetic drama) as a vision of community that can unite to combat modernist angst. People in this community will be able to speak to each other, counteracting the mute incommunicability that was one of the primary scourges of earlier Eliotic modernism.

This continuum, from unsettling wasteland flashbacks in part 1 of *The Rock* to proleptic anticipations of *Four Quartets* in part 2, is not unlike the one previously described in *Sweeney Agonistes* running from "Ting a ling ling" to the knocks and "Hoo-ha's." Obviously, the continuum here is more promising since its terminus is not merely madness and death with some obliquely redemptive vision hovering behind that; the end point now, rather, is the serene, soothing tranquility of Eliot's last poetry. Chapter 1 concludes by discussing a character on the margins of the play who offered a penetrating insight into the world of that drama, the man Sweeney once knew who did a girl in. Here, too, we see an understated but dangerous man, the Plutocrat, who stands as an emblem of the turmoil that a community must guard against and a reminder of the range of a community continuum. Like the murderer in *Sweeney Agonistes,* this man is an incarnation of Sweeney or at least of Sweeneyism. He combines Sweeney's sleaziness and Loot Sam's coldly calculating self-involvement, although he is cloaked in a more respectable facade.

The stage directions given at the Plutocrat's entrance recall the tenor of *Sweeney Agonistes:* he is surrounded by the same sort of speakeasy backdrop, described as "FLASH LADIES, GUNMEN and other shady and rapacious individualists" who, throughout the Plutocrat's two speeches, are "getting lower and lower in class," streaming on "until the stage is pretty full" (45). The exiting stage directions, too, bespeak a Sweeneyesque spectacle: crowds "cheer uproariously and kneel for a moment" to flunkeys bearing a golden calf, "then rise and begin to push and shove and pursue the image across stage. Fall to struggling with each other indiscriminately. The calf is dismembered. Exeunt in tumult" (47). Like Sweeney in his earliest appearance ("Sweeney Erect"), the Plutocrat leaves a tumultuous and disheveled wake of chaos, the pointless terror of a barbaric dithyramb, after he rampages through a scene. Here, the result is social discord rather than an epileptic screaming on a bed, but it amounts to the same thing: a moral horror.

Like Sweeney trying to seduce Doris into life on a crocodile isle, the Plutocrat is trying to seduce the masses into a social condition that appears appealing but is, Eliot feels, ultimately fraught with destructive disaster. Sweeney's slick argot was especially poised to make its impact in the 1920s jazz-age context; the Plutocrat's unctious, corporate paean to capitalistic prosperity is similarly poised to catch the attention of the 1930s world fraught with depression. In *The Rock,* though, there is a Chorus (and not an orgiastic one like Swarts and Snow's) and, even better, a Rock to refute this tempter. The Chorus rebukes the Plutocrat after his first speech, showing that the people, the masses, clearly recognize and reject what he represents: a faux community of (as the Chorus explains) those whose souls are torpid, who serve their own selfish interests and ambitions, who eschew brotherhood with men. The Plutocrat tries once more, "in a conciliatory manner" (the stage direction informs), to insinuate his way into the community's hearts and minds, and to share—compromise—the power of the Church with the power of gold. But this time The Rock himself dashes the Plutocrat's facade to bits, reminding the audience that he lives in an eternally transcendent realm and knows intimately the contest between hell and heaven. Doris had to spar deftly with Sweeney to fend off his constraining vision of the crocodile isle; The Rock simply crushes the Plutocrat and what he represents, rising in an apotheosis of confident triumph:

And the Gates of Hell shall not prevail.
Darkness now, then
Light.

Light. (48)

Sweeney Agonistes blurred the boundaries between life and death, consequently presenting its audience with the troubling possibility of a cloudy and indeterminate limbo. Here, by contrast, terms that are supposed to be incontrovertibly antithetical—darkness and light—are indeed distinctly so. Early visions of torpor in *The Rock* are subsumed by its social component, which is a heady one: it is richly elaborated and developed (historically, economically, artistically, morally) in a way that the potential for communities in *Sweeney Agonistes* was largely only implicit, subliminally lurking. The explicit religious tenor in *The Rock* accounts for much of this social element. The Anglo-Catholic life Eliot chose in 1927 provided him a ready-made community and a prefabricated discourse that infuses that community. But complementing this play's pat Christian discourse is a less explicit focus (which will become more manifest in his last four plays, as the prominent Christian sensibility is relegated to a rather unobtrusive backdrop): the presentation and exploration of the idea of community.

COMMUNITIES OF DRAMA

The importance of a durable sense of community, which the Christian church has offered for centuries in England, is a constant refrain in *The Rock.* Five years after completing *The Rock,* when Eliot delivered the lectures that became *The Idea of a Christian Society,* he wrote that "to understand the society in which he lives, must be to the interest of every thinking person" (6); *The Rock* demonstrates that in 1934 he held these same beliefs. Eliot forthrightly creates in *The Rock* (as he had only tentatively contemplated in *Sweeney Agonistes*) what may be called a community of drama. This is a community that is defined through drama; the dramaturgy itself is the first sign of community and is at the same time an analogical model for an extradramatic fulfillment of community (for which the drama at hand offers incentive, inspiration, and guidance). Eliot presents the extradramatic imperative in *The Rock* straightforwardly and unmistakably at the end of the play. The drama announces its termination and pushes the audience to return to the real world, having learned its lessons; as the Chorus states, "In our rhythm of earthly life we tire of light. We are glad when the day ends, when the play ends" (85). A comforting darkness evolves into a transcendent light, and the Chorus offers its praise to the "Light Invisible" (85). The Rock acknowledges the choral declaration that the play has ended—"You have spoken well" (86)—and consecrates the beginning of an affirmed community.

Toby A. Olshin cites numerous other examples of dramatic self-consciousness:

Ethelbert's song from *Hamlet* and his reference to the Old Vic (11) immediately remind the audience that what they are seeing is the illusion of an illusion. The Rock, too, forces "those who are sitting here silent" (53) to remember that their participation in the "action" is on several levels at once. Blomfield's exclamation "As if a church was run like a theatre!" (54) is followed soon afterwards by the ritual drama of the blessing of the Crusaders (61–4). Mrs. Ethelbert's line purposefully breaks the suspension of disbelief when she reminds her husband, " 'Ere's 'undreds and 'undreds of people all waitin' to 'ear you sing that song what was wrote for you special" (67). (318–19)

Olshin (following S. L. Bethell) argues that this motif points to the omnipotence of an invisible spiritual order that trivializes the impermanent and artificial drama at hand. I heartily disagree with Olshin's inference, based upon the simple logic that people who have chosen to compose themselves as a theatrical audience are unlikely to see the institution of the theater as negligible. (The same holds true, of course, for someone who has chosen to *write* a play.) On the contrary, playgoing is precisely what the audience members have all chosen to do at that given moment in time, so I believe that while part of the dramatic intent is certainly to extol the object of this drama, religious community, another very key part of the equation must be the analogous virtue of this theatrical experience. The prominence of theatricality in *The Rock* is simply another variant of Eliot's preaching to the converted in this play: he strokes the audience of Christian playgoers by lauding the efficacy of Christianity *and* of playgoing—continually reaffirming the virtues of this community of drama.

A vacuum of intellectual, spiritual, and cultural communities pervades *The Waste Land* and can be seen as the ultimate root of every inadequacy therein. Conversely, the presence of an enduring community infuses *The Rock* with strength and endurance. It seems, initially, that the Cockneys will be unable to meet their construction deadlines or to build the church's foundation on marshy ground; the rabble of discontented Unemployed Workers threatens to rise up in revolutionary fervor, as fanned by Redshirts, Blackshirts, Agitators, and Plutocrats; High Church aesthetes threaten to obscure the mission of the urban church with their obsessive attention to ceremony and detail. Nevertheless, the power inherent in a united community is destined to emerge victorious at the end of all this, just as all the ancient types, prototypes, and exemplars—Nehemiah, St. Peter, Mellitus, Rahere, Wren—have succeeded at their own similar enterprises amid the nurturing support of their own communities.

Eliot explicitly preaches this imperative twice in *The Rock,* both times through his Chorus:

> What life have you if you have not life together?
> There is no life that is not in community,
> And no community not lived in praise of GOD. (21; Chorus 2, 154, in
>   *Collected Poems*)

> Can you keep the City that the LORD keeps not with you?
> A thousand policemen directing the traffic
> Cannot tell you why you come or where you go. . . .
> Where there is no temple there shall be no homes,

Though you have shelters and institutions,
Precarious lodgings while the rent is paid,
Subsiding basements where the rat breeds
Or sanitary dwellings with numbered doors
Or a house a little better than your neighbour's;
When the Stranger says "What is the meaning of this city?
Do you huddle close together because you love each other?"
What will you answer? "We all dwell together
To make money from each other"? or "This is a community"? (30–31; Chorus 3,
    156, in *Collected Poems*)

In part 2, the Chorus urges that the citizens learn how to be penitent, then "learn the joyful communion of saints" (75); similarly subtle evocations of community-mindedness (note that Eliot invokes not saintliness *per se* but the *communion* of saints) pervade the pageant.

Eliot's methodology for promulgating community—in *The Rock* as in all his subsequent plays—is, simply, an uncompromised and wholehearted embrace of it: just say yes. Every aspect of his dramas (as of the world outside) relates to the community, has meaning only in terms of it, and is meaningless in the absence of it. This sensibility is certainly the single most significant aspect of Eliot's playwriting career: and so while numerous other critics argue that Eliot did not hit his stride in terms of an established, stable dramaturgy until as late as *The Family Reunion* or even *The Cocktail Party,* I suggest that all of Eliot's last six plays (and to some degree even his first one) are unified by this basic focus, the affirmation and attempted attainment of communities of drama. The community dynamics of the music hall and Christian dramaturgy infuse *The Rock,* assisted by the language of the 1930s style that locates itself keenly poised to speak in a language "where the words are valid": not surreal, convoluted, pedantic, anticommunicative, as in his poetry. Instead, it is accessible, straightforward, unmomentously—but nevertheless sincerely—accepted and understood. Seven lines from the end of the 1942 poem that brings his poetic works to a close, "Little Gidding," Eliot serenely embraces "[a] condition of complete simplicity" (209). This condition has in fact begun almost a decade earlier in *The Rock* and endures throughout his dramatic career.

CHRISTIAN COMMUNITIES?

Obviously, all these manifestations of community are intimately linked to Christianity; one is compelled to wonder whether Eliot believes that a community of drama can exist only within Christianity. This seems to be the case in *The Rock* and in some of Eliot's essays, such as "Religious Drama and the Church," *The Idea of a Christian Society,* and *Religious Drama: Mediaeval and Modern.* He writes in the last of these, for example, that all serious drama, religious or secular, must be more fully infused with Christian faith. And in *The Idea of a Christian Society* he describes modern society as "totalitarian democracy," akin to paganism and marked by "regimentation and conformity, without respect for the needs of the individual soul; the puritanism of a hygienic morality in the interest of efficiency; uniformity of opinion through propaganda, and art only encouraged when it flatters the official doctrines of the time" (18). The sole antidote to this society, Eliot suggests, "the only possibility of control and balance is a religious control and balance . . . the only hopeful course for a society which would thrive and continue its creative activity in the arts of civilization, is to become Christian" (19). Achieving such social unity in England, he adds, depends on accepting the Church of England's central role (37).

Yet what seems in *The Rock* to be a Christian imperative is not doctrinally imposed upon Eliot's later plays. Christianity defines the community he depicts in *The Rock* because it is the one he chose to join in 1927. Christianity is certainly a backdrop in his last four plays; but it is only a backdrop, gently and subtly allusive: the later plays are unequivocally *not* substantially Christian propaganda in the mode of *The Rock*. *The Waste Land* tried to encapsulate a universal condition that Eliot happened to locate (like himself) in London. In the plays, Eliot aims to counter the condition of *The Waste Land* with a similarly universal condition of community, which is similarly centered where he is at the time he writes the plays—that is, in a Christian venue—but which need not stop there or limit itself to this center.

So while *The Rock* manifestly demonstrates that Eliot's ideas of community in fruition originate in historical Christian culture, one can glean from this pageant play, beyond just this point, a methodology for creating community— just as *The Waste Land* and Eliot's poetry taught a methodology for perceiving the reality of the fragmented external modern world and shoring these fragments against the ruins. He writes in *The Idea of a Christian Society* that the paramount concern of the contemporary political philosopher (Eliot's voice in this essay) is not the creation of a Christian state but only of a just state generally. The present secular system must be improved, changed; it is "in the long run unworkable and conducive to disaster" (7). The changes Eliot advocates, "while deducible from Christian principles, can recommend themselves to any intelligent and disinterested person, and do not require a Christian society to carry them into effect, or Christian belief to render them acceptable" (7–8). Such changes, incidentally, may well bring about a Christian society, he continues, but it need not be the primary focus of the changes.

Given Eliot's notorious capability for clever rhetorical *legerdemain* throughout his prose, the astute reader might not take this disclaimer at face value: it sounds like someone cannily trying to allay suspicion that he is carrying out a specific agenda by raising the subject and simply denying that it is his concern. But as subsequent chapters will demonstrate, Eliot's later plays—even the explicitly Christian *Murder in the Cathedral*—indeed bear out his contention here that his primary concern is the depiction of a harmonious community, which happens to be Christian in orientation merely because that reflects Eliot's own particular present experience of community. He defines his ideal community in *The Idea of a Christian Society:* it happens to be "the Christian Community"[9] and its "traditional unit . . . in England is the parish" (23), but its definition transcends sectarian terminology or limitations and describes the communities of drama in all Eliot's plays. "It is the idea, or ideal, of a community small enough to consist of a nexus of direct personal relationships, in which all inequities and turpitudes will take the simple and easily appreciable form of wrong relations between one person and another" (25). Eloquent in its simplicity, this definition recalls Eliot's technique of localization in *The Rock* (as discussed earlier, with regard to his depictions of nearby deserts and literal neighbors) to make abstract ethical issues of community immediately comprehensible and accessible.

—————— 3 ——————

Murder in the Cathedral: "Our Eyes Are Compelled to Witness"

Both *The Rock* and *Murder in the Cathedral* are Christian dramas, sponsored by the same circle of people who promoted religious plays for explicitly Christian theatrical events. Both integrate passages of formal prayer and feature a prominent Chorus, which is arguably the most successful dramatic element and contains the best writing in both plays.[1] The latter play is strikingly more successful, better written, better received. Still, many critics group them together as jointly emblematic of Eliot's newfound and fervent religious commitment, or even regard the two works as a single enterprise.[2] These plays, written a year apart, are seen as representing something Eliot felt he had to make explicit or expunge from his system before going on to write *Four Quartets* and the final four plays, which draw upon a more subtle aesthetic.

But *The Rock* is not fully of a piece with *Murder in the Cathedral*. While *The Rock* offers numerous specific illustrations of historical communities, only in *Murder in the Cathedral* does Eliot begin to manifest an understanding of the general and *real* condition of community, as he will continue to do in his subsequent plays. He works toward a social portrait of the universal human condition, rather than the merely concrete matter at hand of getting a church built. *The Rock* expressed all the right ideas about community—ideas that form the foundation of Eliot's communities of drama—but did so two-dimensionally. The panorama in *Murder in the Cathedral* unstintingly teems with real considerations of human community and its consequent emotions: uncertainty, fear, betrayal, sacrifice, pride.

The play and interplay of emotions comprise a great part of the dramatic manifestation of community in *Murder in the Cathedral.* Eliot increasingly comes to appreciate the dramatic centrality of emotion as his theatrical career advances; the communities he will create must (at least ideally) allow individuals to give play to their emotions honestly and fully. Consider Harry's fervent dialogue with Mary about happiness, hope, and fear in *The Family Reunion*; Edward's lengthy and passionate unburdening to Reilly in *The Cocktail Party*; Sir Claude's heartfelt attempts to establish personal communion with Colby in *The Confidential Clerk* and his later painful endurance of Colby's resentment that accompanies their unleashing such emotionally potent forces. Another example is Lord Claverton's resolution to confront his past personal failures, however painfully, in order to foster honest relations with a community that encompasses those he loves as well as those who resent his past attitudes toward them. Eliot's drama becomes increasingly attuned to such focuses of emotionalism, in contrast to the repression that typifies Prufrock and the gentleman caller of "Portrait of a Lady." Freely confronted emotion is the core—messy, but necessary—of any community that its members will treat as truly meaningful. And, of course, it is the fodder of any drama that an audience will consider insightful and relevant.

Eliot begins to conjoin his philosophical and formal aesthetic agendas neatly in his playwriting with *Murder in the Cathedral.* The 1935 Canterbury production sharply marks his break with what he had come to consider the inadequate poetic that characterized his earlier poetry. I believe Eliot considered this earlier poetic not to be wrong or false but merely incomplete: it could not encompass the entirety of what he now felt his writing had to embody; it depicted the problems of human interaction but not the resolutions of these problems. No longer does he limit his writing with stylized rather than real emotion (such as the characters' affectations and poses in "Portrait of a Lady"), avoidance of emotion (typified by Prufrock's refusal to pose a question or confront a situation that threatens emotional intercourse), or nervously brash parody of human feelings (as in "Hysteria," *The Waste Land,* and copiously throughout *Sweeney Agonistes*). This new poetic—first manifested in *Murder in the Cathedral* and nurtured throughout all his subsequent drama and poetry—marks the most significant fulcrum of Eliot's half-century career. Though written only a year earlier than *Murder in the Cathedral,* and during a period when Eliot's personal and spiritual sensibility were of the same general timbre as when he publicly embarked upon the proliferation of this new voice, *The Rock,* by contrast, makes no firm commitment to this poetic of emotionally laden social interaction. In that play Eliot is content to rely on flat characters from Crusaders to Cockneys; confrontation of any emotional force is fairly irrelevant to the fundraising tableaux at hand. The copious parodies (of labor supporters, the working class, and high church debutantes, for example) displace a more sincere, vital sensibility.

TIME AND THE ARCHBISHOP

In his play about a twelfth-century cleric for production in the fourteenth-century chapter house of Canterbury Cathedral, Eliot expressed a particularly modern sense of his struggle for a language of drama.

"I wanted to bring home to the audience the contemporary relevance of the situation," Alethea Hayter quotes Eliot as saying; he told an interviewer he wrote the play as anti-Nazi propaganda (94). Archival evidence suggests that when Eliot was working on the film adaptation of *Murder in the Cathedral* in the 1940s (an adaptation that stayed close to the spirit of the original stage play), he was pointedly aware of its contemporary relevance. The T. S. Eliot Collection of manuscripts at King's College, Cambridge, includes a précis of various parts of E. G. Coulton's *Life in the Middle Ages* "prepared in connection with the film script," according to the archivists' description (item D1). The précis headed "Book I: Religion, Folklore and Superstition" shows attention to how past and present intersect. In discussing medieval anti-Semitic massacres, the précis notes, "Throughout Europe people were urged to kill and cast them out and forbidden to have anything to do with them unless they were converted to the Catholic faith—an exception in this primitive ages [*sic*] that stands favourable comparison with Hitler's sweeping degradations from 1931 onwards." In the précis titled "Book II: Chronicles, Science & Art": "In England 1346 [the year of English victory at Crécy, the first monumental land engagement of the Hundred Years War] was the precursor of 1940. . . . To defend itself, the nation stood to arms."

Discussing his work on the screenplay, Eliot wrote in a letter to the film's director, George Hoellering (Eliot Collection, item D1), that his intent was to present a vocabulary and structure that were not quite current but would not suggest to the audience any particular period style. Eliot meant his language to be untethered, and consequently fluent, interactive, between the play's twelfth-century setting and the audience's present—and encompassing as well, one supposes, all the times in between. He thus imbued his modern play with the temporal transcendence he admired in medieval drama, which "cared little about anachronisms and a great deal about the permanent elements of humanity," as he wrote in *Religious Drama: Mediaeval and Modern* (page 3 of unpaginated text). Carol Billman writes that *Murder in the Cathedral* adheres to the tradition in which "medieval dramatists make thematic use of departures from linear chronology to point up its long-range insignificance"; Eliot shows a "lack of interest in temporal history for its own sake" (47–48). All this indicates Eliot's intention to write a play that is not of an age but for all time.

An example of the nominally ancient play's easy intercourse with modernity is what Eliot called the Knights' "platform prose" (*Poetry and Drama,* 86)—the discourse of Becket's assassins expressed in a tenor evocative of windy, contemporary after-dinner speeches. Initially unsettling within the context, this conversation is quickly comprehensible as a dramatic statement. The assassins step out of medieval character in a sense, but, the audience eventually realizes, their mock-eloquent prose (and prosaic) cant is no more or less meaningful than anything they could say in any rhetorical style to justify their action—a crime Eliot finds as outrageous for its banality as for its inhumanity and sacrilege. Niloufer Harben calls the Knights' strange speech "a moment of Shavian irony intended to shock the audience out of over-emotional empathy to consider the situation as it relates to them" (105); this view is closely in accord with what Eliot himself said about bringing home the play's contemporary relevance to the audience and also with Eliot's apparent intentions for the work's vocabulary and structure as explained in his letter to Hoellering.

The sensibility of time that the play's language conveys may be understood by reference to the dazzling mobius-strip effect of temporality in *Four Quartets,* especially the meditations in part 1 of each poem. In "Burnt Norton," times present and past are somehow eternally conjoined with each other and with the future. (The poem's opening lines, which offer the most enduring paradigm of time in Eliot's later career, were originally written for *Murder in the Cathedral* but wound up in "Burnt Norton" after they were cut from the play.) In "East Coker," beginnings and endings are identical as time formulates a circular system; in "The Dry Salvages," time exists in a symbolically stylized realm (signified by sea voices and a tolling bell), which defies scientific chronometry or human memory; and at the opening of "Little Gidding," Eliot suggests a constitution of eternal time that both integrates and transcends natural time, moving toward an apotheosis of splendid ineffability evocative of Dante's luminous apex in *Paradiso.* A language that can communicate in and through this vast range of time, across the time span of what Eliot would consider civilized Europe, is well poised to offer a medium of communality for any of these times. Most important for Eliot, the language and the play can achieve this communality for his 1935 audience at the end point of the English and Christian community that had been initiated at places such as Canterbury Cathedral in the Middle Ages.

In *Four Quartets,* Eliot provides the *theoretical* and *philosophical* foundations that define his empowering awareness of what he believes to be the nature of time. (This postulation absolutely undercuts the debilitating skepticism of Bradleyan temporality Eliot expressed in such early poems as "Rhapsody on a Windy Night." There, time can encompass no larger a realm than what is offered by immediate experience, and the value of such experience is trivialized by the poem's exposition of what one actually experiences through such an immediate temporal perspective: 1:30 A.M., sputtering street lamp; 2:30, cat eating garbage out of the gutter; 4:00, toothbrush.) *Murder in the Cathedral* complements *Four Quartets* by offering the *practical* manifestations of the historically and temporally interactive awareness that Eliot would later intellectually crystallize in his final poetic sequence. Eliot meditates on the nature, frustrations, and possible power of time throughout his poetry and drama. Only in

Murder in the Cathedral, though, is time a real, necessary, and pragmatic issue in external, historical, and social realms. Certainly time is a fundamental component of *Four Quartets,* but even when it goes beyond theoretical and philosophical formulations, it does so essentially in a personal sense rather than a social sense. The poems celebrate reaching back in time to the texts and language of Eliot's English ancestor, Sir Thomas Elyot, in "East Coker" I, or the poet's personal communion with the Yeats-Dante specter in "Little Gidding" 2.

In Eliot's poetry before *Murder in the Cathedral,* time is either an aesthetic construct (the seasonal backgrounds in "Portrait of a Lady"; Tiresias' time-traveling cameo appearance in *The Waste Land*) or a nagging technical detail upstaged by modernist stylistic laissez-faire (as in the whimsical temporal fluctuations of "Gerontion" and *The Rock*). In *Murder in the Cathedral,* Eliot's task is to confront an incident that occurred nearly eight centuries earlier, understand the meaning of that incident in its own era, and present it so that it conveys some sort of meaning for the modern age. Throughout his career, time is Eliot's constant nemesis and bogey. *Murder in the Cathedral,* in its forthright and successful confrontation of time, represents the consummate challenge Eliot had to meet to be able to create dramatic communities with confidence: durable, meaningful communities that could withstand time.[3]

The play's initial exposition sets out a microcosm of how Eliot confronts time. As the action begins, Becket had been absent from his country and his people for seven years of exile. They were seven years of ostensible calm, but on a deeper level, the Chorus realizes, they were spiritually and intellectually false, unsettled, barren. Orderly households are all they have to show for the time of Becket's absence; this hiatus must end in a confrontation of weightier matters. The Chorus must understand and finally reject this little and empty piece of time past, in their time present, to prepare for a meaningful time future. Dealing with seven years that are fresh in their memory is a manageable task for the Canterbury citizens; the lessons they learn from it are applicable to Eliot's larger concerns about reconciling one's self and one's community with the nature and reality of time.

Carol Billman notes that *Murder in the Cathedral* prominently associates "time and timelessness . . . through allegorical juxtaposition"; Becket's "development from birth in innocence through sinful life to death and possible afterlife reflects the history of the human race." She offers as an example the Archbishop's confrontation with the Tempters, each of whom "sums up his thinking at a given stage in his life" (50). In the same way, the spiritual leader's seven-year exile represents a parallel allegorical juxtaposition of time and eternity for the Chorus, the community. As Thomas rejects out of hand seductive reminders of earlier times past—his period of worldly exuberance as "gay Tom," for example—he serves implicitly as a model for his Chorus.

All Eliot's subsequent plays are predicated upon a similar consciousness of time. Eliot contrasts a community that foundered in a fixed era of time past with one that is better poised to endure a time future. As in the tenet from the opening of *Four Quartets,* this favorable time future usurps and redeems time past in its renewal, acceptance, understanding. In *The Family Reunion,* Eliot pointedly contrasts the eight past years[4] Harry has been away from Wishwood with a future redeemed because he has confronted his ghosts. In *The Cocktail Party,* time past—the first five years of the Chamberlaynes' marriage, during which they failed to confront their marital problems (a hellish period, as Edward tells Reilly)—combines with the two years of time present (a purgatorio) that the play occupies between the first bad cocktail party and the second improved one; the Chamberlaynes' survival of this messy period betokens their newfound ability to proceed productively into a paradisiacal time future.[5] In *The Confidential Clerk,* an intricate time scheme (compiled as the characters attempt to sort out who did or knew what, when, about births, adoptions, and so forth) chronicles the lying "confidences" of the past, coexistent with Colby's life up to the present, which has been enmeshed in comic deceit perpetuated by unsatisfied egoists incapable of nurturance; this time is contrasted with a future promising truth and anagnorisis. And in *The Elder Statesman,* Gomez meticulously details the past time span of Claverton's deceits, which parallels the chronology of his career; at the close of the play, as Claverton sets his lands in order in the present, he leaves behind him at least the incipient germ of a revitalized family community that his daughter and her fiancé will carry into the future.

MEMORY, EMOTION, FEAR

In the last lines of *Murder in the Cathedral,* the Chorus's final prayer offers an especially modernist coda. The play has been moving toward a point where the audience is poised to carry on with the problems and realities of its own time, thanks to Eliot's having slogged through preceding time. The penultimate strophe offers a lengthy and conventional homage to the glory, omnipotence, and pervasiveness of God's holy and beneficent spirit. The final strophe, though, focuses on the shortcomings of our modern culture, our society, our zeitgeist—very much in the terms established by *The Waste Land*—as opposed to a prayer's more conventional apologia for our tainted mortal shells. The strophe begins,

> Forgive us, O Lord, we acknowledge ourselves as type of the common man,
> Of the men and women who shut the door and sit by the fire;
> Who fear the blessing of God, the loneliness of the night of God, the surrender required, the deprivation inflicted;
> Who fear the injustice of men less than the justice of God;
> Who fear the hand at the window, the fire in the thatch, the fist in the tavern, the push into the canal,
> Less than we fear the love of God. (87–88)

At the play's conclusion, Eliot's Chorus essentially prays: Forgive us our infinite mediocrity, forgive us our modernity. Using the same kind of condensed "Audenesque" 1930s style he had used in *The Rock,* Eliot connotes images of mundane and ubiquitous contemporaneity: isolation, alienation, petty violence both natural and human. Most important—and exactly in the mode of *The Waste Land*—he connotes *fear:* fear of all the specific threats he catalogues and beyond this a general panorama of fear indulged in by tepid and timid humanity. (The play's original title, in fact, had been *Fear in the Way.*) Such fears as Marie's in part 1 of *The Waste Land* are never demonstrably vanquished—these fears are, rather, encouraged and nurtured by such masochistically entrancing expressions as "I will show you fear in a handful of dust" (54); the poem's audience eagerly devours this fearful display. Given an adulating fascination with such fears, *The Waste Land* fails to achieve the spiritual ideal it almost fantastically suggests in part 5, "The awful daring of a moment's surrender" (68). The end of *Murder in the Cathedral* is similarly implanted in human inadequacy, the incapability of—actually, fear of—what the Chorus here calls "the surrender required." In *Murder in the Cathedral,* as in *The Waste Land,* Eliot's subject is the pervasive threat of mediocrity in time present and the relationship between this time present and a time future in which people may fare better or at least improve their lots by developing a more insightful perspective on the immediate moment—its fears, its pettiness. (Despite the fearful failure described above, an improved vision of time future *is* present in *The Waste Land,* in the voice of the thunder: this vision is at least a hope, even if, as suggested, it is unattainable within the terms the poem establishes.)

Murder in the Cathedral seems to conclude as Eliot's earlier poetry did: with pessimistic consciousness of the last twist of the knife, fragments shored against the ruins, a whimper instead of a bang. Besides the anticlimactic final prayer of mediocrity and fear, the Chorus's last speech is laden with recurrent compromise and banality. As they intone to God "we . . . praise thee" (86–87)—seemingly the simplest rote words of praise to formulate—a boggling fifty-four words intercede between subject and verb to dampen what might be an expression of salvation: words of hesitancy and qualification, apposite self-denigration of "we" ("the scrubbers and sweepers of Canterbury, / The back bent under toil, the knee bent under sin, the hands to the face under fear, the head bent under grief"). The Chorus's attempt to pay homage to the site's holiness after the martyrdom is similarly mitigated, cheapened, by copious concessions to, first, the inevitability of violent worldly invasion; next, cultural banality; and finally, vintage inescapable wastelandishness:

> There is holy ground, and the sanctity shall not depart from it
> Though armies trample over it, though sightseers come with guide-books looking
>   over it;
> From where the western seas gnaw at the coast of Iona,
> To the death in the desert, the prayer in forgotten places by the broken imperial
>   column. (87)

Once again, what might otherwise be a simple, formulaic, fairly easy statement
of devotion—hardly very radical—is pathetically compromised, qualified to
near obscurity. *Murder in the Cathedral* ends with the apparent failure of
Thomas's community of faith and courage, a failure to transcend human pettiness and fears. Becket's parishioners, his community, remain unable to lift their
line of sight very convincingly beyond the pedestrian realities of loneliness and
pub squabbles. Replete with unresolved tensions between time and eternity,
mortality and spirituality, the play finally "does not declaim but suggests,"
writes Carol Billman; it bears the firm imprint of modernism "in its incorpora-
tion of puzzling ambiguities and explorations of man's doubt-full struggle to
find his place in history and the cosmos" (54). The author himself offers an
apology for this community's minimal accomplishments: "Human kind cannot
bear very much reality" (69).

But despite all these heavily mitigating strains, *Murder in the Cathedral* rises
above the pessimistic morass that characterized Eliot's earlier poetry. Its final
achievement is neither ideal nor dismal: it is, rather, at a point somewhere in
between on a continuum that implicitly defines both the ideal and dismal end
points. The continuum measures how the community confronts time morally
and historically—how it appreciates time, which indicates how well it is poised
to survive through time. The ideal way of surviving is presented at the conclusion to *Four Quartets,* where all shall be well in a harmony of poetry, philosophy, and spirituality that have matured in time. (The endings of Eliot's works
show his sentiment about the condition of the present and its promise for the
future. The ending represents the last moment in which a reader exists in a
work's "present" and is the closest that the text comes to the future; it is the
springboard, the leaping-off point.) At the other extreme is "Gerontion," representing the abysmal incompetence of the moral intellect to appreciate its place
in time (and its responsibility of existing in time and somehow advancing
within these temporal forces). The title character, a historical spectator, has had
ample opportunity to observe forces moving from past, through present, toward
future; yet he is stodgily determined *not* to use his experience to reform or
improve his interaction with time and history. Gerontion's condition is identical
at the beginning and end of the poem, representing a horrible stasis. Technically, he possesses a working human intellect, as he has made at least "a thousand small deliberations"; yet these result in absolutely no fecund product:
merely "[t]houghts of a dry brain in a dry season" (31). Like Prufrock, Gerontion does not disturb the universe by acting on his perceptions of inadequacy;
much less does he work to resolve them.

The location of *Murder in the Cathedral* on this spectrum of temporal consciousness may be elucidated by recourse to one of Eliot's "Ariel Poems,"
"The Cultivation of Christmas Trees," from 1954; this poem nicely parallels,
in miniature, the point Eliot embeds in the play. In the last lines of that poem
he depicts the nature of an average person at life's end (which is, like the end

of a poem, the perfect place to observe both a moral trajectory and a temporal one: at the boundary between time present and time future):

> before the end, the eightieth Christmas
> (By "eightieth" meaning whichever is the last)
> The accumulated memories of annual emotion
> May be concentrated into a great joy
> Which shall be also a great fear, as on the occasion
> When fear came upon every soul:
> Because the beginning shall remind us of the end
> And the first coming of the second coming. (107–108)

The way Eliot appraises "emotion" as he surveys what endures of a life at its end accords perfectly with his focus on emotions in *Murder in the Cathedral* (and throughout his plays). "Memories of emotion" is an especially appropriate emblem of emotions that have been controlled, captured, fixed, appraised, freed from the volatility of emotions in action. In this sense, the phrase approximates the nature of emotions in drama, where they are similarly controlled and captured (as opposed to the volatile unpredictability of emotions in life). Emotion connotes time present, while memories connote time past; the conjunction of the two situates the poem's reader or play's audience poised to synthesize the two terms of this triad into the third. *Murder in the Cathedral* represents a historical enactment of "memories of emotion"—a study of how, in the cultural "memory" of time past, Thomas Becket dealt with his emotions, temptations, weaknesses, and aspirations in his time present. As in Eliot's subsequent plays, this study of times past and present leaves the audience poised to plunge into time future.

The emotions in "The Cultivation of Christmas Trees" are composed of joy as well as fear, with fear dominant (as the Canterbury women's emotions are pervaded by fears). The poem's last lines show how it, like *Murder in the Cathedral,* demonstrates a social advance embodied beyond the condition of "Gerontion." A lesson has been learned and put into action. Something that happened earlier will "remind" us of something that happens subsequently: this learned action manifests itself in temporal progression. Time moves forward, and the human intellect advances along with it. The verb, "remind," is poetically and intellectually meek, tepid; it does not ring with the tenor of a moral victory over the forces of ignorance or barren dryness. Will those who have been reminded *act* upon their memory of what has happened in the past and use it to act more positively in the future? Eliot makes no promises here, and yet we have (even if only marginally) more cause to be optimistic than pessimistic about this possibility, since the poem has at least transcended the condition of stasis and carries a momentum that is pointed in the right direction.

The ending of this poem functions like the end of *Murder in the Cathedral,* where unconvincing conventional prayer serves as a cover story for more potent modernist fears lurking just beneath. Eliot's saint's play is not a resounding affirmation of uncompromised spiritual faith; it is, rather, a somewhat frail indication that the playwright is willing, for the first time, to attempt to imagine a story whose ending points in a direction that may indicate a morally upward trajectory rather than a wastelandish mire. Just as the signs of a child's first logical development is his ability to establish a relationship between two events or conditions—cause and effect, for example—so Eliot here depicts people and communities who have achieved this state: in "Cultivation," people for whom time past (the beginning) bears a discernable relation to time future, and in *Murder in the Cathedral,* a community for whom a martyrdom illustrates the condition of their present fears and weaknesses and yet sets them in some way poised to use the martyrdom as a guide for their own moral lives: to inspire them to sacrifice, personally, for the sake of the community.[6]

THE SAINT AND THE CITIZENS, MODERNIST STYLE

The play's ending marks it as unmistakably modernist, uncompromisingly mired in the modern world. But, of great importance—and this is the advance in Eliot's social vision over his predramatic sensibility—the play deposits its audience in the modern world, having explored, along the way, not just banality and fear as in *The Waste Land* but beyond these, the life of a saint.

Following Eliot's lead, I must, however, qualify this characterization of Becket as saint. The Becket of *Murder in the Cathedral* is a character historically and institutionally revered as a saint, and not unjustly so in Eliot's view, albeit not especially glamorized here. Traditional hagiographic motifs such as fervent faith and personal atonement for previous sins occur mainly in the play's background, in the historically richer picture of Thomas Becket that Eliot knew a Canterbury Cathedral audience would possess, but not prominently within the drama itself. The play displays not so much a conventional saint as a man, a rather good man making rather good decisions about tough issues— whether and how to choose morality over expediency, resisting temptations. No director of the play should use lighting to suggest anything like a halo hovering over Becket's brow during the action. He is a man making his decisions among a community of men and women, not a community of saints. It is the task of Eliot's modern communities, following in the footsteps of the medieval Canterbury community, to recognize and emulate Thomas's triumph by making rather good decisions. Eliot's original audience was, of course, facilitated in this enterprise by being physically present at the site of the play's climax—a brilliant dramatic effect and one that many subsequent producers have appropriated by performing the play in cathedrals.

It is pointedly the Chorus of citizens, rather than the hero-saint, who speak the closing words. They embody whatever real gains and moral enlightenment are suggested by the experience of this play: the formation of a community based upon common exposure to and adaptation of a common set of values and experiences. Early in the play, the priests affirm this social imperative: when Becket's return to Canterbury is imminent, the Second Priest says,

> The Archbishop shall be at our head, dispelling dismay and doubt.
> He will tell us what we are to do, he will give us our orders, instruct us. . . .
> We can lean on a rock, we can feel a firm foothold
> Against the perpetual wash of tides of balance of forces of barons and land-
> holders.
> The rock of God is beneath our feet. (17–18)

The search for stability and assurance amid the chaos of the surrounding world is successful here, early in the play, for the Priests. This search reenacts Eliot's prototypical modernist quest. Prufrock, gentlemen callers, street wanderers, and numerous other characters from Eliot's poetry undergo the same quest; in those poems, though, the quest is (tormentingly) personal, whereas in Eliot's drama it takes the form of a socioreligious quest for community. The quest here is fulfilled in a way that it is not in the poetry: here the Priests stand upon "the rock of God"; at the end of "Prufrock" the protagonist finds only unstable, ephemeral sand beneath his feet, and at the end of *The Waste Land* the terrain supports no more than fallen towers and fragmented ruins.

The Priests quickly find their social foundation in *Murder in the Cathedral*. (*The Rock,* trumpeting the church's strength to an audience of churchgoers, essentially equaled what the Priests have done in the passage quoted above; Eliot's use there, twice, of the image of *the rock* of God is perhaps a reference to his previous play.) The mission is enormously easier for the Priests, who are already part of the community energized by the Archbishop's return, than for the Canterbury citizens. The Chorus is a harder sell, although, of course, worth the trouble, since it is only their awakening and inclusion that will mark the value of this play's achievement.

CHORUS/AUDIENCE

Like Becket's Chorus, Eliot's own "parishioners"—the community of his theater audience—return to a world that, after the experience of Thomas's devotion (Thomas Eliot's in 1935 no less than Thomas Becket's in 1170), remains essentially as it was before. Given the medieval setting and Eliot's admiration for ritual and tradition, Eliot must be congratulated for having avoided the obvious pitfall of an arcadian and reactionary solution to the problems posed in this play as he wallowed in an arcadian Christian nostalgia in *The Rock*. The deflationary tenor at the end of *Murder in the Cathedral* announces his pragmatic realism. He means for his audience to value the moment of awareness, and of community, that they have had. This experience—"catharsis" is too strong a term—does not magically wipe away oppressively mundane realities, but it informs these realities so the community that has undergone the shared experience may be a few inches closer to using that experience beneficially. From the very first lines, Eliot makes clear that the play is not primarily about Thomas's martyrdom but about the effect on his community of this martyrdom. The Chorus, in the play's sixth line, announces that the impending dramatic action itself is less significant than its effect upon them:

> Some presage of an act
> Which our eyes are compelled to witness, has forced our feet
> Towards the cathedral. We are forced to bear witness. (11)

The nature of the "act" is only vaguely connoted, but the dramatic centrality of the community's role in this act is made paramount by the striking image of compelled witnessing and the rhetorically insistent repetition of this compulsion: "compelled to witness . . . forced to bear witness."

These opening lines have a deeper metadramatic resonance in terms of the issue of witnessing. Eliot makes the Chorus identically coexistent with the play's audience, whose feet in June 1935 have similarly come to Canterbury Cathedral and who also are compelled to witness what is to follow. The etymological root of "martyr" is "witness." In a sense, the real martyrs in this play, with its focus on earthly rather than saintly community, are the Chorus of witnesses who live on to deal with the aftermath of Becket's martyrdom, an event that is not validated until it is witnessed, appreciated, acted upon. This etymology heightens the vicarious connection between Chorus as martyr-witness and audience as pure witness, thus martyr, and by extrapolation the figurative hero of *Murder in the Cathedral*. Eliot fully exploits a Brechtian sensibility: that the essential consequence of a play is its impact on the audience and that dramatic historical analysis must serve to bring the past into the present with an eye toward using its lessons to affect and improve the future.

Niloufer Harben expands on this play's Brechtian motif, writing, "Right through the play Eliot can be found continually distancing the audience from the surface of the action in order to involve it on a rational plane. . . . Eliot is not averse to making the audience aware of its own identity and the fact of performance" (106). Harben explains how Brecht uses drama to promote change and how Eliot does the same: Brecht provides

a complex, multidimensional vision, through his registering of alternative points of view, so that the audience is drawn in to consider a predicament from different perspectives. A world is no longer dramatized mainly from the inside. The point of reference shifts from an internal to an external consciousness, and a situation is held apart, observed, and entered into from the outside. Eliot similarly can be found distancing the audience from the action intermittently, and moving in the direction of self-conscious theatricality in *Murder in the Cathedral*. He too presents the world depicted from the outside, enabling the audience to see the situation depicted in terms of a wider historical reference.

He also includes the sense of a historical situation being overtaken by the course of history and rendered anachronistic by subsequent developments. (111)

At the end of part 1, Eliot (in the mode of Brecht) appeals pointedly to the audience through the Chorus. He engages the playgoer vicariously and insistently, as Becket describes the sense of cosmic interrelatedness that begins to make sense, for him, of the impending martyrdom:

> I know that history at all times draws
> The strangest consequence from remotest cause.
> But for every evil, every sacrilege,
> Crime, wrong, oppression and the axe's edge,
> Indifference, exploitation, you, and you,
> And you, must all be punished. So must you. (45–46)

The obvious referent for "you" would be each Tempter in turn; and a more clever resonance might be the anticipation of the four Knights, and his awareness of betrayal. (In many productions, the roles of the Tempters and Knights are doubled, augmenting this resonance.)

But this reading is not fully exhaustive, not completely attuned to the nature of Becket's character at this point. I believe that Becket has by the end of part 1 already confronted and transcended his fourth temptation (of power, pride, self-obsession). He is, then, no longer primarily concerned with his own fate, his own person—and thus would not be strongly concerned with accusations, revenge, or earthly quibbles with Tempters or Knights. Becket has already begun to prepare the community at large to benefit from his death. (His sermon, in the interlude immediately following this scene, explores the paradox of Christmas being a time of rejoicing amid mourning, alluding to the life that can come out of death, the beneficial that can result from the horrific.)

The most important thing Thomas can accomplish in his remaining few days on earth, Eliot must feel, is to begin to lay the foundation for a community that can endure. Thus, the Archbishop's reference to "you, and you" who must be punished should be directed toward the Chorus: like all descendants of Adam and Eve, the Chorus, as part of a human community, must suffer punishment. They suffer also the punishing trials of the righteous (typologically reenacting the life of the martyr) and, amid the milieu of modernism, simply the suffering and punishment resultant from living in a world turned upside down.

An insightful directorial interpretation of these lines would be for Thomas to speak these lines while vaguely gesturing toward the Tempters (a different one with each "you") who are immediately in front of him; but these individual gestures should suggest that the Archbishop is simultaneously pointing at and *through* a Tempter, to a member of the Chorus behind each one: skewering, as it were, Tempter and citizen at the same time. The morally compromised Tempters are most complicit in the guilt that Thomas announces will be discovered and punished; but equally implicated are the common women who form (in my blocking) a background to the Tempters. The Chorus members are, seemingly, innocent bystanders—part of the society that had experienced (in the historical prelude to the play) personal, governmental, and clerical corruption. The point of including them in Thomas's accusation is that society must accept collective responsibility for its guilt before the sacrifice of a would-be martyr can effectuate a collective salvation.

And to add a final layer to Becket's dramatic force as he announces the involvement of "you, and you" in this community, Thomas might further "skewer" individual audience members through—beyond—Tempters and Canterbury women. "You" becomes us, the audience, although we would have assumed (as the Chorus did) that we were innocent bystanders. The Chorus members would certainly respond with anxious discomposure at being included in Thomas's indictment, sharing a punishment that only the Tempters would seem to have merited. The audience would take its cue from the Chorus: we are at least as unsettled as they are, probably more so, by this unexpected engagement in the play's moral condition.

THE POINT OF A DUBIOUS COMMUNITY

The Chorus shows considerable hesitancy to enter into Thomas's incipient community, which manifestly promises widespread suffering. *Murder in the Cathedral* offers other seemingly unauspicious community visions: each of the Tempters offers his own slick, convincing, albeit morally bankrupt, prescription for establishing what he promises will be a stable community, such as the Third Tempter's promise of "a happy coalition / Of intelligent interests" (33).

Why all these dubious visions of community? A reader-response approach will best explain them: the point of reading *Paradise Lost,* Stanley Fish argues, is avoiding such pitfalls as Satan's compelling attractiveness, thereby demonstrating "proper" Christian values. Eliot's audience, similarly, must wade through a morass of unpromising community visions to appreciate, all the more, the one that will finally work at the end (or beyond the ending). Fish's seminal formulation of reader response in *Surprised by Sin* is worth examining at some length, especially since the intricacies of a text explicitly designed for the moral improvement of a Christian audience form a common bond between Milton's and Eliot's texts. Milton's reader, Fish writes, "is surprised and disconcerted by unforeseen difficulties" (206)—difficulties paralleled in *Murder in the Cathedral* by the seeming paradox of Becket's martyrdom, which is traditionally supposed to be an unmitigated apotheosis, but which is met with a consistently lukewarm reception by its most important witnesses, the Chorus.

Further, Fish continues, Milton's reader is "humbled by the discovery of his inadequacy, revived by a kind word or a momentary success, thrown back again by a new error; and thus he stumbles through the poem. . . . Milton asks us to respond fully to each of his effects and yet be prepared to discount one or all of them in the light of better knowledge" (206–207). Eliot offers his readers this experience through each Tempter, whose rhetorical and dramatic force ensures that we "respond fully to each effect" and whose *more forceful* rhetorical and dramatic undercutting by Becket represents the "better knowledge" that compels the audience to discount them.

"We must commit ourselves and not commit ourselves at the same time," Fish writes, "moving between the immediate experience of the poetry and the acknowledged authority of a 'hard and definite outline,' remaining open to the first while awaiting (not demanding) the guidance of the second" (207). Fish's use of the Bradleyan terminology ("immediate experience") that was so influential to the younger Eliot nicely augments the applicability of *Surprised by Sin* to Eliot's career. *Murder in the Cathedral,* a fulcrum in Eliot's career, draws upon aesthetics and sensibilities present in both the earlier and later phases of his oeuvre. The terms of Fish's dichotomy can be smoothly appropriated to explicate Eliot's tensions, and those of his readers, at this fulcrum. The outlook embodied in "immediate experience," which infused Eliot's pre-conversion poetry, has not disappeared from *Murder in the Cathedral.* But at the same time, the presence of a "hard and definite outline," a phrase Fish borrows from H. R. Swardson, also makes competing claims upon Eliot's audience through the play's compulsions of witnessing, sacrifice, and sanctifying community. This medieval community *does* have a definite outline, as defined by the sacrifice, expectations, and teaching of the Archbishop. Eliot's earlier poetic communities, as mediated by the solipsist's immediate experience, had few (if any) outlines, boundaries, or forces of cohesion.

Milton's readers may well give up trying to understand him in the face of these difficulties, as Swardson argues, but Fish counters that such surrender is only "our temptation, not our duty or inevitable fate" (207)—again, Fish's reference to temptations strengthens the relevance to Eliot's text, which personifies its Tempters. Fish calls *Paradise Lost* "a profoundly disturbing experience which produces something akin to a neurosis; the natural inclination to read on vies with a fear of repeating old errors and encountering new frustrations. In this, the poem is a microcosm of the world and the difficulties of reading are to be equated with the difficulties of the earthly pilgrimage. The reader's sphere of action is the poem, and his heroism, like Abraham's, is in going on (or out), in accepting—on faith—the supposition that local failures and discomforts are preludes to a larger success that awaits him under the aegis of a controlling and inspired mind. Submitting to the style of the poem is an act of self-humiliation"—which I see paralleled by the audience's self-humiliation lurking in Thomas's accusation of "you, and you" at the end of part 1, as they submit to the play they have elected to attend. "Like all heroic acts it is a decision to subordinate the self to a higher ideal, one by-product of which is the discovery of the true self. The imperative is 'read!' and by not giving up, by not closing the book, by accepting the challenge of self-criticism and self-knowledge, one learns how to read, and by extension how to live, and becomes finally the Christian hero who is, after all, the only fit reader" (207). Fish's paradigm perfectly suits my own for *Murder in the Cathedral:* his ideal reader becomes my ideal audience member, ideal witness; given the inherent social nature of drama, Fish's imperative of the text teaching us how to live is all the more relevant to Eliot's imperative for community.

Like Milton, Eliot does not make his audience's task easy. As the audience approaches the incarnation of incipient community, there is nothing like the descent of The Rock, as in his last play, to announce eternal harmony. This play's "triumph" is more fragile and human—weak, but a *brave* weakness for Eliot. In 1935, he dares to make the kind of uncertain and necessarily tentative venture out onto a limb, with no promise of obvious success, that Prufrock was unable to make when he could only mumble, "Do I dare?"—and didn't.

The Chorus initially fears its compelled presence described in the play's opening lines, as, indeed, it will continue to fear it at the end of the play. But it is simply and totally what they must do: it is their function in the play, and it must be their mission (and the audience's) in life, to witness. How they process what they witness takes place outside of the bounds of the play and is less assured—certainly, it is less dramatically presentable—than the thrilling murder.[7]

AUDEN REDUX

The memorable refrain Eliot uses to indicate the Chorus's condition—far from accord with the Priests' smug confidence about their "firm foothold" upon the foundational "rock of God"—is "[l]iving and partly living" (19, *passim*). At the play's opening, the Canterbury women are a recapitulation of all Eliot's earlier poetic personae (who were, at best, "partly living") in the throes of modernism, alienation, incommunicability, anomie. The Chorus might perfectly well be composed of Prufrock, Aunt Helen Slingsby, Professor and Mrs. Channing-Cheetah, and the guests from Sweeney's party.

Eliot portrays this condition of partly living similarly, yet not identically, to the way he portrayed it in his poetry. To amplify his presentation of what it means to be "partly living," he draws strongly and explicitly upon the Audenesque, as in *The Rock,* and with generally the same intent, but with even more widespread application here.

In numerous places, the play's tenor, vocabulary, poetic, syntax, and rhythm are strongly indebted to Auden's early poetry; and plentiful examples of what seem like literal borrowings can be found as well. What an early critic called the " 'Audenesque trick' of the knights' prose address to the audience . . . might well derive from Father Christmas's initial entry in *Paid on Both Sides*" (144), writes Steve Ellis. He characterizes Auden's influence upon Eliot's dramatic prosody, noting

how concerned Eliot was in his dramatic writing of the 1930s to "avoid any echo of Shakespeare" [quoted from *Poetry and Drama*], leading him to eschew the iambic pentameter and introduce light syllables into his lines to break up regular stress in the interests of a "conversational" tone. . . . Writers like Auden (and the classic example would be his poem "Spain") deliberately use the technique in a similar rejection of "poeticality," the preference of the flat over the ornamented voice, impassive and what we might now call "laid back." (147)

Auden's early poetry was strongly influenced by Eliot's, in the younger poet's presentation and adaptation of modernist wastelands and angst. In 1935, Eliot seems to make recourse to his own earlier poetic via Auden, as modified and tinkered with by Auden. (Remember that Faber & Faber published Auden, under Eliot's aegis, so Eliot could consider himself as having a kind of proprietary relationship to the Audenesque.) "[A]ny interchange between Eliot and Auden . . . was two-way" (143–44), writes Ellis. The Audenesque strain of Eliotic modernism confronts Prufrock et al. and their anguishes *not* in the realm of solipsism but in a social setting. The pain Eliot's dramatic characters experience is not egotism (that is, intellectual isolation) but social isolation.

Auden's cast of characters includes spies, soldiers, and strangers, with their sides, teams, countries all broken down into tormenting us-versus-them divisions. They represent barriers to an ideal, clearly affirmed society or even to just some apparition or fantasy thereof. (Auden's social ideal is evoked by, for instance, the "street music" of home that seems, in retrospect, "gracious" in "Control of the passes was, he saw, the key"; the "first garden party of the year" in "Consider this and in our time"; the bonding, storytelling, and camaraderie in "To my Pupils"; and so forth. These elusive ideals are all envisioned, but then somehow withdrawn or dissipated, in Auden's early poetry.) Auden's vision contrasts with the sensibility of Eliot's early poetry, where the barriers created by the modernist condition shut out an abstractly intellectualized vision of European culture rather than a concretely envisioned community. (Eliot's portrait of European culture is as a privileged patriarchal domain which, as Sandra Gilbert and Susan Gubar argue [253–57], no longer actually exists when Eliot writes, even as he belatedly bemoans its decline.)

The Audenesque social isolation represents the fundamental shift of course, then, by which Eliot's poetic relocates, or adjusts, its focus on a "waste land" vision in *Murder in the Cathedral*. Eliot uses the Audenesque to localize his vision (at least relatively) from a barren intellectual landscape that defies a concise physical location to a troubled social venue that is more easily pinpointed and confronted. Explicating Eliot's appropriation of the Audenesque will establish a paradigm of the influence that extends profusely throughout the play. The Chorus laments:

> We have had various scandals,
> We have been afflicted with taxes,
> We have had laughter and gossip,
> Several girls have disappeared
> Unaccountably, and some not able to.
> We have all had our private terrors,
> Our particular shadows, our secret fears. (20)

The girls who disappear unaccountably evoke Auden's poem "To my Pupils" from *The Orators* (1932): "Why, that girl who rode off on her bicycle one fine summer evening / And never returned" (23)—one of Auden's array of "unlucky" ones enmeshed in personal and moral scandals. The kinds of incidents that afflict the Chorus and the way of denoting them in the passage above— "various scandals," "private terrors," "particular shadows," "secret fears" — pervade Auden's poetry of the late 1920s and early 1930s. Compare

- with Eliot's various scandals, Auden's

> banker we'd noticed
> Worried for weeks;
> Till he failed to arrive one morning and his room was empty,
> Gone with a suitcase (23)

- with Eliot's private terrors, Auden's supreme Antagonist, which generates

> rumour, soft
> But horrifying in its capacity to disgust
> Which, spreading magnified, shall come to be
> A polar peril, a prodigious alarm (15)

- with Eliot's particular shadows, Auden's image:

> Beams from your car may cross a bedroom wall,
> They wake no sleeper (1)

- with Eliot's secret fears, Auden's ears that "poise before decision, scenting danger" (1).

Eliot's language is tame, bureaucratically abstract; yet at the same time, his sketchy generalities carry the force of the oppressively Kafkaesque (later, Orwellian and Sartrean) horrors of the age: a terror that is aimless and uncertain but none the less potent for that. Part of the horror is precisely that it *is* so hard to define (and thus combat or defuse) yet readers and audiences accept, on perversely modernist "faith," that the wastelands, the alienating forces, are incontrovertibly extant. Phrases such as "secret fears" and "private terrors" should not patently send shivers up one's spine; they lack colorful, convincing, vivid illustration and characterization. But the language *does,* paradoxically, horrify, precisely in its casually fatalistic sense of abandonment to an unarguable (because unidentifiable) presence. The audience may, initially, mock at the Chorus's complaint of its "afflictions": taxes! How banal and ubiquitous; everyone is afflicted with taxes. But this is precisely Eliot's point: it is those things with which everyone in the community is afflicted that—*consequently*—embody the greatest terror. (What precisely does Eliot think is done with these taxes? It is not too far a jump to surmise that they could be used to fund such public institutions as the judicial system in Kafka's *The Trial;* so, there is indeed potential affliction.)

THE DIALECT OF THE TRIBE

Eliot's primary challenge as verse dramatist in *Murder in the Cathedral* parallels Becket's impatient attempt to put into words—comprehensible to the Priests and the crowds of Canterbury women—a sense of his community mission. Becket's drive to assert the church's independent and divinely ordained power, which will be confirmed in his martyrdom, matches Eliot's assertion of an eloquently confident and "valid" voice of dramatic community. Each is convinced, at the *beginning* of his enterprise, of its fatedness, its possible perfection (although this perfection is dependent upon the quotidian vagaries of mortality and of other people). Both Thomases struggle to deal with the pedestrian details that in many ways come harder to them than the martyrdom. Becket's martyrdom is, of course, literal. Eliot's analogous figurative mission is the crowning touch to what had been going on in his life throughout the decade since he first tentatively ventured into the theater: his is the martyrdom of the confirmed solipsist (which perhaps he always remained at heart, despite his stance of renunciation and communality) who agrees to expose himself, venturing out into the external world, where people can routinely affect him, touch him, hurt him, oppress him, even if their reality remains somewhat suspect to the solipsist.

Both Becket and Eliot finally succeed, finding mortal communication harder than divine but realizing that a divine discourse achieved alone would simply be a higher variant of solipsism, which is as unacceptable to Thomas Becket in 1170 as to Thomas Eliot in 1935.[8] Eliot's desperate line from *Sweeney Agonistes,* "I gotta use words when I talk to you," would fit perfectly early in part 1 as Becket and the Chorus grope for satisfactory expression. Poetically, *Murder in the Cathedral* retains remnants of Eliot's previous styles, especially early in the play. His language integrates what is strongest and most important from his early *poesis,* while at the same time shaping it, making it conducive to his agenda of refining and developing his voice organically (and showing this organic progression before the audience's eyes in the play). The development moves toward what he envisions as the more durable poetic that marks his later work—"where the words are valid." A close reading establishes a paradigm regarding this development: in the second strophe of the play's first speech, the Canterbury women anxiously describe the tenor of their world.

> Since golden October declined into sombre November
> And the apples were gathered and stored, and the land became brown sharp points
>   of death in a waste of water and mud,
> The New Year waits, breathes, waits, whispers in darkness.
> While the labourer kicks off a muddy boot and stretches his hand to the fire,
> The New Year waits, destiny waits for the coming. (11–12)

The first of these lines echoes the seasonal obsession from all Eliot's earliest poetry: there is sullen, subdued resentment at the rhythmically and mechanically amoral cycles of nature, which impassively continue in their procession heedless of anything occurring "beneath" them. These stolid forces of nature mock inept human attempts to create an order that would be analogous to theirs. Think of the bleakly horrible plaint, "April is the cruellest month" (which is even more closely evoked later in the same choral passage: "Now I fear disturbance of the quiet seasons . . . Ruinous spring shall beat at our doors" [12]). Although Eliot has been struggling for over a decade to confront abstract forces of oppression on human terms, he still cannot overcome his conviction of April's vernal cruelty.[9]

Sparked by the first line, this whole passage connotes Eliot's recurrent poetic motif of dislocated natural cycles. Compare the line "I read, much of the night, and go south in the winter" (53), from *The Waste Land*; the menacing and insidious October night in "Prufrock"; the December afternoon, April (but August-like) afternoon, and October night, respectively, in the three sections of "Portrait of a Lady," that seem like conspirators in the Lady's deviously arranged scene: as if the seasons have somehow positioned themselves to taunt the gentleman caller with his alienation from rituals and patterns and his inability to control the large, overarching natural cycles that govern our lives.

Still, while the Chorus's image of golden October declining into sombre November looks back to these fairly psychotic seasonal conceits, it is at the same time more tempered, less manifestly threatening, in its depiction of natural cycles and change. The procession from October to November is at least more chronologically comprehensible and orderly—one month to the next—as compared to the erratic December-April-(August-)October scheme in "Portrait of a Lady." The shift from a "golden" season to a "sombre" one, while devolutionary, is less stark than the outright cruelty of Eliot's 1922 April. And the passage from *Murder in the Cathedral* seems more of a system unto itself, and thus less caustic to the people caught in its wake, than in Eliot's earlier poetry. The image shows nature operating in what is essentially its own self-enclosed domain, with ripening, harvests, and fields. People are delicately excluded, absent by virtue of the poet's passive construction ("apples were gathered"); if they are present, it is only as types ("the labourer")—they are not spotlighted with humiliating specificity as was J. Alfred Prufrock. This is a calmer vision of an omnipowerful nature as contrasted with Eliot's earlier lampoons of people's perverse attempts to enter into the processes of nature, in an endeavor fated to ridiculous, embarrassing failure.

The second line quoted above offers vintage wasteland imagery. Eliot distances, and thus diminishes, a potentially fecund Frazerian image of fruition and harvest: the apples are stored, so they are present, ironically, only in their absence, just as the luxuriant hyacinths in the garden of *The Waste Land* ironically evoke only sterile barrenness. The ensuing landscape is literally morose (brown, muddy waste) and imagistically laden with an allegorically parallel spiritual-intellectual condition: "sharp points of death." Compare a similar image from *The Waste Land*, the deathly modern Cleopatra (whose perfumes "drowned the senses in odours" [56]) in "A Game of Chess": "Under the fire-light, under the brush, her hair / Spread out in fiery points" (57). This image goes back even farther than Eliot's early 1920s wasteland tenor, to his juvenile "The Death of Saint Narcissus." The martyr in that poem—perhaps a prototype of Becket—literally faces sharp points of death: burning arrows. Saint Sebastian was the topic of another early (unpublished) poem by Eliot. Lyndall Gordon notes that Eliot's inspiration for that poem came from three fifteenth-century paintings he saw featuring "innocent, firm-fleshed youths exposed to penetrant arrows" (*Early Years,* 61); Gordon also suggests that the jackknifing Sweeney of "Sweeney Erect," "playful with his razor in the brothel" (62), is another manifestation of Saint Sebastian's character wielding another sharp point of death.

The images of the waiting New Year in the third and fifth lines of this passage denote a surrealistic and devious personification of a temporally abstract concept. Compare this with the yellow fog and smoke that rubs, licks, lingers, slides, in "Prufrock"; Eliot exploits the same basic logical disjunction—a kind of pathetic fallacy—that he nurtured to give his earliest poetry its haunting quality. A New Year, of course, does not breathe or whisper any more than the streets from "Prufrock" harbor insidious intents or lead one to a question; Eliot stretches figurative license to (or even beyond) its limit. The fourth line, with its minimalist abstraction of a working-class tableau, casually understated, evokes the 1930s style used prominently in *The Rock.*

Growing out of the explication above, it seems valid to generalize that in *Murder in the Cathedral* Eliot sustains the fierce attention to the nature of language that he demonstrated throughout his poetry. His language undergoes a metamorphosis: a poetic (predominantly in the earlier sections of part 1) that reenacts, or looks back to, his earlier style, evolves into a new linguistic sensibility—closer to "where the words are valid"—in part 2. Eliot's poetic reenactments are closely evocative of, and indebted to, the original models of his earlier verse, yet with a subtle but significant variation, a kind of softening and maturity. He is building toward some climactic resolution that is more humane, more communicative, more indicative of a continuing dialogue that can grow out of his words, than a blunt terminus such as "[t]he last twist of the knife." In part 2, fulfilling this promise, Eliot refines the language into the serenely cerebral poetry of peaceful acceptance and communal interaction that will infuse *Four Quartets.*

REBOUNDING FROM MALAISE

Having established the nature of the Canterbury community's inadequacies and some sense of its possibility of redemption, the playwright proceeds to unite these disparate conditions through language. As part 1 draws to a close, Eliot announces the beginning of this enterprise by shifting his language—which had been focused until this point on basic narrative exposition and imagistic elaboration of themes—into high gear. It becomes a poetically energized force that is able to dazzle, encapsulate, resolve, unify in the mode of the entrancing opening of "Burnt Norton," where Eliot confidently brokers grandiose metaphysical conundrums in the reins of a deft, measured poetic control.

In a splendid crescendo to Thomas's confrontation of temptations and his resolve to proceed beyond them at the end of part 1, Eliot offers a fusion of three choruses in one, as Canterbury women, Priests, and Tempters, speak alternately. Each group first asks an abstract question about the external environment and protection from it; a second similarly abstract set of questions are more specifically about protection from the fears and threats of the night. The next three statements concern Death, personified, and his mystical powers; and finally there are three statements about man, who appears fairly insignificant, quietly pathetic:

C[horus]: Is it the owl that calls, or a signal between the trees?

P[riests]: Is the window-bar made fast, is the door under lock and bolt?

T[empters]: Is it rain that taps at the window, is it wind that pokes at the door?

C: Does the torch flame in the hall, the candle in the room?

P. Does the watchman walk by the wall?

T: Does the mastiff prowl by the gate?

C: Death has a hundred hands and walks by a thousand ways.

P: He may come in the sight of all, he may pass unseen unheard.

T: Come whispering through the ear, or a sudden shock on the skull.

C: A man may walk with a lamp at night, and yet be drowned in a ditch.

P: A man may climb the stair in the day, and slip on a broken step.

T: A man may sit at meat, and feel the cold in his groin. (42–43)

Though stripped of the manifest hostility and ugliness he would have had in a poem such as "Rhapsody on a Windy Night" or "Preludes," Eliot's "man" here remains as hapless as anywhere else in his canon: fraught with the fears, qualifications, and mediocrities that have always afflicted Eliot's common man and woman.

Since a chorus classically represents the culmination of dramatic power and effect, then this Chorus of Choruses (hyperChorus?) exerts a tremendous claim on our attention. Yet while it is striking and compelling, the passage is also, finally, unsatisfying: it leaves important issues hanging. Why have the three groups—representing every component of the play except Thomas—come together? Why are they telling us this? It must be important, yet what does it mean? Eliot achieves a comparable effect at the end of *The Waste Land:* when the thunder offers commands on how to live—give, sympathize, control—there is a similar compulsion to listen to this fascinating voice, but in that poem Eliot mitigates the compulsion by the enigma of its obscurity. The language of these united choruses bears affinities to another earlier passage in Eliot's work: the questions and answers evoke the surreal, enchanting, fairly nonsensical conclusive lines Eliot wrote for Hallie Flanagan's 1933 Vassar production of *Sweeney Agonistes:*

Sweeney: When will the barnfowl fly before morning?
    When will the owl be operated on for cataracts?
    When will the eagle get out of his barrel-roll?

Old Gentleman: When the camel is too tired to walk farther
    Then shall the pigeon-pie blossom in the desert
    At the wedding-breakfast of life and death. (in Smith, *Dramatic Theory,* 63)

Both passages feature open, pointed questions and peculiar responses (answers?) that are troublingly indecipherable yet nevertheless impossible to dismiss. The tenor is vintage Eliotic: keen, pointed, incisive, yet at the same time elusive, troubling, confusing, eerie, obscure—which is to say, modernist.

The effect is to make the audience aware of the dramatic and rhetorical power available here—the three unified choruses point to the larger unified entity of the play at hand. At the same time, though, this passage bespeaks the need for a tighter dramatic direction, coherence, and focus. Yes, this is tantalizing, but it will not do as a conclusion. (Herein lies an important difference between the passage at the end of Flanagan's *Sweeney Agonistes* and this one. The former was fraught with incompletion, undurability: Eliot never published the Vassar ending with the remainder of *Sweeney Agonistes*; it came as a fragmentary ending to an already fragmentary dramatic piece, lacking closure.) In *Murder in the Cathedral,* though, there is a part 2 ahead. The "hyperChorus" keeps the audience hanging but with something to meet its need for resolving the confusion.

Part 2 opens with the Chorus speaking in the same kind of style as at the end of part 1—"Does the bird sing in the South? . . . The starved crow sits in the field, attentive; and in the wood / The owl rehearses the hollow note of death" (53)—although the language begins to move toward a clearer pattern.[10] While the dialogue at the opening of part 2 maintains a lingering sense of enigma or irrationality as at the end of part 1, it begins to take a shape, drawing on earlier traditions of morally prophetic language, that is more recognizably usable. The line about the starved crow in the field at least vaguely connotes the tenor of an Old Testament dream-prophecy and perhaps, from the New Testament, a wordplay evoking the cock's crow, which, Christ prophesies, will betoken Peter's betrayal. A few lines further down Eliot draws upon the language of Christian paradox, which helps begin to place and explain, to contextualize (especially with reference to the more conventional exegesis in the interlude), Eliot's earlier paradoxes: "war among men defiles this world, but death in the Lord renews it" (53).

REPETITION AND PATTERNS

The rhythms, cycles, and harmonies of Ecclesiastes begin to infuse the speech of part 2: "The ploughman shall go out in March and turn the same earth / He has turned before, the bird shall sing the same song" (54). (This is still from the first choral speech. The Chorus had stymied the audience with its complications at the end of part 1, when its privileged dramatic mode had been usurped, compromised, shared with two other "choruses"; but here it returns to its own position of elegance, balance, and gnosis, implying some restoration of order.) The Chorus begins to implant itself in an emerging discernible pattern, the pattern of this modern play, as it integrates traces of an Audenesque tenor while sustaining the concatenated anaphoric style of Ecclesiastes: "And voices trill at windows, and children tumble in front of the door" (54). Finally, this passage concludes in the serene triumph of repetition:

> What work shall have been done, what wrong
> Shall the bird's song cover, the green tree cover, what wrong
> Shall the fresh earth cover? We wait, and the time is short
> But waiting is long (54)

Repetitions resonate: work, wrong, cover, wait, augmented by other prosodic reinforcements of repeated sounds such as the alliterative "w," the internal rhyme of wrong and song, the assonance of green and tree. Ecclesiastes again serves as a model for a biblical trope of repetition: compare, "A time to be born, and a time to die; a time to plant, and a time to pluck up that which is planted" (3:2). Eliot's repetition is also in the mode of ritually repeated prayer and of similar passages of *Four Quartets* that approach transcendent apotheosis through language (developments on the themes of "time" in "Burnt Norton" 1; "dark" in "East Coker" 3; "water and fire" in "Little Gidding" 2, and so forth). The repetition is, paradoxically, at the same time energizingly dazzling and soporifically entrancing. The audience's response to this range should be to give itself over wholly to the power that manifests this capability: the poet, the language, the drama.

From the grasp on language (as a medium of stability and control) that Eliot thus begins to affirm in the first choral passage of part 2, his words continue to mature and develop as part 2 unfolds. The Priests revel in the repetition of language: a choral refrain of meditations on "To-day" (and note how their repetition, like all these repetitions, naturally evokes a choral sensibility: a symphony of shared voices engaged in a communal quest). "To-day?" asks the First Priest. "To-day, what is to-day?" responds the Second Priest. "For the day is half gone." "To-day, what is to-day?" repeats the First Priest. "But another day, the dusk of the year." And again the Second Priest: "To-day, what is to-day? Another night, and another dawn" (56). The Third Priest goes on to synthesize the nature of "to-day," and to link it with the eternal: "Every day is the day we should fear from or hope from. . . . Even now, in sordid particulars / The eternal design may appear" (57).

Eliot, in his late poetry, similarly reveled in synthesis achieved through repetition: repetition was the acknowledgment that he had said all he had to say, that he had come full circle, that he had confidently ensconced himself in the soothing tautologies of Christian belief. In "East Coker" 3 he proudly announces: "You say I am repeating / Something I have said before. I shall say it again" (187). In her essay entitled "The Rhetoric of Repetition in *Murder in the Cathedral*," M. Geraldine expands upon Eliot's use of the technique in this play: "If Eliot considered that what was worth saying once was worth saying again, either in the same words or new ones, it is not surprising that in a play such as *Murder in the Cathedral,* a play so strongly thematic and ritualistic, he is especially conscious of the peculiar effects achieved by recurrences of figures, phrases, and ideas" (132). Repetitive language contributes to the play's "structure, especially that element of structure concerned with unity and pattern" (136). The Priests' repetition, then, and the Chorus's as they affirm seasonal rituals at the opening of part 2, indicate that the play is moving closer toward unity, patterns, firm clarity of structure.

LANGUAGE AND TIME

Building with greater confidence upon the motif of repetition established by the Chorus, the Priests lull the audience into a state resembling prayer, into the play, into faith in a controlling force. Most prominently, they lull us into poetry, which is, for Eliot, the epitome and unification of the combination of prayer, ritual drama, and faith. The Priests' chorus unifies language—*words*— with *time,* the play's crux from early in part 1. The refrain of "To-day" signifies a temporal bridge between the physical and metaphysical connotations of dramatic time. Calender time (time present) has been shown approaching interaction with spiritual time (time future) in an earlier part of the Priests' chorus that precedes the "To-day" passage: "Since Christmas a day: and the day of St. Stephen," says the First Priest. "Since St. Stephen a day: and the day of St. John the Apostle," adds the Second; "Since St. John the Apostle a day: and the day of the Holy Innocents" adds the Third; and the First Priest returns, closes the circle, *repeating* the formula he began: "Since the Holy Innocents a day: the fourth day from Christmas" (54–56). The First Priest has, to paraphrase Eliot from "Little Gidding," arrived where he started and known the place for the first time. "The place" is 29 December, referred to simply by that date *on* that date, 29 December 1170, for the last time. Hereafter, it, too, will be a temporally transcendent signifier, like Christmas, St. Stephen's Day, and so on: it will be St. Thomas's Day. Tolling the days of the Christian tradition, the Priests bring the action up to the time present of the play: a day that resonates with significance both in immediate terms—this historical drama is predestined to have its climax on this day—and in the longer lasting realms of history and faith. The play, like the day, is here simultaneously time bound and poised to spring into the future, that is, to implant in its audience a sensibility that will endure beyond the end of the day and the play.

Words and time are unified. Eliot's words are able to function in time—to show time present as it becomes capable of moving into time future. I identify this point in the play as its arrival at "where the words are valid," a moment of transcendent dramatic and linguistic success that, I argue, manifests itself with considerable regularity and coherence throughout Eliot's drama. Language is the ideal and exemplary signifier of community; communication is the sine qua non of community, as the story of the Tower of Babel exemplifies. Eliot associates a carefully nurtured language with a confrontation of time—i. e., an attempt to understand, pinpoint, and properly interact with time (as, in part 1, the Chorus's task was to reconcile the seven years of Becket's past absence with his presence in the present and the implications for the future). This attempt represents a unification of the ideal (Eliot's desired perspective on time) and the real (his ability to communicate this ideal). Linda Wyman reinforces the importance attached to the success of language in *Murder in the Cathedral*. Arguing that "language is the chief imitator of the action" here, she identifies the play as manifesting what she calls a "plot of diction"; although the play also portrays change in the situation, character, and thought of the protagonist, "we are shown, in the total design of the language, a meaning more comprehensive than that encompassed by the protagonist alone, so that our final attention is directed to a *complex* of meanings, of which all that we have learned about the protagonist is a part" (135–36).

From the opening of part 2 and the Priests' chorus, and for the rest of the play, the action is clear; the "plot of diction," as Wyman terms it, is intractably established. It is equally clear what the action will mean and how the community must and will deal with it—the consequence of using valid words is precisely that meaning becomes clear. Immediately following the Third Priest's promise of "eternal design," the Knights enter speaking in jumbled, clumsy language evocative of a Marx Brothers charade. The First Knight announces their "business with the Archbishop"; the Second Knight elaborates, "Urgent business"; the Third Knight chimes in, "From the King"; the Second Knight explicates, "By the King's order" (57). The Knights are best remembered for their comically, grotesquely inappropriate language in their tawdry "apologies" for having murdered an Archbishop in his Cathedral. Their prose is sputtering and cliché-ridden—they are unworthy of linguistically joining the other members of this dramatic community in poetry. Paradoxically, their verbal bumbling further augments the ideal of language that develops throughout part 2. The Knights are highly effective at defining by negation the importance of valid words to the establishment of a community: they are fated to be as far removed as possible from the community that their murder has paradoxically helped to create, as their language betrays that they are destined to remain unalterably outside it.

As part 2 progresses, Eliot's characters transcend their earlier communicative inadequacy and malaise, finding a voice. When, for example, Becket rebukes the Knights' intrusive assault on his authority, he firmly declaims, "Never again, you must make no doubt, / Shall the sea run between the shepherd and his fold" (65). He begins to speak with compelling rhetorical flourishes, weaving his impending moral triumph in what becomes a versatile language of fluent, irrefutable eloquence:

> It is not I who insult the King,
> And there is higher than I or the King.
> It is not I, Becket from Cheapside,
> It is not against me, Becket, that you strive.
> It is not Becket who pronounces doom,
> But the Law of Christ's Church, the judgement of Rome. (65)

> I submit my cause to the judgement of Rome.
> But if you kill me, I shall rise from my tomb
> To submit my cause before God's throne. (66)

> Human kind cannot bear very much reality. (69)

> All my life they have been coming, these feet. All my life
> I have waited. (69)

> Peace! be quiet! remember where you are, and what is happening;
> No life here is sought but mine,
> And I am not in danger: only near to death. (70)

The effect is as if, at an American political forum, George Bush were suddenly to metamorphose into Jesse Jackson. The poetry, the rhetoric, the language, all accelerate drastically. Becket emerges as being fully in command in his role as orator, leader, dramatic hero—much more so than he was in his sermon. (In that interlude, he was constrained by imposed conventional rhetoric and the limitations of being, both as Archbishop and as impending martyr, a functionary to a higher authority). As he approaches his death, his character becomes consummately enlarged in its dramaturgical presence. He is a spectacular, heroic dramatic entity, unfettered and unstoppable. As the action, finally, becomes exciting—as the Knights storm the Cathedral—Thomas effuses poetry, the oratory of serene spiritual leadership, an omnipowerful sense of certitude, and the dramatic composure of an unchallenged star at the moment of his unparalleled dramatic height.

As Becket hits his stride, Eliot, in tandem, hits his own. *The Rock* presented a contrived, heavily worked, self-conscious Christian community ("Hey, fellas—or fellow Christians—let's put on a show"). Eliot succeeds in *Murder in the Cathedral* in creating a literary text, as well as a community, that is immensely more vital, more natural, more compelling, and less artificial, less dependent upon the elaborate conceits of a pageant or a music-hall show, or the rhythmically primordial "beating of a drum," than in his previous drama. In *The Rock,* Eliot's attempt to latch onto and convey a sense of a churchly community demanded the embellishment of ballets, ballads, songs and dances, vaudevillean patter. Here the community enterprise progresses with a simple sense of ease, grace, inevitability.

A key factor in Eliot's success is that he has found the right language, a language that is eloquently poetic and profuse. His language is, not coincidentally, in many ways very close to the language of *Four Quartets,* which is a further sign of its fecundity. In *Murder in the Cathedral* Eliot achieves a poetic, a style, a tenor, vital enough for him to nurture not just in this play but also in his final sequence of poems, written during a period of several years he believed to be the apocalyptic moment of Western culture. He must have thought this language very noble and important; he latched onto it as a rare force that could shore fragments against the ruins in the streets and skies of London.

And it was a language that, obviously, sufficed to write a long, *consistently* good play. Eliot had already written, first, a short play full of mostly good dialogue—tight, snappy, jazzy, compelling; and, next, a long play containing occasional effective passages that he later felt had to be excerpted from the morass of a mostly unmemorable script. In *Murder in the Cathedral,* he has written 1,300-odd lines of verse drama—roughly equivalent to the number of lines he had published since the beginning of his career—that do not pale in comparison to his poetry.

The whole of *Murder in the Cathedral* is recognizably and resonantly Eliotic, which confirms that he has hit his mark in writing verse drama. Indeed, many passages easily intermingle with his poetry: one of the most pointed lines from "Burnt Norton" 1 appears first in this play: "Human kind cannot bear very much reality" (*Murder in the Cathedral,* 69; *Collected Poems,* 176). Obviously, for anyone studying the relation between Eliot's poetry and his drama, this line provides a bridge between the two. Many characters speak in the language of *Four Quartets,* especially the Fourth Tempter. (In the film, Eliot himself spoke the lines of this character.) A thirteen-line passage E. Martin Browne had asked Eliot to write for *Murder in the Cathedral,* later deemed unnecessary, was resurrected as the opening of "Burnt Norton," clearly indicating that by the mid-1930s Eliot was writing in a mode, and in a language, that he found appropriate for both drama and poetry. In numerous critical essays from the 1930s onward, he wrote about these two genres in a way that brings them quite close to each other. *Poetry and Drama* (1951) and *The Three Voices of Poetry* (1953) are especially important in terms of establishing a vast common ground between poetry and drama and delineating their interstices in his aesthetic theories.

COMMUNITY AND REALITY

"Human kind cannot bear very much reality" (69)—I take this line spoken by the Archbishop, which I find the most resonant words in the play, as an emblem for the work. I read it not exactly as a moral—it is a bit too clipped, too understated, too mundane for that, and certainly the historical reenactment of a martyrdom does not lack an obvious moral in and of itself. The line is more in the realm of an insight, for Becket as well as for Eliot. For both it is somewhat anticlimactic: Thomas has made more momentous pronouncements about the moral condition of humanity in proximate passages, as Eliot has, likewise, written more spectacular poetic phrases. The line embodies a stance of gentle resignation: coming to terms with the nature of Becket's Canterbury and Eliot's West End (where the play would run after its Canterbury debut), with a tenor that rings truer than anything else either has said. While not the play's highest moment, this acknowledgment is a crucial foundation, representing a crucial awareness, the lack of which would preclude any dramatic development beyond the sensibility of *Sweeney Agonistes* or the rather pallid theatrical talents evidenced in *The Rock.* The line is equivalent to anagnorisis—an essential component of any dramatic undertaking—but its accomplishment is that it takes place on the social level. It is a moment of self-awareness but not merely individually; it betokens an entire community's self-awareness.

The line promises not very much reality but a little, just enough. Eliot, similarly, could not bear very much reality. In his earlier poetry he looked at the world around him, like the streetwalker in "Rhapsody," only out of the corner of his eye; he could not process more than the token detritus of the modern world (a morsel of rancid butter, a slowly creeping rat) that signified the massive horrors shored amid the ruins. For more than twenty years, from the early 1910s to the mid-1930s, Eliot had been progressively creeping farther out of his rat hole. The linchpin that connects his final poetic effort, the serene, majestic, *Four Quartets,* with the initiation of his successfully poised drama, is the line that appears in both: "Human kind cannot bear very much reality."

Despite the manifest anticlimax of this expression, it also signifies a potent triumph. Reality is what Eliot wholeheartedly sets his sights upon from 1935 onwards. Honestly naturalistic and forthrightly confronted emotional childhood memories, regrets and mistakes admitted without repression or bitterness, moments of dappling sunlight mixing with hidden laughter in the garden, replace ontological skeptics laughing "like an irresponsible foetus" (23) in a surreal garden with Priapus in the shrubbery. Eliot is ready to embrace gossipy, somewhat banal, busybodies—Julia Shuttlethwaite, Alexander MacColgie Gibbs, Maisie Montjoy—and obsequious hired help—Denman, Eggerson, B. Kaghan—in intrigues that offer "not very much" or very shocking reality, rather than the kind of societies that culminate in everyman's desire to do a girl in and preserve her in a tub of Lysol.

In *Murder in the Cathedral,* Eliot is delicately aware of the levels and forces of reality that people—from Tempters and Knights to Chorus and even Archbishop—cannot bear. He deftly, sensitively, tolerantly, doses out, with the precision of a chemist, the small amount of reality that each *can* bear: so we get the Knights' largest possible dose of reality, which is hardly any at all (though there is the germ of an insight on the part of the Third Knight, who realizes, as Judas did, "We have much more to lose than to gain. . . . I dare say that we didn't make a very good impression when we came in just now" [79]). We get the fear of witnessing on the part of those who are destined to be witnesses, and—persisting even after the supposedly glorious event, the making of a saint—the lukewarm hopes and fears, couched in the cautious, tepid Audenisms that have replaced the uncompromisingly harsh, jackknifing, critical voice of the early Eliot.

Eliot pointedly writes "human kind" rather than the more common "humankind."[11] "Human" and "kind" do not conjoin easily into a single unified word, perhaps to stress the fact that, as he expressed in his earlier poetry of solipsism, humans are not inherently or naturally kind; nor, in the modern age, are they of a kind (as, he seemed to believe, people had been when they lived in homogenous and clearly focused medieval communities). Eliot did not at first believe that he was in touch with his kind, his kindred. For any person— saint, playwright, playgoer—the connection with the rest of humankind does not happen easily. The space between words denotes the gap that remains in time present, the gap that must be actively and consciously bridged as one works to create and sustain the community that can someday accept humankind more naturally, more easily.

4

The Family Reunion: "The Particular Has No Language"

In terms of his social vision, Eliot seems more intent upon portraying an attempt to escape from community in *The Family Reunion* than in affirming a meaningful community. Throughout the play, Harry, Lord Monchensey, resists and strains against the claustrophobic obsolescence of Wishwood. The "country house in the North of England" (as Eliot describes the play's setting [7]), though a tormenting and hostile venue for the protagonist, does, in fact, represent a long-established community for the Monchenseys. Certain members of this community, most prominently its women, have established a stable, if unpalatable, equilibrium of social existence. Indeed, this play's pointed association of women with a community that must be sundered generates Eliot's most manifestly hostile misogyny in his dramatic oeuvre: the depiction here of women as cloying, constraining, and manipulative evokes the portrayals of women in his poetry from two to three decades earlier.[1] In the final three plays, and especially in *The Elder Statesmen,* Eliot at least implicitly tempers a long-standing suspicion of women. He was later to fault *The Family Reunion* on numerous grounds, retrospectively judging it more harshly than any of his other plays.[2] Though he does not specifically mention the play's misogyny, I speculate that that may have been a key reason why an older and kinder Eliot distanced himself from it and to a considerable extent disavowed it.

Like the feudal sensibility that a manor house connotes, Wishwood's community stability exists mainly in the past and is crumbling before our eyes in time present. (In this vein, Michael Beehler notes that the house will ultimately prove to be "the *topos* of death: the tomb of Amy" [38].) To convey the decline of the present from the past, Eliot opens the play with echoes of his darkest modernism, setting the tenor with his recurrent trope of temporal and seasonal disjunctions and confusions (in the mode of "April is the cruellest month"). Amy, in the first lines, bemoans the emptiness of her life, "Now that I sit in the house from October to June" (11). The sun's warmth, once appreciated for its natural splendor, now taunts her by its absence or unpredictability. "Make up the fire. Will the spring never come? I am cold" (11). Night is feared, she says in her opening speech; clocks cannot be trusted; the coming of tomorrow is no longer assured.

As at the beginning of *Murder in the Cathedral,* the failure here to find comfort or order in a normal progression of time, from past through present to future, indicates a serious breakdown in the community's constitution. Ivy advises Amy to go south in the winter, directly evoking Marie's decadent seasonal dislocation in *The Waste Land.*[3] Carol H. Smith sees Eliot's traditional Frazerian associations in Amy's character, amplifying the resonance of this natural and seasonal symbolism: "The conflict between Harry and his mother . . . is patterned on the ritual plot with its agon between the sin-laden and impotent representative of the old year and the reborn and sin-free god of the new year. . . . Amy represents the old principle which must be destroyed before the new principle can be born" (*Dramatic Theory,* 134–35).

INAUSPICIOUS COMMUNITY PORTENTS: ECHOES OF SWEENEY'S LONDON

Amy's Wishwood is not the sole emblem of community in the play. Charles mentions that he finds London cozy, suggesting another community that might provide an alternative to Wishwood's apparent rottenness. At the least, some other (and quite different) place could offer an instructive contrast: the inhabitants of Wishwood's community might learn something from London. Violet's response to Charles, though, shows her fear of change—a dangerous stance if one's community is inadequate—and the women's determination to cling to the status quo in their manor.

> Well, as for me,
> I would never go south, no, definitely never . . .
> England's bad enough, I would never go south,
> Simply to see the vulgarest people—(13)

she states, evoking the demurrals of Klipstein and Krumpacker in *Sweeney Agonistes:*

Dusty: Why don't you come and live here then?

Klipstein: Well, no, Miss—er—you haven't quite got it
    (I'm afraid I didn't quite catch your name—
    But I'm very pleased to meet you all the same)—

> London's a little too gay for us
> Yes I'll say a little too gay.

Krumpacker: Yes London's a little too gay for us
> Don't think I mean anything *coarse*—
> But I'm afraid we couldn't stand the pace. (117)

Like Violet's aspersion on London, Klipstein's and Krumpacker's hasty disdain for that urban community does not in any way indicate that the men are ensconced in their own satisfactory community; if they were, why would they be cruising for dates and parties with caustic strangers? Rather, Eliot uses the veterans of *Sweeney Agonistes* and the old aunt from Wishwood to voice a caveat: characters' closed-mindedness toward the virtues of a possible alternative community indicates that they are not looking very critically or correctly at their own communities. Parochial, haughty, condescending jibes at other people's communities indicate people who cannot function well in their own social groups. Klipstein does not even remember the name of the woman to whom he is speaking: certainly his attitude forebodes his ill-suitedness to any community.

Eliot further establishes a rhythmic link between his first and fourth plays in Violet's speech explaining her distaste for London, or anywhere away from Wishwood:

> Go south! to the English circulating libraries,
> To the military widows and English chaplains,
> To the chilly deck-chair and the strong cold tea—
> The strong cold stewed bad Indian tea. (12)

Compare the last line and a half with Sweeney's verbal assault on Doris, whom he threatens to convert

> Into a stew.
> A nice little, white little, missionary stew. (118)

The similarities are subtle, perhaps even partly subconscious to Eliot, yet they indicate that he is grounding himself in the mode of the harshest, most dangerous hostilities from *Sweeney Agonistes* as he begins *The Family Reunion* and as he depicts the attitudes of Wishwood's women toward community. Both passages are couplets whose lines end with the same word—"tea" and "stew," in both cases food. Violet uses "stewed" to describe the bad tea, and Sweeney's stew is certainly *bad* as well, especially for Doris who would be a component of it. Both couplets achieve the effect of describing this bad food by repeating modifiers—"strong cold" is used twice in *The Family Reunion*; in *Sweeney Agonistes* "nice little, white little" repeats "little" and the assonance of "i," as well as the ending word. The final line of each is composed of five modifiers, overzealously packed into a line that has run on from the previous one as a description of this bad food.

The rhythm in each passage could be described as banal or sing-song or even neurotic in its concatenation; the final line's six insistent stresses in each instance create a nervously threatening sense of tedium. Violet's is more latent than Sweeney's, but finding an echo of the earlier passage in the later one suggests that Violet's antipathy to her community is just as violent as Sweeney's, only masked with a more conventional social veneer. After all, as a genteel spinster enclosed in the traditions of the country estate, her denunciation of bad tea may be the starkest challenge she could pose to her society. It is a symbol, albeit oblique, of community failure: denigrating the cultural artifact of aristocratic English high tea conveys a semiotic resonance matching the force of Sweeney's cannibalistic bad food. In drafts of these lines (from the T. S. Eliot Collection manuscripts), Eliot had originally described the tea as simply inferior, then weak, then bad; the final version, with sharply precise and relentless modifiers that seem to have been revised four times during composition, shows his obsessive insistence with impugning this tea. It is not too elaborate to read Violet's outburst as angry frustration, pathetically circumscribed, at the limitations of a disintegrating Wishwood society that allows her no criteria for evaluating the world around her, no critical reference points, other than the comparative merits of different teas. With his keen ear for prosody and rhythm, Eliot would likely have recalled a beat he had used a dozen years earlier. His recycling of that tempo and tenor serves as a touchstone to the horrors of his stillborn dramatic community from the 1920s.

Carol H. Smith details further links between *The Family Reunion* and *Sweeney Agonistes:* "One of the most striking similarities . . . is the re-use of the cry of Orestes in Aeschylus' *Choephoroi* when he finds himself pursued by the Erinys. In *The Family Reunion* Harry repeats the cry in his anguished announcement to his assembled family that he, too, is being pursued by his own hounds of hell. . . . The 'hoo-ha's' in the final chorus of *Sweeney Agonistes* are converted into the Furies of *The Family Reunion.* Moreover, the theme of the murdered girl discovered in a Lysol bath in Sweeney's tale is repeated in Harry's drowned wife, and the same sense of mystery surrounds the event" (113–14).

THE CHORUS

The play is predicated upon, and infused with, Eliot's stark preconversion poetic and sensibility. In *Murder in the Cathedral,* the manifestations of that sensibility, fear, fell to the Chorus to address most directly. In *The Family Reunion,* the Chorus (composed of Ivy, Violet, Gerald, and Charles) plays somewhat the same function as in the previous play, banding together to express the fears and timidities of would-be community members oppressed by the seemingly inevitable destructive realities of quotidian life. Here, as in *Mur-*

der in the Cathedral, the potency of the Chorus seems mitigated by self-depre-
cation and a tendency toward anticlimax, but in both plays the audience (if it
is responding "properly") must consider the simple fact that the Chorus has
formed at all as a triumph over the zeitgeist of anomie. It represents, by definition, a community enterprise, even if it is not as keenly energetic a community
as might ideally be possible. Speaking in unison, the Chorus members overcome the tremendous forces of inert silence. Contrast Eliot's Choruses in both
plays, however meek and whiny, with the pervasive absence of effective social
dialogue in *The Waste Land.* The mute and muted crowd flowing over London
Bridge, undone—figuratively encompassing the poem's entire populace—never
begins to approach the possibility of unison, choral community, or speech.

Eliot's 1922 crowds, from what might aptly be called his inferno period,
closely resemble Dante's mobs in hell. Those hordes pathetically try to express
themselves, make themselves comprehensible, argue their causes, or explain
their lives in a language that becomes only increasingly pathetic gibberish as
Dante journeys deeper into that "community," which is really, to the properly
responding reader, the epitome of an anticommunity. (Dante's thirteenth-cen-
tury Florence *seemed* to be a large, important, vitally functioning city-commu-
nity; it was the burden of his poem to show the fallacy of this appearance.
Eliot's country estate of Wishwood, similarly, seems at first like the core of an
archetypal English community, but the dramatic experience will prove otherwise.) The increasing fluency, mellifluousness, and community-mindedness of
the language that emerges as Dante proceeds out of hell and through the rest
of his *commedia* parallels Eliot's developing sensibility in the 1930s and 1940s
of language as a potential force of beneficent communication and as the foundation of a community.

Eliot's Chorus in *The Family Reunion* may be considered as having ventured
just outside hell (like Eliot himself, as he seems to have imagined his life in
the 1930s). It speaks with a tentativeness reflecting this incipient step in a
journey toward an ultimate but distant "paradise," that is, toward community.
In its first speech, the Chorus laments its very presence at this reunion and in
this play:

> Why do we feel embarrassed, impatient, fretful, ill at ease,
> Assembled like amateur actors who have not been assigned their parts?
> Like amateur actors in a dream when the curtain rises, to find themselves dressed
>   for a different play, or having rehearsed the wrong parts,
> Waiting for the rustling in the stalls, the titter in the dress circle, the laughter and
>   catcalls in the gallery? . . .
> Yet here we are at Amy's command, to play an unread part in some monstrous
>   farce, ridiculous in some nightmare pantomime. (21–22)

The Chorus's first four lines convey a sense of haplessness and aimlessness, by
deconstructing the moment at hand—the very moment of drama—as wholly as

possible. (It is, of course, highly paradoxical that the Chorus, which should represent the epitome of dramatic unity, coordination, and syncopation, serves to undercut the dramatic enterprise.) The speakers present themselves as unprepared, unscripted amateur actors incapable of presenting a play—despite the fact that the audience had heretofore assumed it was in the process of watching a play. Eliot's deconstruction challenges the essential realities of the most basic assumptions that the audience would have thought inviolable: the specific dramatic conceits and forms involved in the play that is in the midst of performance. The effect is as compelling as any of Eliot's poetic deflations (*"Not with a bang but a whimper,"* or "The last twist of the knife"), cleverly adapted, or fitted, to the medium of drama.

The fourth line quoted especially engages, and implicates, the audience in this deconstructive abyss: depicted as rustling, tittering, catcalling, the spectators are thus deprived of, or excluded from, the ideal dramatic experience to which they would have thought themselves entitled simply by having purchased a ticket. The moment is a variation on Becket's "skewering" accusation-implication of Tempters, Knights, Chorus, and audience at the end of part 1 of *Murder in the Cathedral,* as discussed in chapter 3 ("Chorus/Audience"). It is even more dramatically successful here, as Eliot dispenses with subliminal subtlety: he explicitly tells the audience that it is having a bad audience experience, not what it meant to have at all. Audiences are not prepared to become engaged in a play to this extent; Eliot startles his playgoers, grasping them, as it were by the scruffs, unaware. Thus he has them firmly in his power: he has implicated them in this scenario, and only through his guidance can they possibly extricate themselves. "Unprepared" actors hovering in a fumbling existential void evocative of Pirandello, likewise, miss out on the drama, the community, the choral unity, which everyone in the theater—on stage and in the audience— had been led to expect pro forma but is disappointingly denied.

Simultaneously whetting his audience's appetite for a community of drama and depriving his audience of it, Eliot compels them to realize how much they crave it. The Chorus's final line locates audience and play in a ridiculous monstrous farce, a nightmare pantomime. Eliot's destruction of the fledgling dramatic construct at hand—the play has been going on for perhaps ten minutes— does not leave the audience simply in a vacuum but somewhere closer to the harshest surreal nightmare farces of his poetic youth: "Mr. Apollinax" or "Hysteria" or even poems that were too grotesque to be written in English such as "Lune de Miel" or "Dans le Restaurant." Like the paralyzed characters in those poems—ill at ease, incapable of ameliorating the miserable situation at hand— the audience of *The Family Reunion* is made to feel that it has had worse than just an *empty* experience but, rather, one in which every playgoer is meant to feel ridiculous, cheapened, reduced to the condition of a tawdry voyeur. The audience is the victim of the crude, Sweeneyesque hoax of having been promised a party, a social encounter, a community—but given, instead, the seat of honor in the midst of Eliot's modernist, jackknifing wasteland.

ENTER HARRY

It is at just this point, with the scene set by the choral deconstruction, that Eliot's protagonist, Harry, Lord Monchensey, first comes on stage: into the shambles the playwright has wreaked of Wishwood, family, community, drama. One imagines that Harry's mission must be to traverse this landscape and to emerge having achieved anagnorisis, catharsis, restoration of order, establishment of community. Given this inauspicious starting point, one imagines that the task will not be easy. In fact, one might well surmise that the task is too difficult for any credible dramatic emergence or success at all (which in many ways this play's reception bears out).[4]

As the play develops, the dramatic task becomes even more difficult, more unlikely: redeeming a character who has no remorse for his wife's death, who in fact may have killed her (or at least wishes he had). Vinod Sena associates the dramaturgical fault lines with the flawed presentation of Harry's supposed murder: Eliot's "radical defect . . . is that while he uses the murder as a necessary means for levering Harry from the secular to the supernatural plane, the moment he has rehabilitated himself there, the reality of the means [i. e., the murder] is denied" (901). Eliot evades a central dramatic aspect of Harry's character. "This failure of artistic integrity, this Fletcher-like opportunism exploiting momentary effects while avoiding their consequences, ruptures [the play] at the very point where everything else is expected to meet and integrate. Not only is the audience confused, wondering if Harry really committed the murder or not—an irritation that is not easily overcome—it also creates an intriguing and mystifying position regarding the nature of sin and its expiation" (903), Sena complains. The trouble with Eliot's device "is that by reducing Harry's assumed murder to an illusion it knocks the bottom off the spiritual scheme at the play's center. If Harry's murder is illusory, so, too, must be his torments" (903–4).

A playwright who has amassed some degree of experience, as Eliot had in 1939, might be expected to beg off from this infelicitous scenario,[5] but I surmise that Eliot decided to plod on because it was for him more than a play: it was his life. He knew that in his characterization of Harry he would draw upon wider resources than just the craft and imagination an author regularly metes out to construct a fictional dramatic creation: the protagonist would have, in addition, a direct line to the author's soul. Harry is, in many ways, the younger Tom: the would-be loner and solipsist; the desperate wanderer in the mode of "Prufrock" and "Preludes."

The Family Reunion is the culmination of Eliot's transition from private poetry to public theater; and Harry takes the starring role in this endeavor in addition to, and parallel to, his function as protagonist in the play. Harry brings with him all the baggage from Eliot's 1920s sensibility but nevertheless appears on stage. While the play is often (as Eliot admits) a dramatic muddle, it is nevertheless a play, so Harry is by definition ensconced in drama and thus in at least a nominal community. Harry would be the best of all Eliot's dramatic or poetic personae to examine if one had to pick a single character to epitomize the whole of Eliot's career. He embodies a fusion of both Eliot's poetic and dramatic impulses, both the earlier scorn for the social world and the later awareness of the need to resolve this scorn, to compromise, to come to terms with his community.

In populating this play with male characters (Harry's brothers and uncles) who are more strikingly absent than present, Eliot shows how easy it would have been for Harry, likewise, not to have attended the "reunion" himself. But Harry *has* chosen to come—however doubtfully and however much he remains, despite his literal presence, in many ways figuratively absent. This marginality surrounding Harry's presence is another way Eliot denotes the fragile tension in this play: the forces of isolated, alienated solipsism confront those of dramatic community, with the forces of community achieving an exceedingly tentative victory. If an unworkable character, Harry is still a fascinatingly and engagingly volatile one because so many of his creator's fears, anxieties, dogmas, and prejudices are packed into him. Nevill Coghill, introducing his edition of the text, nicely adjudicates the paradox of a play that is so rich and yet so troublesome: "*The Family Reunion* is the most carefully worked, and yet the most deeply flawed, of all Eliot's plays, perhaps of all his writings. The flaws pierce to the heart of the play; yet the things attempted in it are so arresting, original and courageous that even its flaws are better worth discussing than the merits of many a more successful, more ordinary piece" (11).

Lyndall Gordon, conjecturing why Eliot abandoned the theater for nearly a decade after writing this play, disputes Eliot's stated reason—the difficulty of putting on plays during the war—noting that *Murder in the Cathedral* was often successfully revived. She suggests instead that Harry's exit line in his penultimate appearance, "I must follow the bright angels" (111), indicates Eliot's own mission, which was to retrieve a sense of grace he had glimpsed at Burnt Norton; and at the same time she notes that Harry's line is "a difficult one for an actor to deliver with any conviction" (*New Life,* 93). From this observation, one can extrapolate a step beyond her excellent biographical appraisal of Eliot at the time of *The Family Reunion:* certain passages in the play, such as Harry's exit line, are in fact *not* an actor's lines—they are not Harry's but Eliot's. In the event, it proved dramatically unsuccessful for Eliot to merge himself with his character in this way; yet it remains instructive to disentangle from this play Eliot's posture on community and the way in which he inscribes this vision (often, as here, with strong autobiographical referents) into *The Family Reunion.*

Eliot in 1939 was struggling to rid himself of the demons of a failed marriage from which he had escaped but not distanced himself. This play is itself a crucial act of distancing for him, reinforcing the compulsion he must have felt to embark with Harry upon the unpalatable dramatic task that lies ahead at his first entrance. Harry's ghosts are Eliot's. (Of Eliot's comment in a letter to director E. Martin Browne that Charles was the character most like himself [reprinted in *The Making of T. S. Eliot's Plays,* 106], I can only regard this statement as evidence of Eliot's inveterate proclivity to toy with his colleagues—or perhaps, more deviously, to test whether they were reading his work correctly—by striking false or obfuscatory poses.)

"The timing of the play's composition forecasts events in Eliot's life with remarkable closeness," Gordon writes. "In the play Harry is said to be 'psychic,' in that he knows in advance that his wife will be destroyed"; Eliot finished the play in June 1938, and "during the next two months, July–August, Vivienne was institutionalized" (80). Virginia Woolf (who was well acquainted with the Eliots' marital situation), after seeing the play, described the family as stiff pokers and wrote in her diary, "The chief poker is Tom" (in Gordon, *New Life,* 83). "The description of the wife in *The Family Reunion* is an accurate picture of Vivienne as others saw her at this time," Gordon writes, "an excited, irresponsible woman who would never leave her husband alone" (64). Noting her flirtation with suicide in the mid-1930s, Gordon adds: "A physical accident, she whispers to Eliot, might befall her at any moment. She cast herself as a doomed wife, the living replica of the doomed wife" in *The Family Reunion* (72).

"Martin Browne told Eliot that he found Harry baffling," Gordon writes, and Eliot replied with a "long analysis of Harry that sounds like a private testimony" (83). She paraphrases this letter: Harry, Eliot said, "was partially desexed by the horror of his marriage. He could be 'stirred up' by a lovable woman but, because of his state of mind, was unable to develop this feeling into a stable commitment. His attraction to a particular woman warred with the general idea that all women are 'unclean creatures.' His solution is to find refuge in an 'ambiguous relation' " (49; biographically, Gordon shows that this "ambiguous relation" is with Emily Hale). The play's central event, Harry's wife's death, echoes and confirms the autobiographical fantasy revealed in the lines from *Sweeney Agonistes:* "Any man has to, needs to, wants to / Once in a lifetime, do a girl in" (122). Charles, discussing the drowning, voices the identical sentiment: "In any case, I shouldn't blame Harry. / I might have done the same thing once, myself. / Nobody knows what he's likely to do / Until there's somebody he wants to get rid of" (34).

A detail in the play's typescripts indicates that Eliot's depiction of Harry's trials seems to relate to something outside the play, something that happened in "real time." The play refers to Harry's having left Wishwood, forsaking his family and ancestral home to marry, eight years earlier. In two drafts (T. S. Eliot Collection, items D4 and D5), however, Eliot refers to the event as being seven years past (in Amy's and Agatha's references that appear, in the published text, on page 17). These drafts are from 1938, and the play was presented and published in 1939. Eliot's changing of the event's date, then, may point to something that happened seven years before 1938 and eight years before 1939, that is, in 1931: something, it seems reasonable to conjecture, to do with his

own lamentable marriage. Eliot may think of 1931 as a time at which he felt
he had made some fateful and momentous step: a figurative departure on a
journey, away from the conventionally placid yet smothering institutions of his
past, that would culminate in his own torment and his wife's being "pushed
overboard," over the edge.

Eliot effectively separated from his wife in 1932, after many years of extremely difficult relations. *The Family Reunion* seems to be his attempt at confession (however oblique) to having pushed her into isolation, into madness—
into a kind of death. Though details remain incomplete about the final stage of
the Eliots' marriage, biographers agree that the poet bore some degree of com-
plicity for driving his wife away and committing her to institutionalization in
Northumberland House in 1938, where she remained until her death in 1947.
(Edith Sitwell is reported to have said that Tom went insane and promptly had
his wife certified.) Michael Hastings details this scenario most vituperatively in
the introduction to the text of *Tom and Viv,* his speculative though well-re-
searched play about the horrors of their marriage.

Eliot's biographers offer no specific elucidation on what might have happened in 1931, although certainly it was a time when his marriage was drawing
dramatically closer to collapse. There was little personal closeness between the
Eliots for most of their marriage, but by the early 1930s Eliot was moving
toward absolutely ending their relationship. Peter Ackroyd notes that in his
1931 essay on Thomas Heywood, Eliot quoted as a valedictory the lines, "O
God! O God! that it were possible / To undo things done; to call back yester-
day." He also writes that "in December of that year [Vivien] was describing to
Ottoline Morrell the unpleasant time she had had with her husband and, two
weeks later, complained that their Christmas had been a most unhappy one"
(188–89).[6]

THE TROUBLE WITH HARRY

Stylistically, this play is the most poetically resplendent of Eliot's four West
End drawing-room comedies. In a 1959 *Paris Review* interview, Eliot called
the play his best in terms of poetry (60), and in "T. S. Eliot as Dramatist"
Browne concurs: "Of the four modern works, *The Family Reunion* is poetically
by far the finest" (43). Eliot's fine, often entrancing poetic voice masks the
trouble with Harry. Eliot burdens the play with extraneous or unresolved material: The subplot about Harry's possible romance with Mary, a conventional
love interest, is incomplete and tangential to the matter at hand. The titular
reunion itself is unconsummated; two brothers never appear. Amy's death is
curiously irrelevant. The dramatic hook, or interest, in the murder mystery from
part 1 evaporates. All these facets, handled properly, could have generated ve-
hicles, or foils, or expository opportunities, for Harry. But as it stands, Harry
remains at sea: my own loaded metaphor, but one that fully describes his condition in this play. It is as if part of Harry's guilty contrition is to remain figuratively adrift, as his drowned wife has literally been relegated to this fate.

And Eliot, taking Harry's plight as his own, seems as much at sea in this play as Harry does. In *The Making of T. S. Eliot's Plays,* Browne's chapter on *The Family Reunion* extensively details copious revisions to the script, which nevertheless failed to overcome its basic and considerable dramatic problems. Gordon's intricate description of ten layers of composition (*New Life,* 277–78) details Eliot's five-year struggle with the play. Vinod Sena, incisively cataloguing the play's failures, charges that it finally "fails to cohere as a work of art, adding up at every level, thematic, structural and verbal, to an exercise in disintegration and discontinuity" (896). I suspect that Eliot sensed that he was incapable of ever writing this play properly. He was aware of structural imperfections that are diametrically antithetical to the deft craft and pacing of *Murder in the Cathedral.* But because of his interest in Harry, I believe, Eliot carried on with the project to completion despite misgivings and indications of inadequacies.

If the end of *The Family Reunion* suggests any sort of successful community statement or awareness, it does so only through the lens of the later plays: Harry's vague escape, apotheosis, anagnorisis, become more coherent if considered in the contexts of the resolutions of later characters. Celia Coplestone, Peter Quilpe, the Chamberlaynes, Colby Simpkins, Monica Claverton-Ferry, and Charles Hemington all do, finally, shed the tedious tokens of time present: lies, patterns of counterproductive interaction, emotional and social inadequacy. They experience, and dramatically present, a coherent emergence from their paralysis, finding (as Reilly terms it in *The Cocktail Party*) their "ways" or "*metiers.*" But of course those characters had not yet been imagined in 1939, so the question lingers: What is Eliot doing with Harry? What does the character's portrayal signify? Charles certainly speaks for the audience's interests when he states, after his nephew has departed from his first bizarre appearance on stage,

> My purpose is, to find out what's wrong with Harry:
> Until we know that, we can do nothing for him. (35)

Harry is a Jamesian exile, a wanderer, a passive victim of his times, tentatively awaiting what Henry James characterized for John Marcher in "The Beast in the Jungle" as "something rare and strange, possibly prodigious and terrible . . . altering everything, striking at the root of all my world and leaving me to the consequences" (71–72). Likewise, in the Jamesian mode, Harry is destined to fail in his endeavours or, at best, to attain only a Pisgah view of Palestine. The Jamesian tenor clearly infuses the play through Eliot's copious allusions to "The Jolly Corner," another ghost story about an exile who returns "after years abroad" and "meets his deformed other self lurking in the old family home," as Gordon aptly characterizes the parallel (88).[7] Eliot's ghostly nightmare play, with specters appearing by windows, evokes James's *The Turn of the Screw* as well.

Eliot's earlier poetic characters are laden with excuses for their inaction and inertia. Unlike Gerontion, though (who defers social responsibility because he "was neither at the hot gates / Nor fought in the warm rain / Nor knee deep in the salt marsh, heaving a cutlass, / Bitten by flies, fought" [29]), the Jamesian Harry *was* there: he was there at the drowning in time past, and unlike his blissfully absent brothers, he is there at Wishwood in time present. And unlike Prufrock, Harry *does* ask an overwhelming question: How does he balance his conventional social position and obligations as country gentleman, master of Wishwood, with the compulsion to do a girl in? How can he manage to do all the things that he knows are good in a theoretically moral way, aspiring to the ideal of community, when he has such bitter inner hostilities and a profound sense of individual and social iniquities? (This ideal of community is an especially vital one in the late 1930s as the absence of European community hurtles the world toward an inferno of which it knows precisely, from twenty years earlier, the horrendous nature.)

In contrast to Eliot's earlier types, Harry offers no excuses, no intellectual sidestepping or rationalizing. *The Family Reunion* presents a moment of truth for Eliot in 1939, which he seems compelled to undergo in a final assault on his personal animosities, hostilities, wastelands. In Eliot's earlier plays he had been hopefully attempting to acclimate himself to an Audenesque social demeanor. He tried to adopt a sensibility that acknowledges community responsibilities and awareness and the difficult yet necessary imperative to forsake the role of the spy, the stranger—a task especially hard for Eliot, a master poseur and voyeur. His heavy integration of an Audenesque tenor implied that his dramatic ideal was a selfless collective commonweal, as indicated by the individual's desire to become a member of a community of nurturing friends. (Auden's memorable formulation of this condition: "Equal with colleagues in a ring / I sit on each calm evening" [29].) From the perspective of 1939, it appears Eliot judged that *The Rock* and *Murder in the Cathedral* unnaturally repressed a darker solipsistic reality, masked it beneath the Audenesque demeanor; and that his fourth play would have to address the interstices of dramatic community and Hobbesian individualism.

Eliot's program for addressing this dramatic challenge may be examined and understood, once again, with respect to Auden. In his poem from *The Orators* that begins "Though aware of our rank and alert to obey orders," Auden surveys a generic battlefield's eager participants and asks, "What have we all been doing to have made from Fear / That laconic war-bitten captain addressing them now?" (22). Eliot's emotional landscape throughout his marriage, and as he writes *The Family Reunion,* is constituted of very different dangers from those of Auden's warscape. Still, Auden's language aptly suggests the central query that this play poses (and, in a manner, resolves): what has Eliot been doing to have made all this—his and Harry's hostilities, failed marriages, crimped emotional lives—from hatred, from miscommunication, from what boils down in Auden's poetic to Fear? Auden's question is embedded in a poem that concretely represents a war, meticulously inspecting the details, social patterns, and rituals of human behavior amid an unapologetically vivid depiction of a military regimen. In the same way, Eliot uses *The Family Re-union* to examine the etiology and nature of Harry's Fears, embedded in what figuratively articulates a personal battlefield as much as Auden's poem embod-ies a literal one.

Like Auden, then, Eliot chooses to confront and expose an array of solipsis-tic anticommunal torpor and to locate it in a schema that upholds more than it undercuts Harry's Fears. (That is to say, the play itself is fearful of asserting and embracing a viable or credible community. Eliot's later plays do not repeat this model: *The Cocktail Party* ends with the promised cocktail party; *The Fam-ily Reunion* does *not* end with a family reunion.) Auden makes his task more difficult by inserting his incisive social challenge into what is very pervasively a war poem, rather than a poem about a less drastic and ominous topic. He does this, I surmise, because it would have been too easy, and too artificial, to write those lines into a pacific poem. They are more difficult to resolve but more mimetic of the condition of the world outside—thus more valuable and more meaningfully resonant. The war poem distastefully but honestly evokes the realities of nationalism; authoritarian (and implicitly fascistic) social groups; the nature of war, and people's perverse attraction to it. Similarly, it might have been easier, smoother, for Eliot to write a character such as Harry into one of his last three plays, in which a fairy-godmother-like beneficence prevails and Harry would ultimately be much less aggravated by ghosts, guilt, and the lack of a nurturing community. (One might think of Eliot's final plays as emotional "peace-plays," as opposed to the fiercely "war-like" combativeness of *The Family Reunion*.) But the result would have been less real for Eliot, less valu-able. Certainly it would have been less relevant to the situation that afflicted his own life.

With its willful embrace of dramatic difficulty, it is unsurprising that this play should have proven to be less than successful: Eliot's old sharp edges and his wary, defensively closed postures, transposed into Harry, largely prove to stymie dramatic community. It is fitting that Eliot should have taken a ten-year hiatus after committing to the public stage this anticommunal dramatic state-ment, this bundle of hostilities against family, against traditional English com-munities, against emotional, personal, or community bonding of any sort. The play is an intentional abomination, for which *Four Quartets* embodies a kind of penance. Eliot sentences himself in "Little Gidding" 2 to "the rending pain of re-enactment / Of all that ʲou have done" (204)—this is what *The Family Reunion* consummately represents. (All dramatic performance, of course, is re-enactment; this expression in "Little Gidding," then, might be read more gen-erally as Eliot's disclosure that all his drama is a penance, to which he con-signs himself, for whatever "things ill done and done to others' harm" [204] he had committed throughout his life.) The antithesis to this painful reenact-ment is also contained within *Four Quartets:* in "East Coker" 1, it is por-trayed as

> daunsinge, signifying matrimonie—
> A dignified and commodious sacrament.
> Two and two, necessarye coniunction,
> Holding eche other by the hand or the arm
> Whiche betokeneth concorde. (183)

It is a vision of tightly harmonious community, set in Sir Thomas Elyot's Tudor tongue to the primal rhythms that Eliot believed infused all drama. These lines summarize what Eliot means to present—a paean to community, matrimonie, concorde—in his three final plays written after *Four Quartets. The Family Reunion* fails to manifest or develop, externally or in its own internal dramatic terms, the moral that I think Eliot would like to have been able to communicate by writing this play: that no matter how bleak one's past, one can determine to shed the shackles of time present and set a course toward atonement and redemption in time future ("follow[ing] the bright angels"). Yet the experience of writing the play seems to have been a kind of personal (if not a public, dramatically effective) catharsis for Eliot, enabling him to work out his antipathies toward families, communities, the mundane obligations of living in the present. His final three plays, especially *The Elder Statesman,* show his resolution of the personal and community quagmires that pervade this play.

FURIES, FEARS AND FELICITOUS FAILURE

Read in this light, the family reunion-that-is-no-reunion becomes the subject of a play whose strongest value (in the dramatic quest for community that I take as the ultimate imperative of Eliot's playwriting career) is its negative exemplariness. The reunion remains an unconsummated cipher, and the family itself is more of a deconstructed void than a real entity: Harry's father is long dead, only fuzzily remembered (and as a clumsy construct rather than a credible character). Harry's (nameless) wife is similarly dead, flat, an unconvincing blur in everyone's memory. Agatha and Mary are permanently without the prospect of their own mate or family, painfully marginalized within Wishwood's supposed "family community" as it stands. Harry's brothers are absent caricatures (and Eliot fully intended this sense of absence, resisting Browne's attempts to make them more concrete characters), while his ineffectual uncles might as well be; the seemingly pointless presence of Gerald and Charles betokens the vacancies Arthur and John would have manifested even if they had come to the reunion.[8] The ideas of family, reunion, Wishwood as community, and the entity of drama itself are all, in tandem, enmeshed in the enterprise of this play, which is implacably fated to be a resounding failure.

Another slant on why this play is and indeed should be a failure is offered by Richard E. Palmer's analysis of the play's existentialism. He finds a rich existential vein in the play's underlying mood of angst; its fundamental ontological assumptions about the pervasive inevitability of Harry's anxiety that are evocative of Sören Kierkegaard, Martin Heidegger, Karl Jaspers, and Jean Paul Sartre; its structure of values; and Harry's situation and pattern of action (174). "The anxiety of the family is clearly an existential anxiety," Palmer writes; "it has no precise object. It is more than an uneasiness in a particular situation; it is a sort of ultimate uneasiness. They do not know why they should be anxious" (175). I believe Palmer is correct that the Monchenseys keenly signify the resonant presence of the existential(ists') world, so it is not surprising that the drama of their reunion should be a morass of vacancy, uncertainty, irresolution, all of which is, in conventional dramatic terms, a failure.

Amid this setting, Palmer writes, the protagonist likewise is an exemplary token of the existential condition: Harry's "stance is that of a heroic confrontation of non-being: he is face to face with what he calls 'the nightmare'—in himself and in the world. His situation is thus the basic existential situation of the self in quest of a true self, and he is faced with the challenge to exist authentically in an inauthentic world, to find a way out of inauthenticity, out of spiritual meaninglessness and emptiness" (185). Given all this, the supposed faults of *The Family Reunion* may simply be explained as an illustration of dramatic form following function: if the plot, classical analogy, characters, denouement, dramatic consciousness, and confidence, all seem to hover in an existential void, that may be exactly Eliot's intent. (The same holds true for *The Waste Land:* the poem's devolution of conventional form is itself a statement on the condition of the modern world that the poem asserts.)

Palmer's reading, while providing a sort of aesthetic defense of this play's apparent problems, does not excuse its public dramaturgical failure. Certainly Sartre, Jean Genet, and Samuel Beckett demonstrated that one can write successful existential plays, but *The Family Reunion* is not redeemed by casting it in the context of those playwrights. Though it shows strong traces of existentialism, it does not come close to achieving the formal or structural unity of a play such as *Waiting for Godot* or *No Exit.* Eliot's merging of a partial (*not* complete or thorough) existential sensibility with conventional popular form is, then, yet another irreconcilable dramatic maneuver that this play attempts. The play is affected by all the malaise, uncertainty, and ambiguity that accompany the existential sensibility but without benefit of a consequent ameliorative (or instructive) aesthetic. The plays of Beckett, Sartre, and Genet teach their audiences something about how to exist in an existential world; *The Family Reunion* does not. Like the other incomplete or unsuccessful motifs that pervade this play—deconstructed (and unreconstructed) drama, voided characters, diffused plot and denouement—existentialism simply offers one more pothole in the road that makes Eliot's figurative path that much bumpier.

Harry is not stupid—especially to the extent that he represents the self-inscription of a writer not known for his humility. If Eliot fills Harry's character and the scenario in which he operates with flaws, there must be a reason for it. Harry must somehow learn from his mistakes, as Eliot hopes to do as well. As playwright, Eliot does indeed learn from the failures of past experience in his final three plays. (In his personal life, too, Lyndall Gordon suggests that Eliot's second marriage and his calmer later years represent a fairly conscious re-working of his earlier failures.)

Beginning its final speech (which I find one of the most memorable and haunting passages in Eliot's drama), the Chorus states, "We do not like to look out of the same window, and see quite a different landscape" (127). That unsettling experience is metaphorically what happens to Eliot in *The Family Reunion.* He looks out "the same window" as in all his plays—looking at various lives through the constant focus of aspiration to dramatic community. Out that window Eliot sees, for example, the seeds of a Christian community growing from Becket's martyrdom in *Murder in the Cathedral* or the seeds of a secular community rising from the ruins of the Chamberlaynes' marriage in *The Cocktail Party.* But in this play, through this window, he sees a very different landscape, a disconcerting one for playgoer and playwright alike. Instead of the potential for community, Eliot and Harry see here lingering bitterness that ends only in death or in a cowardly and selfish escape. In other plays, through other windows, Eliot finds a small piece of common ground, with the potential for building a discourse of shared communication leading to community, and an inspiration to persevere in this effort. Here, Eliot and Harry find the task of rebuilding a reinvigorated community on the ruins of the old one daunting, dispiriting, impossible.

What Harry literally sees out of the windows in this play, of course, are the Furies. What exactly are the Furies? No one in the play knows; though Harry ventures at interpretations, his character does not compel the audience to regard these as reliable—and in any case, he never explains his nature clearly enough to make his ghosts comprehensible. Eliot knew that the dramatic manifestations of these ghosts was always ludicrous: describing the presentation of the Furies at a 1948 Swedish performance, he said that they "had appeared as a sort of rugby team of fifteen huge leprous giraffes, swarming out when the bookshelves parted in a library that looked like St Pancras Station" (in Gordon, *New Life,* 87–88). Elsewhere he described various attempts at portraying these ghosts: "We put them on the stage, and they looked like uninvited guests who had strayed from a fancy dress ball. We concealed them behind gauze, and they suggested a still out of a Walt Disney film. We made them dimmer, and they looked like shrubbery just outside the window. I have seen other experiments tried: I have seen them signalling from across the garden, or swarming on to the stage like a football team, and they are never right" (*Poetry and Drama,* 90).

Browne never knew what the Furies were or how to stage them; nor did other producers. Browne notes that Harry faces a group of figures who neither speak nor move and thus have no life for the audience. "This is a grave mistake; and Eliot is right in saying that none of the devices that either he or I have used or seen others use has overcome this handicap. The Eumenides, whatever they look like, however eerie the sounds or lighting effects which accompany them, cannot involve the audience in an experience which cannot be seen [because Harry must be facing upstage, toward a window and thus away from the audience] upon the face of the character who alone can mediate it" (117).

Gordon assumes the Furies are supposed to be terrifying, but "such terror was never achieved in Eliot's lifetime by all accounts of productions on both sides of the Atlantic. In fact, reviews mention the Furies surprisingly little, which itself suggests their feeble impact. . . . In an Illinois production in 1949, the Furies looked like toy puppets or jacks-in-the-box: not scary, rather fun. In October 1958, at the Phoenix Theatre in New York, they had red pupils glaring from enormous white eyes, as they peeped coyly through the draperies of the living-room" (87–88). In 1951 Eliot finally decided, as he writes in *Poetry and Drama,* that the Furies "must, in future, be omitted from the cast, and be understood to be visible only to certain of my characters, and not to the audience" (90).

Based upon this barrage of evidence from playwright, director, critics, and reviewers, it is safe to state that the Furies represent the single largest and most obvious dramaturgical blunder in the play. As throughout *The Family Reunion,* such a problem announces the presence of fascinating and important issues, although rarely the satisfactory treatment and resolution of these issues. (Remember, again, Coghill's perception of the play's arresting and courageous flaws.)

What is it, then, that Harry or the Chorus or Eliot sees out the window? Generalized Fear—probably petty fears, which is how Auden (who shapes Eliot's choral portrayals of fears in his previous plays) would see it. Worse, the view out of the window embodies inexactitude, ambiguity, uncertainties. In Eliot's earlier poetry, he would have had a field day with these uncertainties. He would have wryly transformed them into "the damp souls of housemaids / Sprouting despondently at area gates" (19), as he portrayed his uncertainties about quotidian urban life in "Morning at the Window," or into surreal dark turns amid vacant, windy, depraved spaces, as he depicted the uncertainties of European cultural history in "Gerontion." By the time he embarks upon his dramatic career, though, Eliot intently seeks the kinds of Aristotelean certainties that "Little Gidding" 5 invokes: simple, common, formal precision; clear sentences, clear images, clear moralities. Dramatic manifestations of these certainties in his later plays are the Euripidean complexities that unravel and resolve themselves in anagnorisis, or loosely Christian "mysteries" that find resolution in the eternally unchanging reality of the savior. And so, again, it is fitting that the Furies—antithetical to Aristotelean entelechy—are such a mess, both in terms of Eliot's conception of them and various directors' attempts to stage them; just as it is fitting that Harry's character be unactable. If it is disconcerting to look out the same window and see a different view, Eliot teaches himself in this play, one must re-vise: not the kind of mechanical revisions manifested during the five years Eliot spent tinkering with this play but a revision in the fullest etymological sense of the word. Eliot must see again; clear his mind; finish *Four Quartets* and take a decade-long respite from the theatre—wiping the slate clean—before embarking upon another play.

VALID WORDS 1: AN UN-COWARDLY FAREWELL TO AUDEN

The Audenesque voice and tenor in *The Family Reunion* functions as in *The Rock* and *Murder in the Cathedral*. It appears, again, most prominently and suitably in Eliot's Chorus—because Eliot is drawing upon Auden as a touchstone of communal concern—as, for example, when it declaims,

> Why should we stand here like guilty conspirators, waiting for some revelation
> When the hidden shall be exposed, and the newsboy shall shout in the street?
> When the private shall be made public, the common photographer
> Flashlight for the picture papers: why do we huddle together
> In a horrid amity of misfortune? why should we be implicated, brought in and
>   brought together? . . .
>
> We like to appear in the newspapers
> So long as we are in the right column.
> We know about the railway accident
> We know about sudden thrombosis
> And the slowly hardening artery. . . .
> We only ask to be reassured
> About the noises in the cellar
> And the window that should not have been open. (42–43)

The Audenesque devices, briefly, include vague, abstract moralism (about guilt, conspiracy, revelation, exposure) set off against an understated specific, immediate, quotidian tableau (the newsboy's shout in the street); the constant compulsion to extrapolate a human situation to its ultimate social culmination (as the group huddles, jointly implicated and brought together); the ironic juxtaposition of the momentous and the ubiquitous (the railway accident and hardening arteries), lampooning our unwillingness to distinguish between events of real external import and our own private obsessions. At the culmination of this thumbnail sketch—a small slice of a sociomoral panorama—Eliot, like Auden, identifies the roots of all this as childish insecurity (needing to be reassured) and the banal essence of fear (imagistically localized, reduced, to noises in the cellar).

The Audenesque, though, is on the way out of Eliot's drama by 1939. *The Family Reunion* marks Eliot's final sally at the fierce social challenges Auden poses, the challenges that pervade Audenesque language. Eliot's final three plays are more attuned to an individual rather than a social outlook. They retain Eliot's community-minded focus but from the perspective of each person's attitudes and conditions, in contrast to the earlier plays' keener attention to the overarching social dynamics of community. (As an emblem of this shift, note that the Chorus—the literal manifestation of community as a mass social group—which is so integral to Eliot's first four plays, is considerably minimized in the fifth and absent from the last two.) In the later plays, Eliot diminished the institutions and rituals of community behavior that had previously played such a central role: Sweeney's party, ritualized jazz patter, music-hall evocations, historical tableaux reinforcing archetypal social and spiritual patterns, mass-experienced martyrdom as the basis of an ecclesiastical community, the institution of the manor at Wishwood as a community for the gentry.

Instead, Eliot will depict in his final plays rich and fully individualized characters who explore their own personal relationship to, and need of, community. It is not too extreme to suggest that in his first twenty-three years of playwriting, from 1926 until *The Cocktail Party* in 1949, Eliot failed to create such fully rounded, satisfying, self-sufficiently individualized dramatic characters; failed to produce a character that transcended flat formulaic types or (like Harry) overdetermined composites.

The more pronounced dramatic stylistic resonance in the final plays will derive from the easily and self-consciously dramatic atmosphere best embodied in the plays of Noël Coward, certainly a less ponderous influence to handle than Auden. Eliot might reasonably be expected to have allowed himself a transfer to Coward's camp as a sort of reward for having traversed, to his own moral satisfaction, the keenly demanding Audenesque landscape of community and ethics by the time he had completed *The Family Reunion*.

Indeed, *The Confidential Clerk*—especially evocative of Coward's drama with all the intricacies and complications that confront a refined high-society couple—contains what may be a subtle allusion to Coward. Lady Elizabeth left an infant son (who turns out to be B. Kaghan) in the town of Teddington, then lost touch with him because she forgot the town's name. When she hears in act 3 that a Mrs. Guzzard from Teddington is coming to see them, her memory is triggered. She recalls where she has left her son, and consequently, all the convoluted, obscure, and deceitful family dynamics that have plagued the Mulhammers begin to clear up. Teddington, Middlesex, is also Coward's birthplace. If the allusion is intentional, Eliot is paying homage to a dramatic model who considerably influenced the style and tenor toward which his later plays evolve. For Eliot, as well as for the Mulhammers, Teddington represents a place linked to the resolution of complex obscurities, and the enabling of a life the eschews an Audenesque ethical morass in favor of a more navigable condition. When Eliot and his characters "remember" Teddington, they are rewarded by being able to function in communities that transcend obstacles to tolerant interaction. Under the influence of Coward, Eliot creates communities of drama that may experience a bit of turbulence at first but are destined to achieve, finally, a calm and harmonious conclusion.

Drafts show Eliot's inclination even in this play to write in a voice like

Coward's, though some such tendencies are effaced before the final version. At one point, for example, after Charles says, "I'd like to ask Downing" (35) about something, he goes on (in both drafts D5 and D4) with a wry but pointless quibble on the servant's name, playfully describing Downing as a downy bird. And at one of the play's most serious moments, when Harry bloodlessly announces that he pushed his wife overboard, draft D5 includes two lines that chattily amplify this statement but without adding any substantial content. In the final version, the response to Harry's statement is tightened: Violet simply responds, "Pushed her?" (29).

Both these eliminations from the drafts, like several other cuts Eliot made, remove dialogue that is clever in the mode of Coward: pleasant, harmless, but empty. In Eliot's later plays, such coy, garrulous snatches of dialogue fit easily—consider, for instance, much of the chatter in *The Cocktail Party*. In *The Family Reunion,* Eliot draws upon but later edits out the tenor of Coward. The sharp, tensely stylized, sometimes existential tone that infuses the play nevertheless retains traces of an influence that will appear in his subsequent plays.

The scene in which Harry announces his supposed murder is a crucial dramatic exposition of a tremendously significant event. After the two lines of Coward-like repartee were cut, only two words remain in the final text: the effect is minimalist, clipped, understated, eerie. Violet's two-word response, as opposed to the more conversational dialogue Eliot had originally written, emphasizes Harry's tortured and interiorized mind. This speech offers an example of how Eliot begins to establish a community sensibility in *The Family Reunion* but fails to develop the initiative to its logical conclusion. This play will *not* be about how a drawing room of people, a community, responds to personal horrors. (*The Cocktail Party,* by contrast, *is* exactly about that.) Eliot undercuts social voices, and a social sensibility. He scents the lightly verbose and interactive patter that will flourish in his final three plays, which characters will use to talk about themselves and work out (rather than repress) their problems. But his instinct in 1939 is to squelch that language one last time.

VALID WORDS 2: IN YOUR OWN LANGUAGE

The play's consummate insight into Eliot's grappling with language takes place at this moment when Harry claims to have killed his wife. As he fumbles to confront the ghosts of Wishwood, Agatha implores him to explain what is on his mind: "Talk in your own language, without stopping to debate / Whether it may be too far beyond our understanding" (28). Harry gropes, not very successfully, for a concrete response. Amid a profusion of untethered surreal images (creatures wandering directionlessly in a smoky vapor, automatism, and flickering anaesthetised consciousness), he attains one isolated moment of clear communicative breakthrough: "I talk in general terms / Because the particular has no language" (29).

Both Agatha's and Harry's references to language were late interpolations to the rest of the surrounding dialogue: both were added after the 1938 Eliot Collection drafts, indicating that the role of language became a cohering focus for Eliot toward the end of his composition process. He consciously wove into the text, amid an especially murky scene, explicit statements about how he viewed the function of language amid a tenuous community in turmoil.

Stripped of the dense surrounding dialogue, Harry's statement about his language embodies the play's essence, its success and failure. Certainly the failure thus revealed is considerable. The absence of a language for the particular, to a poet as precise and particular as Eliot, is a damning lack. But this lack is mitigated with a tentative success—an ability, a determination, to speak in at least a general language if that is the only option. The later plays will considerably amplify this success as they increasingly lay claim to the language of the particular, moving closer to where the words are valid.

Agatha's point is simply that Harry must break his eight years of silence. He must speak, because he is a dramatic character, onstage in a play. He cannot ponder and ruminate to himself ("stopping to debate," as she puts it, which would be an interior debate with himself, not a communicative endeavor), as so many of Eliot's earlier poetic personae did to avoid social interaction. Agatha will not allow Harry to take the air in a tobacco trance. Imploring him to speak whether or not he is immediately comprehensible, she signals a break in the patterns of muteness that so overwhelmingly pervaded *The Waste Land* and Eliot's other poetry of horrific modern ineffability. Later, Harry can worry about honing, shaping, what he has to say, but the necessary first step is simply to begin speaking.

As it progresses, the play offers indications that Agatha's strategy has begun to work. Learning of John's automobile accident, Ivy and Violet chastise Harry for failing to express an appropriate sentiment. What they consider his lack of suitable language, he responds, is not a sign that he is unconscious; rather, he is hyper-conscious, living on several planes at the same time, although unable to express this consciousness because he cannot speak with multiple voices simultaneously. (This explanation essentially restates his initial complaint about communication, that the particular—his exact polymorphous state of consciousness—has no language.) But he embellishes upon this, thus moving beyond implacable muteness. He does indeed have appropriate feelings about his brother, he announces. "Only, that's not the language / That I choose to be talking. I will not talk yours" (85). Harry explicitly puts into action his earlier expression to Agatha, speaking *generally* if unable to speak of, and in, the particular. He is not speaking his family's language, and they do not understand him here (though remember that Agatha had assured him it did not matter if he is not understood). But clearly, he is speaking *some* language, and so it only remains for him to find a place where this language, these words, are valid.

Another indication of progression toward improved communication: Denman—Harry's servant, so an extension of his master—tells the family not to worry about Harry after he has announced his intention to go off somewhere; he feels Harry will not need him for much longer. He senses that Harry is off to some realm where the world's cares and ghosts that have oppressed him for most of his life will no longer do so. Denman cannot prove, or concretely explain, exactly what will happen to Harry: "I've no gift of language," he says, "but I'm sure of what I mean" (124). Eliot means to reassure the audience that Harry has some version of a happy ending, serenity, in store for him, even though it is not precisely informed of this ending in language. The words, clearly, are *not* yet fully valid to convey whatever condition of grace or re-demption Harry attains at the end of the play, but that is not an obstacle to moving some measure in the right direction, *toward* a place where the words will be valid, where Harry could explain what has happened to him in time past and how he will mediate time future, even if he is not yet exactly there. Meaning exists before language, Eliot informs us through this line of Den-man's; Agatha knew this when she told Harry to speak in his own language without worrying about whether the rest of them would understand it. She knew his words would still have some, if not complete, validity, because they would reflect the fact that he had some meaning, some sense of something he wanted to say, in his own mind, even if it could not (*yet*) be understood; communal understanding will come later. Such understanding does not seem to happen within this play: certainly it does not for Amy, who dies before she even gets a chance to try to understand Harry's future life; probably it does not, either, for any of the other characters (though perhaps Agatha has a glimpse of it), or for the audience. Desmond MacCarthy confirms this in his review: "If I had grasped" the point of the play "while in the theatre instead of only when on my return home, I should not have been so perplexed by the play."

Harry, for his part, explains his failure to speak in the medium of communal-ity that Eliot's other plays attain. The "general" terms in which Harry says he speaks very much connote the language of Eliot's poetry: the passage sur-rounding that statement is replete with echoes of all the major phases of his work from "Prufrock" through "Burnt Norton."[9] Harry himself characterizes what he is saying here as "trying to give you / Comparisons in a more familiar medium" (28)—that is, the medium more familiar to Eliot, the language of his earlier poetry. "The particular," for which there is no language, would offer a way to identify and explain Harry's problem: a way of saying, particularly, that he had a miserably failed marriage and was incapable of sustaining a human relationship, rather than just generally acting obliquely brooding, antisocial, put upon. If one can particularize one's ghosts, one's hell, then one can isolate it, confront it, and proceed on with the rest of the things in the general world, which need not all be affected by one's particular anguish (as they were when Prufrock or the gentleman caller in "Portrait of a Lady" took a walk, felt some particular source of oppression that he could not express, and thus envisioned the entire surrounding world as full of malaise and torpor).

Harry's greatest insight in this play is that the particular—*this* particular set of circumstances, for him, here and now—has no language. His "muteness" in terms of being able to speak a specific language in this play is foreshadowed, if not predetermined, when the Chorus, in its first speech just before his entrance, refers to itself as "actors who have not been assigned their parts" or who have "rehearsed the wrong parts" (21–22). Actors, on stage, announcing the absence of a proper script, foster a dramatic atmosphere in which one is not surprised to find that a character such as Harry has no specific language.

When Harry tries vainly to explain his emotional condition to his family in part 2, scene 1, he exasperatingly states, in necessarily futile language, that he needs another language to facilitate social intercourse between him and Wishwood: "Oh, there *must* be another way of talking / That would get us somewhere. You don't understand me. / You can't understand me" (90). And Eliot further asserts this theme, a total lack of workable language, when Harry tells his family (or actually, is unable to tell them) why he is leaving them and where he will go: "I cannot explain it to anyone: / I do not know the words in which to explain it" (109).

Eliot reverts to a mode that pervaded his earlier poetry and characterized much of high modernist literature. As I describe in *The Language of Modernism,* a central motif of literature from the early modernist period was the complaint that the modern condition simply differed so drastically from that of any earlier period that there was no language that could contain or convey its traumas, its ironies, its aesthetic. This plaint of an imperative muteness was both a call to arms for the creation of a new (or at least radically altered) language and a justification for the modernists' writing in their language that often verged on the obscure and impenetrable.

It is surprising, though, that Eliot is still making excuses for the limitations of language as late as 1939—surprising and, perhaps, erroneous: once again, there arises another way of explaining the failure of *The Family Reunion.* By 1939, Eliot has been able to craft and implement a complete, wide-ranging, usable language for himself by shoring fragments against the ruins of the old poetic tradition. The plaint of muteness would seem to ring hollow; it is even a bit gratuitous, or contrived, for a man who has become one of the world's most prominent poets to complain that there is no language for the particular: how, then, has he been able to generate such a bitingly particular and widespread poetic appraisal of the modern age? Additionally, by 1939 Eliot had seemed to move away from a view of the world as conspiratorily and ubiquitously hostile to any meaningful communication; in his previous three plays he has clearly accepted that there is some possible condition of community that includes a communicative language.

In *The Family Reunion,* Eliot offers his quintessential complaint about society, about the world, that he has been tirelessly repeating for three decades—he cannot speak in it. But his reponse to this condition now, finally, is not merely to bemoan the exhaustion of old language or the society that has stupidly lost the ability to use its gift of meaningful speech; nor is it bitterly to celebrate the demise of the old language with a harsh, new (but similarly anti-social) substitute for it. Rather, since the particular has no language, Eliot rejects this particular. He keeps the language; the discourse he crafts in *The Family Reunion* looks forward to the language he uses in his last three plays (dramatic verse dialogue in rhythms that unobtrusively approximate normal speech, as he often described it) more than back to the language of the previous three. The play demonstrates the beginning of a trust in language that is new to Eliot's poetic. He accepts that there is a way of talking, a discourse, a medium, that can be valid. The language is fine; it is the particular that must go: particularly Harry and the unpalatable lingering remnants of an Eliotic sensibility that he must increasingly come to see as obsolete. As deft as Eliot became at the genre of popular, light verse-comedy (with a kick) over the next two decades, the presence of another character like Harry could have sundered the enterprise at any turn. Eliot's solution: no more Harrys. Earlier, Eliot would have found this solution unconscionably false, absurd. By the time he completes *The Family Reunion,* though, he has apparently dealt with his Furies, his Harrys, adequately. The play copiously expresses the need to confront one's ghosts and to come to terms with their power to haunt because of their knowledge of one's mistakes from time past. After 1939, Eliot's ghosts, though never absent from his plays, could no longer torment him; they could no longer render the dramatic enterprise inert, or solipsistically mute, as Harry nearly does here.

——— 5 ———

The Cocktail Party: "Where the Words Are Valid"

More critical material—and more outdated critical material—has been written about *The Cocktail Party* than about any of Eliot's other plays. Eliot's drama enjoyed a burst of attention during the 1950s and 1960s, when critical writing tended to be more affirming of his enterprise than not, although there was also mitigated praise and disapproval; but the scholarship is largely vague and impressionistically belletristic, minimally useful to later scholars. (A striking exception is Carol H. Smith's 1963 *T. S. Eliot's Dramatic Theory and Practice,* a seminal study that transcended the limitations of her critical generation. It is still eminently readable; my study is the first play-by-play scholarly monograph since Smith's, and even three decades later I do not presume that my work supersedes hers.)

This chapter largely sidesteps the accreted annals of scholarship on *The Cocktail Party.*[1] I take on, though, one representative critic, J. L. Styan, whose pronouncements from *The Elements of Drama* will be opportunistically exploited as a springboard for my own contextualization of the play. I offer no apologies for making Styan a whipping boy for his generation of critics; his era still largely shapes the critical discourse on Eliot's drama, and their attitudes need to be displaced.

WHAT'S PAST IS PROLOGUE: *THE WASTE LAND,* REDUX, WITH A TWIST

Styan's work, a study of dramaturgical technique, analyzes *The Cocktail Party* in a chapter called "Passing Judgment" (275–84) as an example of how to examine a play critically. Styan finds the play technically haphazard, imbalanced, and unintegrated; its "nebulous and complex" examination of happiness encourages the audience "to find values in this play that do not in fact exist there. . . . Because it cannot chronicle all the human gradations existing between a Lavinia and a Celia, the play opens enough windows for its audience to flirt with its subject in vague terms" (275). The play's "lucidity may lead the audience to take . . . symbolic solutions at face value without regard for the overtones of meaning Mr. Eliot was working for. This scarcely makes for authoritative drama" (275). Styan complains of the characters' lame, naturalistic response to Celia's death; I quote at length to give a sense of his generation's reading of Eliot's drama, which this passage typifies.

The failure of integration of the two patterns of the play becomes striking when the news of Celia's death on an ant-hill is disclosed. At this crux, the play might be said to collapse. It was necessary to remove Celia from the scene in order that attention might be refocused on the Chamberlaynes. It was also necessary to provide a vividly physical shock to stress that Celia's martyrdom is not a fantasy of doubtful reality. Mr. Eliot electrifies us into sudden awareness of the actuality of her situation. He also wishes to bring her, as it were, vicariously back to life, that we do not forget her contribution, but feel her presence. . . . Edward and Lavinia are represented in theory as having returned to our level, though not quite to the level of the first scene. But in practice they have not. Their reaction is naturalistic: they can neither understand the new Celia nor what her death means. As a sacrifice, it seems to them one of appalling waste. . . . Lavinia and Edward together stumble along with ineffectual remarks that stress their comparative littleness: it would seem they understand each other and that is enough. But naturally, though shocked like the Chamberlaynes, we do not respond as they respond. They cease to be our mouthpiece. Unlike them, we know from Reilly what Celia undertook. . . . Our reaction, therefore, is one of greater understanding than theirs, and again, therefore, we are unsympathetic with them. We remain several moves ahead of them as they fumble toward the understanding of her "happy death." If we do respond in part to their admirable humility, we must detach ourselves from Celia and view her as distantly as they do. She then becomes so much a creature apart, that her significance for us is restricted by the measure of that distance. In Act III *The Cocktail Party* becomes two plays to which we give divided allegiance, and in doing so damage and destroy the meaning and value of both. (281–82)

I suggest that the passage Styan identifies as sundering the play is, on the contrary, one of the play's most important and effective in terms of establishing the sensibility Eliot intends. It begins when Peter, who wants Celia to meet the casting director for a film he is planning, asks cocktail party guests: "Can you tell me where she is? I couldn't find her / In the telephone directory."

JULIA

Not in the directory,
Or in any directory. You can tell them now, Alex.

LAVINIA

What does Julia mean?

ALEX

I was about to speak of her
When you came in, Peter. I'm afraid you can't have Celia.

PETER

Oh . . . Is she married?

ALEX

Not married, but dead.

LAVINIA

Celia?

ALEX

Dead.

PETER

Dead. That knocks the bottom out of it.

EDWARD

Celia dead. (173–74)

The dry tone anticipates the late modernist (or perhaps postmodernist) avant-garde theatrical sensibility that would emerge in England over a decade later. *Beyond the Fringe,* Joe Orton's dark farces, Harold Pinter's drama of haunting understatement, *Monty Python's Flying Circus,* all enact the tenor Eliot presents here: it is typified by the missed beat, hyperbolically underplayed; the tame and low-key morbidity; the inappropriate social disjunction handled with quintessentially English aplomb yet still, beneath the surface, remaining awkwardly unsettled. It is a sensibility, too, with affinities to even earlier writing of Eliot's: remember the offputting ironic disjunctions of characters from *The Waste Land.* Madame Sosostris "[h]ad a bad cold, nevertheless / Is known to be the wisest woman in Europe" (54); compare Celia's crucifixion, very near an ant-hill, nevertheless . . .

Celia is indeed a type of "the wisest woman in Europe." The cocktail party guests appreciate this fact, as does Eliot, who nevertheless cannot forbear giving her the deflationary equivalent of the famous clairvoyant's bad cold, crucifying her near an anthill. He embraces his old familiar trope of ironic-pathetic mock tragedy, marked by a deprecatory lack of seriousness, lack of stateliness. A similarly pervasive assault on order, propriety, and dignity pervaded and deflated the dramatic cast of *The Waste Land:* Mr. Eugenides, the typist at teatime, et al.

Celia's tawdry and anticlimactic death scene evokes another moment in Eliot's drama: the Knights' ludicrous display after Becket's assassination is very much in the same vein. As in *Murder in the Cathedral,* Eliot bombards his audience in *The Cocktail Party* with the pervasive banality of the community that survives the martyr. He demands that the saints be understood not in the abstract but with the concrete recognition that the world out of which they emerge is, if not a pure reenactment of his 1920s waste land, at least still nursing a severe hangover from that condition; a world in which a head cold is more prominent, and more immediately momentous, than the apogee of European wisdom. *The Waste Land,* incidentally, *was* about the wisdom of Europe, despite the fact that wisdom's lame, purported embodiment, Madame Sosostris, is a comic caricature. The satirical construct nevertheless seriously illuminates that which is satirized. Celia's death, by the same token, retains its meaning of wisdom and sacrificial spiritual inspiration for her community, and it is all the more pertinent in that it fits the pedestrian tone of the community as it is presented. If, as Styan might prefer, the party guests joined together in a somber chorus of dirgeful spiritual lamentation, then Celia's death would be irrelevant in terms of the community Eliot has been establishing.

By the time of *The Cocktail Party,* the eerie modernist angst of *The Waste Land* is tamed, but it is still cloyingly, messily present. For much of the play (until its last movement finally transcends this messiness), the nature of marriage is cast in essentially identical terms to its portrayal in the middle section of "A Game of Chess" in *The Waste Land:* as a neurotic, noncommunicative, torturous forced conjunction of "finite centres" that can never interact with each other. Despite the power of this wastelandish sensibility, though, and despite its irreverent manifestation at the moment when the audience learns of Celia's agony, the vintage Eliotic strain is concommitant with the foundation of a community of drama: for a community foundation is the immediate consequence of the party's learning of her death. The remainder of the play pointedly involves nurturing and codifying an incipient community; putting the finishing touches on it; making sure that the acting community and the audience community see, know, and appreciate what has been accomplished.

The triumph of the community of drama that emerges after Celia's death is not an ability to wish away, or act away, the grotesqueness it has connoted (most vividly via cannibalism, offering an unsavory throwback to the last dramatic cocktail party Eliot gave in *Sweeney Agonistes*). Rather, the play's triumph is that it can continue for another ten minutes from this point and continue in the unruffled dramatic patter evocative of Noël Coward, rather than reverting, as Sweeney finally did at his party, to the frenzied chorus of dithyrambic "Hoo-ha's" evocative of Fritz Lang. *The Cocktail Party* continues beyond Celia's death: it continues to shore fragments against the ruins, and it does so not (as at the end of *The Waste Land,* which is more about fragments than shoring) at the eye of a stormy nervous breakdown in process. Here there is no haunting refrain of "Hieronymo's mad againe," warning of the ominous likelihood of another bout of the madness that has just been traversed. Granted, there remains the possibility that Edward's mad again. But this possibility is averted, diffused, in a calming sense of commonweal, easy social interaction, that fits much more naturally than "Shantih" seemed to at the end of *The Waste Land*. There, the word was an arcane, far-fetched construct: foreign, incomprehensible without the endnote (and even then enigmatic). Here, where the words are valid, the ending is soothingly free from intellectually wrenched affectation.

Such aversion of madness, restoration of order, is not poetically deft or stunning; it is mechanical and unmomentous but necessary. This commitment to a quotidian endurance evokes Eliot's stolid determination in "East Coker": "each venture / Is a new beginning. . . . There is only the fight to recover what has been lost / And found and lost again and again. . . . For us, there is only the trying" (189). To return to the occasion of my prefatory tirade: Styan's analysis does little more than confirm that *The Cocktail Party* was written by the author of *The Waste Land* and *Four Quartets,* rather than by, say, Terrence Rattigan. The play is, as Styan terms it, imbalanced, unintegrated, and unauthoritative, because it is a mimetic representation of such a world—the world out of which it emerges and toward which its message is directed; a world in which Eliot *had* lived, solipsistically, and *will continue to* live, communally.

PARTY TALK

The Cocktail Party opens amid a profusion of storytelling. Though the audience catches only fragments of stories, even these dregs (something about being up in a tree with the Maharaja or in the pantry as Lady Klootz rinses her mouth with champagne) bespeak a wide range of adventure, experience, and interaction shared and vicariously relived at this party. The beginning of act 3 parallels this opening scene, reenacting the parodic cocktail party jabber with shards of eclectically flying conversation (intrigues in distant "primitive" lands, destructive monkeys, heathen sacrifices). Here, the party talk more discernibly, though still obliquely, anticipates the play's story line. Under Alex and Julia's guidance, the scatterbrained chatter eventually comes around to Celia's martyrdom in far-off Kinkanja, among "heathens" and destructive elements of an exotic landscape.

These two cocktail parties frame the complex and enigmatic social challenge at the play's core: a married couple's quest for harmony, succor, and communication. The parties are apt paradigms for the nature of community as Eliot envisions it in this play. The free, fluent chatter indicates that the community is more successful, better composed, better able to foster interaction among its members, than any of Eliot's communities heretofore. Absent are the kinds of fears posed by the timid chorus in *Murder in the Cathedral*—averse to any venture that might lead to involvement within a functioning community, and undercutting the force of even the most saintly action. Instead, here, voices merge and contribute equally to the perpetuation of nothing more momentous than the parties and their small talk: but this is enough. The topics are inane, insipid, but they pose no threat to anyone. Eliot's cocktail parties provide safe havens. They are occasions for taking care of and feeding people; checking up on social concerns and contacts; ensuring that people's careers are on track, that they are in touch with each other, that their marriages are functioning. The gatherings generate trust (asked how she knows that a man could hear bats' cries, Julia responds, "Because he said so. And I believed him" [14]) and epistemological certainty (Celia interjects, "There isn't much that Julia doesn't know" [14]). In terms of dramatic form, the parties offer an easy, natural, fecund realm of rapport, development, and unlimited possibility. In *The Life of the Party: Festive Vision in Modern Fiction,* Christopher Ames characterizes the nature of the party in modern society and as it is reenacted in literature: "Our increasingly isolated existence . . . renders parties all the more essential in providing some concrete sense of a society capable of being experienced with immediacy. And though the exclusive nature of invitations may reinforce class distinctions, parties can still dissolve barriers within the newly created community" (12).

But contrary dynamics affect the parties as well: as the plot unfolds, hidden agendas and subterfuge surface. Edward's wife, Lavinia, is absent because she had left him just hours earlier; her cold, impulsive departure suggests that their marriage, despite its mannerly facade, had been in fact a shallow mockery. Celia, it becomes apparent, has been having an affair with Edward, a liaison that itself comes to seem loveless and shallow. Similarly, Peter has been having an extramarital fling with Lavinia but yearns for Celia. In retrospect, it becomes clear that several party guests had been, to say the least, holding their cards close to their chests: consumed with their own subplots and subtexts and considerably less engaged than they appeared to be in what had at first seemed the easily dramatic community free-for-all paced by Julia's incontinent volubility. After the fact—after the audience begins to realize what the drama is about, what kinds of forces are in play—the cocktail party may well be reappraised as pointless. As the postparty realities, unpleasantnesses, and contradictions manifest themselves, Julia's seemingly polite attempts to find out about people and prod them to talk about themselves increasingly appear to be the work of a conniving, meddling busybody, a mission that is apparently pointless and a failure.

Both these contradictory visions of a party are meant to frame this play and the Chamberlaynes' marital struggle at its center. Party and marriage are infused with a dialectic tension between communal harmony and personal combativeness. Communities can be nurturing, natural, smooth. They can be deceitful, devious, intrusive. And, finally, they are both at once. The married couple is a microcosm of the community; Eliot's depiction of the community as defined by the cocktail party guests is a backdrop for the Chamberlaynes' travails, and the Chamberlaynes' quest must be to orient their lives to fit within Eliot's double-edged vision of community.

LET US GO THEN, YOU AND I

One might go even further than "double-edged," in characterizing the pathology of Eliot's community vision in *The Cocktail Party*. Peter, returning to speak with Edward after the party, explodes:

> This evening I felt I could bear it no longer.
> That awful party! I'm sorry, Edward;
> Of course it was really a very nice party
> For everyone but me. (37)

Peter's expression is not technically schizophrenic, since the final line qualifies the seeming contradiction that a party could be at the same time an "awful party" and a "very nice party." Nevertheless, the audience's subliminal sense is still that the statement is manifestly illogical, insane. (In *Is There a Text in This Class?* Stanley Fish discusses a similar and familiar trope in Milton's sonnets: the audience processes the contradiction, then its explanation or resolution, but this treatment does not diminish an initial and predominant experience of contradiction.) The inability to think and express oneself logically, which Peter's outburst suggests, indicates schizophrenia. It becomes apparent during the post-party return to Edward's flat that several characters might describe the party as Peter has done, with a schizophrenic reaction to a schizophrenic experience.

The play's characters manifest several different "personalities"—which take the form, here, of different stances toward harmony and community—vying for expression at a given moment, in a given situation. A schizophrenic's myriad personalities are not under the control of a governing ego. Rather, various characteristics appear, disappear, mutate, replace one another—haphazardly and unpredictably—to the detriment of the sanity and mental stability of the person manifesting these fluctuations. A single self is not (as for a sane person) a substantial center; the schizophrenic exhibits alienation and dissolution, loss, undoing, estrangement, fragility of ego boundaries, and mutations of a discrete and continuous selfhood.

Schizophrenia is characterized by progressive deterioration, which marks the characters' increasingly untenable social and personal stances late in act 1 and through most of act 2. Symptoms include peculiar behavior (such as that which Edward extensively exhibits at his party); inability to care for oneself (which Eliot depicts through the Guardians' perception of the need to feed Edward); and loosening of associations (connoted by the dissolution of the Chamberlaynes' marital microcommunity, and Edward's general inability to interact in the social association at his flat, i.e., the constant sense that he does not fit in, or belong, at his own party). The patients' general behavior as they undergo Reilly's "treatment" in act 2 manifests such schizophrenic signs as digressive, vague, overelaborate speech (especially Edward's long-winded and fairly irrelevant self-defenses); odd and delusive thoughts (Celia reveals that she perceives the entire world around her to be a delusion); unusual perceptual experiences (about the patients' egos, their relationships, their patterns of life, the unity of their past and future); a deteriorating sense of self, identity, purpose for living (shown by all the characters—most prominently Celia—in their sessions with Reilly).

Other lesser or corollary personality disorders add to the schizophrenic milieu: especially, borderline personality disorder, sometimes called "stable instablity" and characterized by chronic difficulty in regulating mood and maintaining a consistent self-image; impulsive and self-damaging behavior; unpredictable moods; brief outbursts of anger, irritability, sadness, and fear; a sense of suffering from chronic emptiness; and chaotic interpersonal relationships. These symptoms, widely attributable to the play's characters, round out Eliot's smorgasbord of psychiatric dysfunctionality.[2]

The application of a schizophrenic diagnosis to Eliot's schema may seem sketchy or offhand; by way of excuse, I note that a concise, comprehensive definition eludes psychiatrists themselves. Schizophrenia is

the most enigmatic of mental disorders. . . . The attention lavished on this condition seems not, however, to have fathomed its many mysteries; and to this day we remain largely ignorant of the causes, the underlying psychological structure, and even the precise diagnostic boundaries of this most strange and important of mental illnesses. . . . It is in the realm of schizophrenia that all the vulnerabilities of taxonomic classification seem to be multiplied. . . . [the condition cannot] be described in terms of a single theme . . . or standard model. (Sass, 13, 25)

For Eliot in *The Cocktail Party* (as for anyone with a tendency toward instability of ego who wishes to remain perceived as sane), the challenge is finding and fixing the boundaries of a viable personality. In this vein, consider the image from "The Love Song of J. Alfred Prufrock," which depicts the horror of being fixed, trapped (by women who come and go), in Prufrock's various *incorrect* personalities, his insincere and untenable poses:

The eyes that fix you in a formulated phrase,
And when I am formulated, sprawling on a pin,
When I am pinned and wriggling on the wall. (5)

Indeed, Eliot had been confronting the prospect of fluctuating personalities, poses, personae, masks, since his earliest poetry. He rarely alighted upon one that worked in this poetry; rather, he fidgeted nervously among an array of unsatisfactory variants: "Shall I say, I have gone at dusk through narrow streets . . . I should have been a pair of ragged claws" (5); "I must borrow every changing shape / To find expression . . . dance, dance / Like a dancing bear, / Cry like a parrot, chatter like an ape" (12; Eliot's ellipses).

The depiction of dramatic character in *The Cocktail Party* may be linked with Eliot's profuse depictions of poses in his early poetry. One may kindly describe these poses as experimental, for the younger man seeking his aesthetic and emotional niches; or they may be characterized, less tolerantly, as pretentiously affected, ludicrous, outrageously offensive, outside the bounds of normally acceptable sane behavior (as in, especially, "Hysteria" and "Mr. Apollinax"). Eliot is obsessed with these thick and often pathetic poses and is apparently unable to appreciate the profound inappropriateness, indeed derangement, of these personae, whose deviant, hostile solipsism he presents as a viable—at times (as for the gentleman caller in "Portrait of a Lady") even heroic—response to the modern condition. All these poses suggest a constant strain of schizophrenic and arbitrary delineation of character-facades throughout his oeuvre.

Medical specialists cite as a fundamental distinction between schizophrenics and nonschizophrenics the fact that the schizophrenic defies empathy: the patient, distanced from the normal course of reality, cannot comprehend, share, pity, or in any way relate to the experiences of another; nor can that other person do so with the schizophrenic. This aspect of the condition is especially germane to Eliot's sensibility in *The Cocktail Party*. Lack of empathy is, of course, quintessentially anathematic to his vision of community and its imperative foundation of valid words—communication that can be, and is, shared—bespeaking an empathetic network of shared humanity.

The task for the community as a whole is to learn to recognize its different possible manifestations and opt for the right one. This is true both with regard to *The Cocktail Party* and, more generally, in the increasingly elaborate prescriptive manifesto for community that is being woven through Eliot's drama. The community, like the schizophrenic subject, must fix itself upon the right "personality" and dismiss, or at least firmly repress, any other conflicting personalities that would generate dissonance.

Reilly explains this paradigm to Celia, whose saintly mission will be a microcosmic representation (or at least one variant) of the mission confronting the community as a whole. Celia expresses her discontent with the community around her, which she represents as being detached from reality, delusional (i.e., what I have characterized as schizophrenic). "A delusion is something we must return from," Reilly replies. "There are other states of mind, which we take to be delusion, / But which we have to accept and go on from" (134). This is Reilly's (and Eliot's) response to the fluctuating, mutable, erratic personalities that have pervaded the play, and to the analogously schizophrenic community sense of purpose, coherence, morality. The force of delusion is not challenged; it is accepted, but it cannot be allowed to be a terminus—everyone must, simply, deal with it. Reilly counsels Celia to go on from delusion to something that will implicitly be more solid, more real, more meaningful.

Community members must recognize that, like its metonymic representation as a cocktail party, the community can be awful or really very nice. The perceptions of these two conditions, as Peter shows by blurting them out in the same breath, may be quite close to each other: they are similar reflexive reactions to the same situation, though obviously they are, ultimately, significantly different. Ideally, one should aspire to dismiss the awful aspects of community and learn to formulate and perpetuate the sensibility whereby it appears really very nice. This lesson will be Eliot's mission for the Chamberlaynes' marriage and for the community of drama as established in this play and in his ensuing drama.

THE SCHIZOPHRENIC INDIVIDUAL AND COMMUNITY: CASE NOTES

Eliot characterizes the play's parties and the communities they betoken as schizophrenic. Most prominently, consider Reilly's hovering involvement in the play's sordid goings-on and his own unstable character(s)—Unidentified Guest and Sir Henry Harcourt-Reilly, doctor and Guardian. The blind are leading the blind—that is to say, the schizophrenic are treating the schizophrenic. Early in the play, as the Unidentified Guest, he tenders the ideas and terminology of a schizophrenically split sensibility, the "loss of personality" he associates with the dissolution of a marriage: "you've lost touch with the person / You thought you were" (29). Following up on this statement when he returns to visit Edward the next day, the Unidentified Guest magnifies the dimension of schizophrenic mutation amid imperfect community. People are constantly changing, he asserts; they cannot maintain any stable perception of each other but only artificial constructs fixed in their memories. For the sake of ostensible manners (which are, however, actually delusory), we "pretend that they and we are the same" as "a useful and convenient social convention," but "[w]e must also remember / That at every meeting we are meeting a stranger" (72). Edward sees that "I myself must also be a stranger"—to other people and, the Unidentified Guest rejoins, "to yourself as well" (73). Edward is, then, fairly lost in the chasms of schizophrenia.

Peter, Celia, Edward—the characters laboring under the trauma of unrequited or inadequate communion—are all very different people, different personalities, when they are at the cocktail party proper as compared to when they are discussing their problems individually outside the party. Though *The Cocktail Party* represents Eliot's most optimistic vision to date of the durability of community, the vision is still tempered and imperfect. Reilly describes the mundane life, the status quo in a community left to its own inadequate devices, as "stale food mouldering in the larder . . . stale thoughts mouldering in their minds" (146): as bleak as the darkest forebodings of communal void in *Sweeney Agonistes* or *Murder in the Cathedral*. The key symptom of this imperfect community is instability or mutability of character and personality. Lavinia needs to determine, Who, really, *is* Edward? (as does Edward himself, for that matter)—and so forth for all the others, the supposedly sane Guardians as well

as the "patients." This murkiness of identity confirms a lay image of schizophrenia if not a rigorously medical one, but it essentially indicates the same
ultimate significance and consequence as real schizophrenia: distancing, and
eventually withdrawal, from reality. Throughout his poetry and drama, Eliot has
reenacted the stance of withdrawal in the face of unsatisfactory externality—in
the form of solipsistic introversion in his earlier poetry or intellectually haughty
dismissal in his later poetry, earlier drama, and many critical essays.

When Edward asserts that Peter is lucky because an incipient affair with
Celia never materialized, he warns of the dangers of average romance—which
he feels is inherently wastelandish and barren—in terms that suggest schizophrenia as the consequence of imperfect communion between two people:

> In a little while
> This might have become an ordinary affair
> Like any other. As the fever cooled
> You would have found that she was another woman
> And that you were another man. (45–46)

The prospect of a person turning into another person indicates unstable definition of the boundaries of a single self. At the first cocktail party Edward indicates that he has perceived schizophrenic tendencies in his wife (which would
be an appropriate symptom, following Eliot's schizophrenic symbolism, to explain the dissolution of his marriage): "Lavinia always had the ambition / To
establish herself in two worlds at once" (43). When Lavinia later explains to
her husband the consequence of their marital breakdown, she indicates that her
ego is in flux: "As for me, I'm rather a different person / Whom you must get
to know" (95). Likewise Edward, in the throes of marital failure, says when he
is trying to explain the failure, "Have I not made it clear / That in future you
will find me a different person?" (100); and, when he is resigned to such failure, "I have ceased to believe in my own personality" (110). Celia, looking at
Edward as she finally realizes her former lover to be devoid of love for either
her or Lavinia, sees him schizophrenically metamorphosing in front of her eyes:

> Twice you have changed since I have been looking at you.
> I looked at your face: and I thought that I knew
> And loved every contour; and as I looked
> It withered, as if I had unwrapped a mummy.
> I listened to your voice, that had always thrilled me,
> And it became another voice—no not a voice:
> What I heard was only the noise of an insect,
> Dry, endless, meaningless, inhuman—. (66)

"The man I saw before," she realizes, "was only a projection" (67); her analysis
of what underlies this projection is an incisive literary description of schizophrenic devolution, comparable to schizophrenics' own reports of their states

of mind. It has become increasingly accepted that Eliot's earlier works, such as *The Waste Land,* serve as valuable documents, or artifacts, of psychiatric distress, like letters written home from the (psychotic) front lines. Eliot's later drama, too, seems to perform a similar function.

To explain Lavinia's unexpected absence from the party in the desperate initial spasms of their failed marriage, Edward is driven to invent a character out of thin air—the aunt whom Lavinia is supposed to be visiting—indicating a delusional appraisal of personality. Fittingly enough, even this fabricated personality is cloaked in schizophrenic fragmentation, mutation, contradiction: "Julia: Is that her Aunt Laura? Edward: No; another aunt / Whom you wouldn't know. . . . Julia: Her favourite aunt? Edward: Her aunt's favourite niece. . . . Julia: . . . I feel as if I knew / All about that aunt in Hampshire. Edward: Hampshire? Julia: Didn't you say Hampshire? Edward: No, I didn't say Hampshire. Julia: Did you say Hampstead? Edward: No, I didn't say Hampstead. Julia: But she must live somewhere. Edward: She lives in Essex" (18–20), and so on, as a running gag throughout the first act. And later, when Edward protests that Alex has used up all the eggs Lavinia's aunt sent from the country, "Alex: Ah, so the aunt / Really exists. A substantial proof. Edward: No, no . . . I mean, this is another aunt. Alex: I understand. The real aunt" (48–49; Eliot's ellipses).

The play's opening is prominently infused with recurrent reminders of delusional comprehension of character. An unstable profusion of real and unreal characters and character attributes bounce around in the Chamberlaynes' flat as its forces of community cohesion, like the Chamberlaynes' marriage, verge on sundering. Eliot creates the aunt to fill the vacuum left by reality (i.e., by Lavinia's so-far inexplicable departure, which signifies a failure of microcosmic community). The unlikeliness of this aunt's fluctuating, dubious existence, and the carelessness with which Edward only partially creates her, are analogous to the dangerous instability of the play's "real people" amid these conditions of personal and community failure.[3]

Eliot himself has been accused of what might be characterized as schizophrenic literary sensibilities by critics unable to reconcile the creation of, say, the characters of Sweeney and St. Thomas Becket, or Madame Sosostris and Julia Shuttlethwaite, as being the work of a single, sane, unified mind. Bernard Bergonzi writes that it is "a common opinion that Eliot's theatrical development in the fifties was a move in the wrong direction, after the promising dramatic experiments of the twenties and thirties" (*Eliot,* 189). William Barrett laments "the embarrassing and delicate situation of the master at the height of his fame and influence at the very moment when his creative powers and energy appear to be at their lowest ebb" (359). A *New Statesman* writer mocks *The Cocktail Party* in a parody of Eliot's own verse: "This is the vulgarist success, blasting / A hitherto immaculate reputation, / The voice / *Par excellence* of the waste land and the wilderness. / Can the exalted oracle rejoice / Who, casting / Pearls before swine, wins swinish approbation?" (In Browne,

Making, 247). And Alan Brien, reviewing Eliot's final play a decade later, describes his audience admiring an unclothed emperor: "They are so afraid that they will miss the point that they desperately make all the points he muffed. They rewrite his plays for him. They magnify his puppets into people. They create an imaginary genius called 'T. S. Eliot—playwright' and clamber over each other to worship at the shrine of the Invisible Dramatist" (305). All these attacks reflect the critics' sense that Eliot, at the peak of his playwriting career, is not the "real" Eliot, the personality they had fixed via his poetry, but some false or deviant construct—as Brien puts it, an imaginary genius. To them, the writer seems to have undergone the same kind of schizophrenic mutation that the characters in *The Cocktail Party* are themselves experiencing: as if Eliot has become, like Lavinia, "rather a different person / Whom you must get to know" (95); and, like Edward, has "ceased to believe in my own personality" (110). Many of his earlier admirers were compelled to admit that meeting Eliot in this play affirmed Reilly's unsettling admonition "[t]hat at every meeting we are meeting a stranger" (72).

IT'S A MAD, MAD, MAD, MAD WORLD

Eliot's early tenets and styles manifest schizophrenic affinities, which corrolate with a generally pervasive schizophrenic strain among modernists, argues Louis Sass in *Madness and Modernism: Insanity in the Light of Modern Art, Literature, and Thought.* The idea expressed in "Tradition and the Individual Talent" that poetry is "an escape from personality" (10) bespeaks an unstable sense of personality on the part of Eliot as poet—a perception that personality is like a mask, an attribute that is not firmly fixed to the person "wearing" it. Eliot's characterization of the cultural condition he called "dissociation of sensibility" is, Sass writes, "remarkably close to Emil Kraepelin's and Erwin Stransky's classic definitions of *dementia praecox* [an early term for schizophrenia]—as 'a loss of inner unity of intellect, emotion and volition, in themselves and among one another,' or as 'disturbances of the smooth interplay' between the ideational and emotional layers of the psyche" (357).

Sass likens the general tenor of high modernism (as promulgated by Eliot and others) to medical assessments of schizophrenia. "Modernist art has been said to manifest certain off-putting characteristics that are reminiscent of schizophrenia: a quality of being hard to understand or feel one's way into. . . . inspiring works that, to the uninitiated, can seem as difficult to grasp, as off-putting and alien, as schizophrenia itself" (8–9). Like schizophrenic illness, modernist works are characterized by "the uncertainty or multiplicity of their point of view . . . by a certain fragmentation and passivization, by a loss of the self's sense of unity and of its capacity for effective or voluntary action" (30–31).

The Waste Land, for example, projects "a desire to occupy, if only for a moment, as many points of view as possible"—a simultaneity of different perspectives—in the mode of "the multiperspectivism of analytic cubist painting" (137), Sass writes. "The consequence of such proliferation is, however, the loss of any single, overarching perspective, any selective principle or hierarchy of significance, which results in the conjuring of a world where anything can stand for anything" (138). Sass, who is a clinical psychologist, finds

an analogous perspectivism in the thinking of many schizophrenics, where the simulta- neity of or vacillation among perspectives is often associated with a particularly acute and in certain respects subjectivist awareness of the mind's role in constituting the world. . . . Like modernist uses of the crossfade technique [i.e., two interfused objects merged into a single object which could exist only in some mental or inner universe], some of the contaminations and incongruous combinations in schizophrenic Rorschach records suggest a subjectivist focus on experience-as-such. (139)

The subjectivist attempt to break the world down and reconstruct human ex- perience without reference to objective reality, Sass argues, is a shared charac- teristic of modernist artists and schizophrenics, both of whom exhibit acute self-awareness complemented by a profound sense of detachment from the empirical world.

In his creation of a schizophrenically mediated community in *The Cocktail Party,* then, Eliot draws on a strain of psychological dysfunction with which he seems quite familiar: generally, through a modernist zeitgeist that is enmeshed with motifs and symptoms of schizophrenia and specifically, through his own poetry that is itself considerably schizophrenic (and which scholars increasingly consider to have significant autobiographical roots and connections). Relatively tamed, genteel manifestations of schizophrenia in *The Cocktail Party* appear in sharper relief when regarded against the backdrop of Eliot's earlier work.

BEYOND SCHIZOPHRENIA: ON THE COUCH, TAKE 1

In *The Cocktail Party,* Eliot initiates a focus on mental dysfunctionality that continues throughout his final plays. Though these plays have commonly been viewed simply as light, harmless West End comedies with a faint Christian leitmotif, they have a deeper and darker strain woven through them: they all contain studies of some incidence of individual mental ill health. Those af- flicted face the task of conquering their illnesses (which are both literal and allegorical) by accepting the external forces of community stability and integra- ting themselves into them.

One might include the previous play, *The Family Reunion,* in this thematic grouping of Eliot's drama[4] but only to a certain extent. It seems warranted to make the simple observation that Harry appears to have been "crazy" (whatever that means; the play does not elucidate) during whatever happened on board the steamship with his wife. But that play's psychological elements do not justify more intricate analysis than this. Unlike Eliot's final three plays, *The*

Family Reunion does not offer fodder for exploring the nature of a diseased mind and the importance of restoring it to health so that it may perform within a healthy community. The obliqueness that confronts an audience's attempt to analyze the psychological details surrounding Harry's behavior is analogous to the obliqueness surrounding the specific incident with Harry's wife. (As suggested in the previous chapter, the play offers more insight into the nature of *Eliot's* afflictions—psychological, emotional, and otherwise—than of Harry's.) One might venture that the state of Eliot's own mental health was still too uncertain when he wrote *The Family Reunion* for him to be able to give any substantial, explicit, or objective perspective on its role in the dysfunctions, and ultimate return toward health, in that community. By the same token, Eliot in the mid-1920s seems to have been immensely further beyond the pale in terms of his emotional and psychological stability than he was in 1939, so that in *Sweeney Agonistes* a pervasive psychotic flair is simply and unquestioningly accepted as the norm in that community.

In *The Confidential Clerk,* the manifestation of psychological dysfunction and rehabilitation appears with regard to Lady Elizabeth's experiences of thought and mind control—more elaborate in Eliot's drafts than in the final text—which are discussed in the next chapter. This psychological treatment is much akin to what Eliot seems to have experienced during his own nervous breakdown in 1921. In *The Elder Statesman,* the psychological dimension takes the form of severe depression, also with autobiographical reference to Eliot's experience as a literary elder statesman afflicted by the unsavory repressions of his past—the disaster of his first marriage—and cured by love.

In *The Cocktail Party,* the schizophrenia is merely a jumping-off point into a community racked by delusion, repression, and psychological ill health that are rampant behind the facades of genteel bourgeois existence. One might expect the play's atmosphere, its social milieu, to be free of the burden of dark, somber, distrustful hostility and danger that pervaded *The Family Reunion* (written during the low, dishonest decade of the 1930s, as the ominous shadow of fascist aggression spread across Europe); in fact, though, this play seethes with profuse mental instability.

First of all, the possibility of a "nervous breakdown," as a consequence of disrupted microcosmic and macrocosmic community, skulks throughout the play. Like "schizophrenia," the term is vague and myriad as it filters through the popular sensibility; but certainly for Eliot, who had experienced a severe case himself, the possibility of breakdown carried with it a very real meaning. The play's opening establishes the causes, or precipitators, of mental illness: insecurity, alienation, loss of control, psychosocial instability. Subsequently, the illness itself begins to proliferate throughout the play, establishing a densely psychiatric milieu; the prospect of breakdown emerges. In act 1, scene 2, Celia tells Edward he is on the verge of a nervous breakdown (61), and Lavinia repeats this observation to him nearly verbatim at the end of the act (99). When Edward reports these diagnoses to Reilly in act 2, the doctor responds that he never uses the term "nervous breakdown" because "[i]t can mean almost any-thing" (110). He does repeat the term he claims never to use, though—with the same implicit qualification—to Lavinia in discussing the precipitation of "what you called your nervous breakdown" (120) and again when he tells Celia that most of his patients "are quite sure / They have had a nervous breakdown" (131).

The term can indeed mean almost anything—or everything—that goes on in *The Cocktail Party.* The conditions it describes are, as Reilly says, seductively all-encompassing. Both Edward and Lavinia seem to hope that others, espe-cially Reilly, will simply accept the momentous import of those two words and whisk them away to the happy sanctuary of a "sanatorium." But Reilly implic-itly believes (and Eliot will explicitly show in *The Elder Statesman*) that such an artificial refuge guarantees no respite from the real aspects, challenges, and issues, of the community.

While the proclivity toward nervous breakdown is ubiquitous in *The Cocktail Party,* Eliot (via Reilly) means it to be seen more as a red herring than as a metaphorical etiology of the community problems at issue. This intention sug-gests that Eliot himself had moved beyond the desperation of his own nervous breakdown (which seems to have been in *The Waste Land,* as it still is here, an emblem of nihilistic stasis). He has begun to demand consideration of more intricate root causes of the problem at hand, beyond the bounds of the solipsis-tic nightmare that—based on the documentary evidence he provided from that illness in *The Waste Land*—characterized his breakdown.

A sanatorium would be only a facile and mechanical solution to the problem of unstable community: it would be a place one pays to attend, where the messiness of community inadequacies are regulated by hired staff. (In *The El-der Statesman,* Badgley Court is exactly such an institution and is shown to be worthless.) A sanatorium would sidestep what Eliot ultimately demands: work-ing out, oneself, one's own metier and a path toward community vitality. Though the community in *The Cocktail Party* is constantly moving toward the desired end of self-amelioration, the alternative of the sanatorium is always in close proximity to the range of action. Indeed, Celia *is* told that she is going to a sanatorium, but because of her calling and her path, she is an exceptional case. The sanatorium does not represent for her what it would for the others. In sending Celia, but not the others, to the sanatorium, Eliot must intend a strong resonance of the word's Latin etymology—*sanare,* to heal. Celia, in her Kinkanja mission, indeed heals, and is healed of her worldly scars. The others, on the contrary, envision a sanatorium as a place not of healing but of escape and of repressing the necessity of healing.

The sanatorium's presence offers an entrée to a wider and deeper range of extreme medical illness. Conditions that would necessitate treatment at a sana-torium include, at the extreme end, as drastic a condition as full-blown "insan-ity." (Even if the patient sent to the sanatorium were, like the Chamberlaynes, not fully insane, that person could still find himself or herself "acquiring" in-sanity—as, for example, may have happened with Eliot's first wife, Vivien, who had died in a kind of sanatorium less than a year before Eliot began working on *The Cocktail Party*.) One should consider the play's treatment of insanity with the same caveats about popularized medical approximations that were raised with reference to schizophrenia and nervous breakdown; Eliot uses these mental illnesses with the same casually vast scope with which a writer of half a century earlier might have described the incidence of "nerves" or "neurasthenia."[5]

Eliot was circumspect in his depiction of full-fledged insanity in the play's final edition. A late version of the play (Eliot's copy of the acting edition: item D6 in the T. S. Eliot Collection), though, shows the idea of insanity potent, not far beneath the surface. About forty lines before the end of act 1 in the published text (99), the long confrontation between Edward and Lavinia becomes increasingly hostile, depressing, squalid. The extent of Lavinia's "medical analysis" of Edward is her statement that she believes him to be on the verge of a nervous breakdown and knows a doctor she thinks could help him. But cut from the acting edition are ten lines in which Edward accuses his wife of trying to convince him that he is insane, and Lavinia's response: while she does not think he is insane, he is in a psychological morass that he cannot handle on his own and that requires a specialist's attention. This passage in the acting edition explicitly uses the word "insane" twice, although the final text leaves the passage more vague, not as pointedly pathological. Eliot may have found the passage as it was written in the acting edition—probably cut as the play was in rehearsal—too flagrantly forthright. Director E. Martin Browne reports that Eliot tried to avoid religious terminology for as long as possible in the play (*Making,* 213). Perhaps he downplayed explicit medical terminology for the same reason: because the play is not most prominently about religion or psychiatry but, rather, about community. Still, there are seething depths of Eliot's emotional and psychological sensibility to be plumbed in this play: and we have yet to hit bottom.

TO BE OR NOT TO BE

An even darker element, similarly cut from Eliot's acting edition, is suicide. After Alex tells Reilly that Edward is enjoying his illness early in act 2 (106), there were five lines in which Reilly asks if Edward had discussed suicide; Alex responds that he had hinted darkly at suicide but was finally convinced that, given the extent of his illness, it would be advantageous to live and experience the rewards of his illness. The word "suicide" is explicitly used twice. It was suggested earlier that the psychological resonances in Eliot's final plays seem to be, to some extent, affiliated with his own state of mind; one wonders if the references to suicide are similarly descriptive of his own uncertainty. In the late 1940s Eliot was attempting to fix, to settle, his personality during a lonely and transitional period in his life, which was marked by forces pulling in drastically divergent directions. Though biographers do not generally regard this period as the most troubled or traumatic time of his life, Lyndall Gordon admits she cannot surmount an opaque barrier:

Almost all accounts of these years sound curiously empty. . . . The man is simply not there. Did he go dead in the late forties . . . or did the prophetic soul live on, burning, inscrutable, behind the facades? The whole truth depends on holding a balance of two almost antithetical selves. There is the man who was burnt out, and accepting fame to the further depletion of his vitality; and there is a public hermit. (*New Life,* 192–93)

Gordon's characterization, like mine, suggests a schizophrenic schism of selves, of Eliot's conflicting personalities. She notes that during this period of his life, as in his youth, he retained his proclivity to strike and cultivate poses, adopt aliases, and mull name changes (212), all reflecting an unstable or mutable personality. He was susceptible to outbursts of personal horror, seemingly indicative of an enduring psychiatric disorder, as he had been during the 1900s and 1910s in Cambridge and London. In 1951 at an American sing-song in Hampstead, Gordon writes,

Suddenly, he felt that he was in a cage with wild beasts, and, going white, he burst out: 'Do you know the Song of the Reconstructed Rebel?' Then he began to sing in a loud, raucous voice, with extreme violence, until Mary [Trevelyan] got him into a taxi. (206)

Freed by Vivien's death of his ties to her, he nonetheless sustained a personally-imposed penance, living a monkish austere existence with John Hayward; he continued the habits of isolation he had followed for much of his life. Awarded the 1948 Nobel Prize for Literature, which pronounced him one of the world's greatest living poets, he had turned—schizophrenically?—to a very different and uncertain writing outlet, drama, as his *only* literary forum.

Eliot's personality at this time, then, seems as fragile, tenuous, and potentially wracked with uncertainty or despair as at any period of his life. Gordon exhaustively recounts in *Eliot's New Life* a period of over two decades, from the 1930s to the late 1950s, when Eliot was heavily occupied by relationships with two aggressive women, Emily Hale and Mary Trevelyan, that were emotionally turgid, laden with an almost constant uneasiness. There is no biographical evidence that Eliot was indeed suicidal at this period, but Alex's reference to Edward's thoughts of suicide lead me to speculate, guardedly, that Eliot himself may have considered suicide. Such thoughts would not have been incompatible with the interpretation posited here of his personality—an interpretation, again, that must be made only tentatively, given the smokescreen that faces scholars and biographers. But one must note that Eliot frequently, if not always, inscribes himself with considerable detail (especially psychological detail) in the personae of his male protagonists: Prufrock, the gentleman caller in "Portrait of a Lady," most of the male speakers in *The Waste Land,* Sweeney, Tom Becket, Harry Monchensey, the elder statesman Lord Claverton . . . there is no reason to omit Edward and his psyche from this procession.

The prospect of suicide is raised, too, in a few other places in Eliot's plays. In his postmortem speech for the Archbishop he has just slain, the Fourth Knight in *Murder in the Cathedral* argues that Becket, a monstrous egotist (and, as suggested in chapter 3, a loosely autobiographical incarnation of martyrdom for Eliot), was himself responsible for his death: "I think, with these facts before you," he says to the audience, "you will unhesitatingly render a verdict of Suicide while of Unsound Mind" (84). In *The Family Reunion,* Charles wonders about the real cause of Harry's wife's death and asks Downing if he thinks it might have been suicide. Though Downing responds that he considers this unlikely, Charles follows up: "Did she ever talk of suicide?" (38), and Downing admits that she did, from time to time, though he believes she did it just to frighten people. When Michael decides to abandon his family and go off with Gomez in *The Elder Statesman,* his sister Monica calls it an abandonment of self, "a kind of suicide" (117).

None of these instances is an actual suicide, yet each proposes suicide as a possibility, even if unconvincingly, as in the Fourth Knight's ludicrous charge. The incidence in *The Elder Statesman* yokes the suggestion of suicide with that of schizophrenia, i.e., the loss of self. The conversation from *The Family Reunion* forces the audience to consider suicide as being part of the atmosphere of the hostile and dysfunctional family gathering: despite Downing's demurral, no other cause of death is definitively suggested for Harry's wife, so the cause *might* have been suicide as much as anything else. Like the suicidal strain in Eliot's mind that was an element of (though finally withdrawn from) the formative process of *The Cocktail Party,* the issue of suicide in these three other plays serves at least to introduce the possibility of massive danger, self-destruction, as a component of the drastic nature of the dramatic contest at hand. An allegorical psychomachia takes form, with commonweal and community beneficence at one pole and schizophrenia, breakdown, sublimated suicidal impulses hovering—darkly, vaguely, yet nonetheless extant—at the other.

As the references to suicide were eventually cut, so were other especially macabre touches. Browne describes the shocked reaction at the play's Edinburgh debut to a quite graphic account of Celia's death, which explicitly recounted the advanced stage of decomposition in which her body was found and the speed with which a corpse deteriorates in the tropics (*Making,* 225–26). In the same vein, the Cambridge copy of Eliot's acting edition includes lines, eventually cut, in Alex's discussion of cannibalism (164) that make Celia's death seem more vividly gory and less, as in the final text, a sort of stylized, symbolic fate. Alex expands upon the discussion of cannibalism in the acting edition by suggesting that there are some especially horrible ways of preparing the victims, who begin to cook before they die. Such dark moments in Eliot's plays have been effaced, or at least muted, but they nevertheless recur—palimpsestically or subliminally or marginally—with some consistency and illustrate the stakes that infused Eliot's dramatic agons.

THEM THAT HELP THEMSELVES

The Cocktail Party is rampant with psychologically centered dysfunctionality. Yet a literal clinical diagnosis, etiology, or treatment is ultimately elusive. The agent of healing initially seems to be some sort of psychiatric specialist or therapist, yet this presumption becomes increasingly dubious: Reilly's professional identity does not become clarified as the play proceeds, and two other characters with no claim to professional medical status, Julia and Alex, seem to be his equals in terms of their roles in treating the "patients." Reilly's prescriptions and behavior are far beyond the bounds of medical practice; he resists a precise characterization as a doctor.

The play, then, first seems to evoke a pronounced medical orientation but then undercuts initial expectations. As intricately as I have tried to examine and document, medically, these characters' conditions, I arrive, finally, at an inconclusive impasse. This inconclusiveness is not to diminish the importance of Eliot's paradigm, in which individuals' pervasive mental dysfunctions herald the dysfunctionality of inadequate community. Eliot firmly plants in his audience's minds the prominence of psychiatric disorders as a symptom of the problem—indicating the drastic threat an imperfect community poses to individual health and welfare—but finally, he directs his dramatic focus *away* from a medically bounded resolution.

The recent discourse of American self-help literature provides a better way of determining and describing these characters' ultimate resolution of their afflictions. Self-help books manifest a sensibility that is, like Eliot's, somewhat indeterminate, fuzzy. They manifestly *seem* medically oriented at first, although this facade is deconstructed upon closer consideration. They offer an appropriate analogue for *The Cocktail Party* and an idiosyncratic but useful ingress to its workings.

In the 1980s the self-help movement flourished in the publishing industry, the media, and the popular cultural zeitgeist. It created such medically tinted conditions as "codependency" and "the Wendy dilemma"; psychiatrically tinted pathological profiles such as "women who love too much" and "men who hate women and the women who love them"; therapeutically tinted entities such as "inner children"; and remedial therapeutic practices such as "affirmation." A scientific and medical orientation frequently cloaks self-help books, involving terminology, symptoms, and schemes of diagnosis and treatment that are associated with clinical therapeutic practice; authors augment the perception of medical authority by flaunting their advanced degrees and professional qualifications.

Actually, though, self-help books embody a sensibility more focused upon what Wendy Simonds calls "the *cultural* consumption and transmission of ideas about . . . selfhood, and interaction with others" (2; emphasis mine). Her study, *Women and Self-Help Culture: Reading Between the Lines,* "offer[s] insight into the patterns embedded in the tangled webs of human interaction" (3) that self-help literature betokens; these tangled webs and patterns, similarly, demarcate the terrain on which one should appraise Eliot's vision of community. Self-help books address themselves to "conditions" that might be more easily treatable if they really were personality disorders or suicidal depression. The conditions or complaints for which self-help readers seek solace, though, actually reflect the sufferer's more intricate discontent in society. This discontent is more nebulous and more difficult to treat because some sort of social change is necessary—a change outside or beyond the individual who is suffering and thus outside his or her ability to control, to mediate.

Books about codependency and the cycles of therapy seem well tailored to Edward and Lavinia's condition. The Chamberlaynes' needs as individuals are not being met within their marriage. They suffer from bad communication; the consequent dynamics include harsh, bitter, circular, unproductively drawn-out arguments. Their relationship is scarred by game-playing, petty combativeness, dishonesty, and distrustful guardedness. The Chamberlaynes (especially Lavinia) would have been a prime target audience for books such as Louise Hay's *You Can Cure Your Life,* Melody Beattie's *Codependent No More,* Harville Hendrix's *Getting the Love You Want: A Guide for Couples,* or Barbara De Angelis's *Secrets About Men Every Woman Should Know*—had such titles existed then.

Eliot anticipates the sensibility that would proliferate in these books of the 1980s and 1990s; he crafted for himself a proto-self-help paradigm, to address inadequacies that kept people wallowing in their own anticommunity self-obsessions.[6] His brand of self-help is meant to teach his "patients" to fit in better, to toe the line of a community demeanor, to get beyond themselves and accept that the essence of their problems involves not just their personal dissatisfactions but their relationship to the larger social world outside them. Reilly himself resembles a self-help book come to life: he more closely approximates one of these best-selling authors than a psychiatrist or a spiritual guardian. As he instructs and inspires his charges on how to find their own ways, his pronouncements have the tenor of self-help platitudes coated in vatic profundity: "The best of a bad job is all any of us make of it" (126); "Your business is not to clear your conscience / But to learn how to bear the burdens on your conscience" (128); "Compassion may be already a clue / Towards finding your own way out of the forest" (138); "You understand your *metier,* Mr. Quilpe—/ Which is the most that any of us can ask for" (177); "You will have to live with these memories and make them / Into something new. Only by acceptance / Of the past will you alter its meaning" (186).

Contemporary self-help books promise a "cure for what ails us, collectively, as a culture" (227), Simonds writes. She calls this promise ultimately illusory, mainly because the "therapy" is excessively mediated, and tainted, by its cultural commodification—that is, its unrealistically impossible attempt to affect the lives of millions of readers; to be all things to all people; to provide, for the price of a cheap lunch, a road map to human fulfillment. Still self-help books imply ideals, even if they are unreachable within the limited confines of the books' approaches: ideals for a mode of human and community interaction that readers feel does not proliferate but should. *The Cocktail Party* works as a self-help text by trying to instruct its audience how to seize control of their own lives, relationships, and marriages and eliminate the pettiness, the pride, the selfishness, the dysfunctionality; how to reshape their values and behavior in a more sensible, more desirable way.

And even if the ultimate value of self-help is diminished by its commodification, still, commodification embodies part of its significance to scholars of culture. Self-help is appealing to emotionally needy people—people like the Chamberlaynes and audience members who empathize with them—precisely because a primary manifestation of the inadequacies confronting the victim of a depersonalized commodity culture is the craving for easy and buyable answers. The Chamberlaynes, in their snazzy West End flat, are ensconced in a bourgeois commodity culture of their own time analogous to the one that has generated the explosive self-help phenomenon in America.

The Cocktail Party was a spectacular hit, running for 325 performances on the West End and 409 on a Broadway run that garnered three Tony Awards. Many critics made the point that the play was, fittingly enough, the talk of the cocktail party circuit. (James Thurber's *New Yorker* article "What Cocktail Party?" wryly parodies the conversation at a typical cocktail party about *The Cocktail Party*; it is an informative illustration of how the play easily intermingled with the culture it depicts.) Eliot was addressing the bourgeoisie, whom he had once lampooned and disdained, on their own turf. Decades earlier, he had steadfastly refused to go into the drawing rooms of this community (in "The Love Song of J. Alfred Prufrock") or fled from it sanctimoniously (in "Portrait of a Lady"); now, he inveigles his way in, ingratiates himself (or panders, according to the more vituperative critics) with the Edwards and Lavinias of the audience. He speaks to them on their own terms, in their own language: in words that both he and they find valid common ground. Eliot's most commercially popular play ever reflects what the masses wanted to see and wanted to get out of a play. In the same sense, Simonds concedes, the American self-help publishing bonanza, with scores of titles appearing on bestseller lists and individual works selling several millions of copies,[7] clearly indicates a pervasive condition that grabs the attention of mass culture, as well as a fervent desire to "treat," or ameliorate, this condition—whether or not such treatment finally offers all it claims.

The Cocktail Party is embedded with psychologically loaded signifiers and tropes in the same way self-help books are. Both Eliot's play and self-help literature aspire to imbue themselves with the kind of authority craved by an audience eager for guidance. Both present themselves to a decidedly *mass* audience and present advice in a way calculated to satisfy a "lowest common denominator" of needs. The "point" (the moral, the solution) must be to some extent simplified and spoon-fed so that it is not missed. It must make the audience feel good, or at least better, about the problems presented and about themselves.

Like self-help books, *The Cocktail Party* taps into the mass-cultural, popular zeitgeist. Neither a self-help book nor *The Cocktail Party* will change the world in and of itself, but their existence is at least a first step in the right direction (in terms of the agendas propagated by Eliot and the self-help authors): a sign that people recognize the need for change and are willing to change. "Even though this reading does not necessarily lead to any radical change," Simonds writes, "it does provide its readers with, at the very least, a momentary respite, a chance to be self-reflective and evaluative" (48); this experience may enable readers, then, to express dissatisfaction with the status quo of social construction and to aspire to a better condition.

Simonds warns, though, of a crucial caveat to an optimistic interpretation of the self-help phenomenon as a sign that society is committed to helping itself surmount its problems. Publishers' marketing demographics demonstrate that *women* are receptive to change—the millions of women who buy and read these books—but men are not as obviously interested in addressing the dissatisfactions of heterosexual relationships (which are the mainstay of these self-help books), and it takes two to tango. Similarly, one must ask if Eliot's audience is sufficiently receptive for his drama to be an effective tool for establishing community. Real-life types of Lavinia and Celia, today, might read self-help books, but would Peter and Edward? If not, Lavinia's aspirations will be frustrated, and even Celia's cannot be properly appreciated, valued, within the community left behind if there *is* no such community.

Are the Guardians (who evoke the Community of Christians Eliot had described ten years earlier in *The Idea of a Christian Society*) merely preaching to the converted? Is Celia's path viable, meaningful, outside the self-enclosed discourse of religious faith? The limitations of the recent self-help movement (which are prominent in the pervasive mockery accorded by the press, by comedians, by intellectuals, and by many men) suggest problems inherent in *The Cocktail Party*. Is the self-help sensibility—both Eliot's and that of present-day American culture—finally lightweight, Pollyannaish? Perhaps; but even so, people are reading the books and attending the plays—in both cases, hearing the words, the language—in significant numbers. Even if the content verges on pap, people "buy" it, signifying ultimate approval by the standards of commodity culture. They thus make some *movement* toward developing and advancing a community of shared interaction—not unlike what Stanley Fish characterizes as an Interpretive Community—thereby eschewing the numbing inertia that pervades the modern age. Made aware of the play's schizophrenic community, the audience attunes itself to the attitude promoted in self-help books: making the best of a bad job. Even if *The Cocktail Party* cannot fully address and remedy the spectrum of ills afflicting postwar, postcolonial, nuclear-age English society, the play's packed audiences confirm that Eliot has their rapt attention. The audience listens, titters, and finally empathizes with the Chamberlaynes. It understands; it is drawing close to where the words are valid.

SED QUIS CUSTODIET IPSOS CUSTODES?

The effective validators of these words, as has been suggested throughout this study, are playwright, actors, audience—the community of drama that the words create and sustain. In *The Cocktail Party,* the nominal validators of these words are the Guardians, the beneficent team of overseers composed of Reilly, Alex, and Julia, about whom little has been said so far. Like the Chamberlaynes' marriage, the Guardians' association is to be taken as a microcosm of Eliot's community vision. But while the audience is privy to every tiny and sordid detail of Edward's and Lavinia's relationship, the nature of the Guardians' community remains mysterious, sketchy. Indeed, the mystery of their interaction provides one of the play's minor comic themes. The nature of their intricate network gradually unfolds as the play proceeds; its extent appears increasingly far-reaching as Eliot exposes their covert para-intelligence webs. Still, the specific details of this alliance are never fully explicit. At the play's end, the audience senses a secret society conducted mostly beneath the surface of the drama—just offstage or otherwise out of the playwright's and audience's scope of perception.

Provocative though they are, the Guardians are not the focus of Eliot's dramatic attention. It follows, then, that he does not intend to depict them as the microcommunity that most fully embodies the paradigmatic and essential values of his community of drama. He carefully, and successfully, ensures that the Guardians do not upstage the main concern of the community of drama he promulgates in *The Cocktail Party.* None of them is Prince Hamlet, nor was meant to be; they are attendant lords—dramatic facilitators; they swell a progress, start a scene or two, deferentially advise. Reilly is often full of high sentence, but all three are also a bit obtuse, almost ridiculous, almost the Fool. Their function in Eliot's dramatic schema is succinctly concentrated in one crucial moment, the delivery of one line. Yet it is a line Eliot has been rehearsing for most of his career; and his Guardians do not now forbear, as his Prufrockian Polonius had done, to *act,* to play their parts. They dare to disturb the universe—Eliot's solipsistic universe that must be profoundly disturbed by his new and more hopeful universe of dramatic community.

WHERE THE WORDS ARE VALID

The Guardians unite in a ceremonious passage of incantative choral prayer at the end of act 2. As in Eliot's earlier plays, choral drama signifies the concord and coordination of the community of drama (or, at least, it evokes the *ideal* of such concord that the chorus would signify in an ideal realm of clear and valid signification). The briefness of the choral component in *The Cocktail Party*—these two dozen lines comprise the only passage resembling traditional choric form—reflects a refinement over the choruses Eliot has presented in all his earlier plays. In part, he is so stinting with the chorus in *The Cocktail Party* because he has accomplished most of his aspirations for choral drama (extensively discussed in various of his critical essays[8]). At the same time, and perhaps somewhat contradictorily, he may be phasing out the role of the chorus in his plays because choruses have always posed a problem for him, a dramatic problem that hindered the fruition of communities of drama. The potential ideal force of the chorus often, in practice, contributed a dissonant note to Eliot's plays. The frenzied, devolutionary chorus in *Sweeney Agonistes* was uncontrollably psychotic. In *The Rock,* the pageant's deft Choruses sapped the spirit from the remainder of the script, which was, in contrast, far more pedestrian. The Chorus was fearful, constrained, in *Murder in the Cathedral.* And in *The Family Reunion* it was intrusive, catty, conspiratorial—like much of the play, it was not smoothly performable, reflecting the fact that its function as a community of drama was somehow out of kilter.

In *The Cocktail Party,* Eliot affirms the traditional role of the chorus in a dramatic community only this once, in the Guardians' invocation, which is accompanied by drinking—what Reilly calls "the libation" (149)—emphasizing its significance as ritual celebratory performance. The passage is clipped, imagistic, tightly controlled by Eliot and Browne. It is more a stylized and diminutive rememberance of a chorus than (as it would be in the traditional choral mode) an exuberant assertion of a community's substantial presence. Browne discusses how, from the first draft to the final text, a "very large (and in itself fascinating) amount of mystic symbolism was greatly reduced" from this invocation, because it was felt to be tonally inconsistent and too heavy-handed (*Making,* 188). (Imagine: the author of *The Waste Land* worried about excessive symbolism.) Eliot constantly guarded against the temptation for the Guardians, or the chorus, to become too prominent, and too strikingly apart from, or above, the main plane of the drama. In Reilly there is, perhaps, one potential loose pistol, a volatile element that might somehow hearken back to Eliot's problematic choruses; but the eminently harmless Julia and Alex outnumber Reilly, and thus ensure a placid choral presence.

Generally in verse drama and specifically in Eliot's earlier efforts, choral declamation offers the most vivid platform for high poetry; and poetry, too, is something Eliot keeps firmly reined in in this play. The poetry in the Guardians' invocation is the play's only consciously poetic moment. Another passage of poetry, nine lines from Shelley's *Prometheus Unbound,* is explicitly *quoted* by Reilly: it is therefore a distinct interpolation into the play, rather than part of the play itself. Before declaiming, Reilly cautiously begs Lavinia's permission to quote poetry at her party—as if it were something inappropriate, which in fact it *is* in Eliot's new and more straightforward, pedestrian community. Tellingly—confirming the play's antipoetic leanings—Browne cut Shelley's poetry from the play's Broadway debut, worried that Americans would not recognize the source and would be confused. A contemporary recording made by the play's Broadway cast (Decca Record DX-100, 1950) rarely sounds poetically intoned at any point: Eliot's careful verse-dramatic prosody and his meticulous attention to the actors' declamation during rehearsals do not prevent the play from sounding predominantly like normal (i.e., unpoetic) dramatic conversation. *The Family Reunion*—in many regards written in the same dramatic style as *The Cocktail Party*—had been wrought with consciously worked, sharp, thoughtful, weighty verse. But a decade later, Eliot's play shows him to be no longer primarily a poet. The words that are valid for him in 1949 are plain and commonplace—no longer (as his poetry, and his poetic, had always been) painstakingly intellectualized.

The occasion of this chorus of Guardians at the end of act 2 is the imminent resolution of the play's personal complications and intrigues. The chorus indicates an upswing in momentum, a turning point, a kind of community peripeteia. Until now, the characters had been profoundly immersed in their own personal hells. In act 2, they have sought counsel and solace; they have talked through their conditions, their stagnation, their stubbornness. They indicate an understanding and even begin to show signs of an incipient control over their previously chaotic lives. They demonstrate the germ of a willingness to work together, cooperatively, to venture outside their finite centres. Lavinia offers to bring Edward some clean shirts at the club where he had been staying since abandoning the flat; Edward, in turn, decides he might as well return home (to the normal locus of the couple's microcommunity); Lavinia suggests that they could share a taxi to be economical. Celia identifies her affliction, a sense of sin, and chooses, without fear, to surmount her former hell; she manifests a form of redemptive faith, although it is expressed only backhandedly ("I don't in the least know what I am doing / Or why I am doing it" [144]). The characters' signs of emergence from their wastelands are vague and tentative, but their trajectory is clear. The Guardians reconvene to confirm and execute their plans, but Reilly notes that "There is one for whom the words cannot be spoken" (150). Peter is that one, and "the words" are the poetic invocation—the sole choral expression—that has been offered for Celia, Edward, and Lavinia: words of protection, guardianship, community benevolence, and progress toward commonweal.

In the play's first draft, Eliot had not yet inscribed in this passage what I suggest is his consummate dramatic awareness, his epiphanic acknowledgment and fulfillment of the dramatic mission he had begun two decades earlier. In response to the reminder that Peter is not yet taken care of, Alex responds, "There are things beyond our powers / Which must be left to the mystery and the mercy" (in Browne, *Making*, 188), a view that is diametrically opposed to the path that the text finally identifies for Peter. In this first draft, Eliot depicts Peter's ultimate redemption, his establishment within a community, as being potentially effectuated only in some realm of spirituality beyond human interaction, beyond the literal realm of the community itself. The change Eliot makes for the final script is simple but momentous:

REILLY

There is one for whom the words cannot be spoken.

ALEX

They cannot be spoken yet.

JULIA

You mean Peter Quilpe.

REILLY

He has not yet come to where the words are valid.

JULIA

Shall we ever speak them?

ALEX

Others, perhaps, will speak them.
You know, I have connections—even in California.

[CURTAIN]   (150–51)

Peter has not yet—but *will*—come to where the words are valid. Someone *will* speak them ("we," or "perhaps," "others": "perhaps" modifies the speaker; it does not qualify the act of speech). The answer, the meaning, the words, are no longer cloaked in unapproachable mystery. There remains some uncertainty—who will speak them? where will they be spoken?—but the mystery does not compromise the definite prophecy (as it had in the first draft) of Peter's "valid" future functional life in the world, among people. In draft, it is a disembodied, abstractly Christian sense of mercy that accompanies and enables Peter's transcendence of his banal condition. This original solution for Peter begs the question of precisely what practical force will manifest mercy or whether Peter will experience it in this world or the next—perhaps Eliot had envisioned an anthill with Peter's name on it. In the final draft, Eliot substitutes a sense of precise promise and pragmatic implementation: the Guardians will make connections as necessary, even in California! California signifies a glitzy, cinematic, decadent-fantasy milieu. Certainly the Hollywood movie industry is as far as one could go from Eliot's genteel West End verse drama, although, as ridiculous as the implicit caricature may seem, through the Guardians' invocation, Eliot nevertheless affirms Hollywood as being part of the same dramatic community as Shaftesbury Avenue. His community sensibility is thus strikingly inclusive rather than elitist or separatist. California also resembles Kinkanja— similarly heathen and foreign but redeemably meaningful, as even the heathens' cannibalism and crucifixion are meaningful within the context of a vital community such as the Chamberlaynes' final cocktail party betokens.

Since the beginning of his career in the theater, Eliot had been steadily moving his drama toward this point—trying to "come to where the words are valid"—and continues to do so for the rest of his life. Whether or not it actually arrives at this place, this condition, is of less significance than the assurance that its momentum is propelling it in this direction. (Compare Moses on Mount Pisgah: his people will certainly attain the promised land, whether or not he lives to see it; his mission, thus, is successful.)

Eliot's "word" resonates with connotations in both the spiritual and secular communities. Yet it is, finally, the words of Eliot himself that I find most momentous. Like Peter, Celia, and the Chamberlaynes, Eliot is moving toward where the words are valid. Remember Harry's parting valediction to his family in *The Family Reunion:* "I know what I am doing, and what I must do. . . . But at present, I cannot explain it to anyone: / I do not know the words in which to explain it" (109); and the response to the hyacinth girl in *The Waste Land:* "I could not / Speak, and my eyes failed, I was neither / Living nor dead, and I knew nothing" (54). These passages represent Eliot's constant struggle with language up until 1949: a struggle plagued by inadequate communication, limited meaning, the solipsism of the finite center. The lines that Reilly and Alex deliver about Peter's future bespeak an easy certitude, confidence, that words can be valid—that meaning and meaningful communication within a community are within the realm of possibility. As such, I see these lines that close act 2 as the simple and central apotheosis of Eliot's literary career. Though a brilliant wordsmith, Eliot had been working in a medium, with words, that had always been suspect, deceitful, mitigated, barren, ineffable—always, somehow, *invalid.* Now, Eliot announces, his medium has finally become a respository of meaning that can be worked with, spoken, communicated, understood, used in the foundation of a community. In his final plays, he uses a valid language—or, at least, a language that he has affirmed, as never before, *can* be valid.

The Confidential Clerk: "Mind Control Is a Different Matter"

Colby Simpkins, confidential clerk to the Mulhammers, briefly tries (and fails) to mold Sir Claude's ward, the exuberant and flighty Lucasta Angel, into a culturally polished woman. She has never been to a concert, she informs him, but she often went to the opera: not to listen to the music, but "I just enjoyed going—to see the other people, / And to be seen there!" (56). This offhand remark anticipates the play's ideal: to foster a sensibility of pure enjoyment and engagement in community. Lucasta's attraction to the theater is heedless of whatever happens to be taking place on the operatic stage. Elementally, she perceives the essence of drama to be the audience: seeing and being seen; being among people in the community that a performance enables.[1]

Critics do not generally place *The Confidential Clerk,* replete with confusing artifices and contrivances, in the top rank of Eliot's drama. On one level, Lucasta's message serves Eliot's predicament in a troublingly constructed play: Do not worry too much about the drama at hand, he informs the audience via Lucasta. Think about yourselves, your role as an audience, rather than the pyrotechnics and occasional impenetrabilities on stage.

When Lucasta speaks of seeing and being seen by other people early in act 2, her attitude is not (yet) effectively established as the play's moral: she does not yet speak for her community of drama. Eliot casts her in the broad and heavy-handed role of a vulgar comic tart, not a dramatic or social arbiter. Before a community can share Lucasta's epiphany (which I take it to be, however understated), it must surmount the forces of deception. Deceptive intrigues, self-delusions, lies, pervade the play. They pose obstacles that must be removed before an expression of community awareness such as Lucasta's can be stripped of its irony and taken as sincere. Eliot and his characters must attack two realms of deception simultaneously: external, or social, or community deception; and internal deception, lies to oneself, interior psychological static—what I term individual deceit.[2]

Eliot appropriates the first of these deceptions wholesale from Euripides, reveling in the scope and complexity of the confusions from the *Ion,* his classical model. Community deceptions in *The Confidential Clerk* arise in relation to such matters as who slept with whom, who took charge of and supported the offspring, and who can expose various genealogical mysteries. Community deceptions involve repressions; lies of omission; confusions of identity (on a *community* rather than an individual level—i.e., not a matter of a person's being confused about who he is but four other people's uncertainty about his identity); attempts to mislead person A about person B, with ensuing deceitful consequences for persons C, D, and E. These consequences erupt in painful scenes. When Colby discovers that Lucasta is (as he believes) his sister, he gasps in alarm but refuses to divulge why, which she takes as a rebuke of her illegitimacy. Similarly, Sir Claude spoils his wife's joy at rediscovering her own son when he reveals that Colby is in fact his own son; he had never acknowledged Colby's supposed parentage because he was sure she would then think he had an infinite number of secret offspring. Eliot handles these issues methodically, formulaically, very much in the mode of Euripides.

Individual deceit—internal, psychological confusion of identity—is handled more subtly. It generates Eliot's more original material and, I think, his more interesting themes—more important, in terms of the trajectory of his drama and indeed of his entire canon. Eliot appraises the masks, falsehoods, and inadequacies of identity in everyday life—that is, before "induction" into a community of drama. This appraisal continues a theme that reaches as far back as his earliest poetry and infuses his entire corpus. Eliot explores and highlights the motif of individual deceit in Prufrock's insecurity, lack of vitality, lack of sincere personality, and ultimate protean devolution; in the gentleman caller's poses and shallow pretentions in "Portrait of a Lady"; and in the fragility of any meaningful persona, and consequent descent into the horrifically banal, in "Hysteria," "Lune de Miel," and "Mr. Apollinax."

The unstable array of mad voices in *The Waste Land* epitomizes Eliot's appraisal of inadequate and untrue identity: each voice chimes pathetically, like those of the damned in Dante's hell, trying to assert its viability, its personality, its character, and constantly resorting to deceit and distortion. Each of these individuals is fated to failure. On a larger scale, *The Waste Land* is a city of the damned, a failed chorus (He Do the Police *in Different Voices*—devoid of unity). It is thus destined not to be supportive of its individuals, to be, instead, harshly anticommunity. Eliot's poetry, especially *The Waste Land,* illustrates by negative definition what Eliot sees as the point of a community (in real life) and a community of drama (in literary life): there must be a stable "exoskeletal" structure to support the stability, sanity, and viability of an individual therein.

Voices founder desperately in *The Waste Land* and finally expire, precisely because its community—whether considered as an intellectual, political, poetic, or emotional community . . . any or all of these—is deranged, disconnected, fragmented, masochistic. Characters (or sensibilities tentatively suggestive of a character type) appear for an instant, only to disappear into an eerie, surreal, hellish void.

In *The Confidential Clerk,* this personal confusion and delusion of identity is given a simple dramatic "tag," an easily accessible and recurring theme: Sir Claude's desire—failed desire—to have been a potter. He wanted to be an artist, to make something with his hands, but he was unable to embrace the simple life and succumbed to the temptations of wealth and aristocracy. Parallel to this failure, although slightly less manifest, is Colby's quest for a calling, so far unfulfilled. Although softer in degree, Sir Claude's and Colby's situations are no different in kind from the torment of false and empty identity exhibited by Marie, the typist at teatime, Sweeney, the modern Cleopatra, or any of the other inhabitants of *The Waste Land.*

In Eliot's next play, *The Elder Statesman,* this same issue of lying to oneself (as Sir Claude has done) and needing to set right these lies before one dies, is the overt theme of the play. The idea of self-deceit that is carefully developed in *The Confidential Clerk* is taken as a donnée in the next play; Eliot straight-forwardly asserts there what self-deceit is and how it makes Lord Claverton unfit to join any community. In *The Confidential Clerk,* though, while Sir Claude does offer an ingress to this theme, the rather benign fact of his missed vocation as a potter is essentially a cover story. The playwright encrypts a deeper exposé of individual deceit on a more personal, interiorized level. Eliot examines the importance of internal psychological integrity by covert recourse to his own history of internal psychological breakdown and reassociation. This theme explicitly appears only briefly in the play (and more extensively, though still fitfully, in Eliot's drafts), in terms of Lady Elizabeth's Swiss treatments for mind control.

COMMUNITY DECEPTION

Community deception in *The Confidential Clerk* is straightforward and obvious and need be discussed only briefly. Its dramatic function is twofold. First, it represents a situation that must finally be rectified—the characters unde-ceived, the truth discovered—if a cohesive and honest community is to exist. A deceitful community, where words, stories, facts, are made up arbitrarily and with intention to mislead, is patently undesirable: confusing and anxiety-ridden. (This characterization of confused anxiety perfectly describes Eliot's poetic, and its consequent anticommunity inclinations, until the 1930s.) Such a condi-tion simply points out the need for its antithesis, a community where the truth is paramount, where the words are valid.

Second, the deceitful community is a visible, obvious, comprehensible ana-

logue to a deceitful individual. The idea of a deceitful individual is a complicated one, difficult to manifest dramatically. This difficulty is especially thorny
since Eliot grounds his portrayal of individual deceit in the intricately dense
angst from his own life in another era (in another country, and besides, the
wench is dead . . .). That earlier poetic proved dramatically impotent—solipsistic, interiorized, pervaded with mute ineffability, and consistently anticlimactic. Consider such poetic endings as *"[n]ot with a bang but a whimper"* or
"[t]he last twist of the knife." These endings not only forestall dramatic denouement and resolution but actively oppose it, defuse it, refute it. This sensibility
had to be reshaped into the dramatic material that would later provide fodder
for Eliot's community vision. When Eliot presents community deceit as an
analogue for individual deceit, he depicts people meddling with each other or
deceiving each other; this deceit is more performable, more demonstrable to an
audience, than internalized individual deceit. "In *The Confidential Clerk,*"
writes Robert A. Colby, "the grab bag of parents and children on which the
plot swings is obviously Eliot's means of dramatizing the larger issue of alienation and kinship among human beings in general" (792). Colby thus confirms
my description of an analogous relationship between individual and community.

Eliot's technique here repeats the one he used in *The Cocktail Party,* where
the Chamberlaynes' marriage was a microcommunity reflecting the issues that
affected the coherence of a larger community surrounding them. Carol H.
Smith's theory of parallel dramatic levels in Eliot's drama applies here. She
describes Eliot's plays as portraying the competing claims of two different
worlds in a "multi-level drama" (*Dramatic Theory,* ix). She terms these two
levels the spiritual and the secular; similarly, I argue that the community and
individual sensibilities often interact in the same multilevel fashion. At different
times in the plays, the individual and the community, or the local and the
general, alternate in the roles of what Smith calls "ordinary" (secular) and
"transcendent" (spiritual) reality—depending on which seems more accessible,
and which more elusive, to Eliot in a given situation. The two realms mirror
each other, so that if a given situation is comprehensible in one realm but more
opaque in the other, the drama of levels allows the playwright and the audience
to work out the situation on the easier level and then make the application to
the more difficult one. Finally, though, the quandary is resolved in both realms
at the close of Eliot's plays. Eliot aspires to portray, ultimately, a well-functioning individual in a well-functioning community, two entities which nurture each
other symbiotically.

Community deceit occurs as Sir Claude rehearses Eggerson about how Colby's hiring should be presented to Lady Elizabeth. If she objects to the clerk's
being hired while she was out of town, Eggerson must say that he had to leave
his job hastily on medical orders; Colby was hired so quickly, they should
pretend, because he had another offer; and Lady Elizabeth should be induced
to believe that she actually chose him herself. Of this introduction to the house-

hold, and Sir Claude's plan eventually to adopt him, Colby later remarks that he feels unsettled with the Mulhammers because "what you've had in mind still seems to me / Like building my life upon a deception" (43). The play's atmosphere of deception is pervasive: when Colby performs for Lucasta, flattering her by telling her it is the first time he has played for anyone, she replies, "Don't be such a fraud. You know you told me / The piano was only delivered this week" (56). As the characters begin to unravel their deceptions toward the play's end, they do so with a firm sense of how tangled and deceitful their behavior has been. When Sir Claude finally tells Lady Elizabeth that he believes Colby to be his son, for example, his confession acknowledges his history of deceit and a dawning awareness of how useless the deceit has been: "I should have told you one day. / I've always loathed keeping such a thing from you. / I see now I might as well have told you before" (94).

INDIVIDUAL DECEPTION: BREAKDOWN

Besides partaking prolifically in a community of deception, each character in this play except for Eggerson is also individually deceitful. Eggerson is the exemplum—a man who is able to serve in his career with diligence and integrity and then retire with a sound, untroubled mind, to his wife, his garden, and his simple clerical community. He may participate in the community deception when instructed to do so, as part of his job, but he shows no interest in such duplicity on his own time.

Everyone else's character lacks complete integrity, honesty. In examining *The Cocktail Party,* I identified several characters' flaws as a contagious occurrence of at least a roughly schizophrenic psychological dysfunctionality. Here, too, the condition that afflicts the play's individuals and challenges their successful entrance into harmonious community can be traced to a common etiology. Eliot depicts the condition as what I call individual deceit, and he does so by drawing upon his own 1921 mental collapse. This breakdown was the result of his inability to perceive and maintain the integrity of his psyche, to be true to himself. Eliot, incidentally, was working at that time as a "clerk" for Lloyds, and his breakdown might be diagnosed as the result of his being unable to keep his troubling "confidences" (about the nature of his life, his poses, his real character) bottled up inside himself. This explanation only offers a tentative suggestion for a titular autobiographical resonance, although Lyndall Gordon offers a specific piece of corroborating evidence: Eggerson's character "was based on a real-life clerk, a Mr. McKnight who had been Eliot's first colleague at Lloyds Bank" (*New Life,* 225). More generally, too, she supports an autobiographical reading of *The Confidential Clerk.* Noting that the play's hero is "a man in search of identity, abjuring father, mother . . . so that he might fulfill a devotion to God alone," she offers the parallel of Eliot's statement to Mary Trevelyan, soon after finishing the play, that "a man who has not known his parents is fortunate, and that his own parents had seemed distant, like 'ancestors' " (*New Life,* 239). In his psychoanalysis of the play, John D. Mitchell also sees autobiographical connections. He calls the play an "unconscious striving . . . to resolve repressed inner conflict." Colby's quest to discover a place where he belongs and is accepted, Mitchell writes, dramatizes Eliot's own longing for such gemeinschaft as a consequence of his exile from America (263).

As all scholars of Eliot's work have noted, his breakdown was of central importance both personally and professionally, strongly affecting the course of his life and his career. (It has jokingly been called the most productive nervous breakdown in literary history, resulting, as it did, in the completion of *The Waste Land.*) When, therefore, Eliot sends one of his characters off to Switzerland for mental therapy in *The Confidential Clerk,* one cannot underestimate the significance of the autobiographical allusion he is tendering. It may be meant as a hint for his more dogged scholarly audience or merely intended as a private testament to his experience with Dr. Roger Vittoz. In any case, to understand the unsatisfactory nature of the individual personality and psyche as Eliot depicts it in this play, one must approach that crux by examining what is known about Eliot's own troubled mind in 1921.

Eliot made his famous visit to Vittoz in Lausanne to be treated for nervous breakdown. It has never been fully clear what happened there; *The Confidential Clerk,* I believe, gives as good an insight into this situation as any of Eliot's writing. (Other than this play, two passages from *The Waste Land* have seemed the most revelatory about what happened in Lausanne: "By the waters of Leman I sat down and wept"[3]—Leman was the old name for Lake Geneva, on which Lausanne sits—and "These fragments I have shored against my ruins.")

Eliot describes his condition, sketchily, in several letters. He writes to Richard Aldington on 6 November 1921 from Margate, on his way to Switzerland:

My idea is to consult, and perhaps stay some time under, Vittoz, who is said to be the best mental specialist in Europe—now that I have a unique opportunity for doing so. I am satisfied, since being here, that my "nerves" are a very mild affair, due, not to overwork, but to an *aboulie* and emotional derangement which has been a lifelong affliction. Nothing wrong with my mind. (486)

Eliot's emotional upheaval does not jibe with his composed outward persona; hence, individual deceit. Even in discussing the ailment, Eliot is drawn into the patent self-contradiction—deceit—of characterizing his condition at first as trivial when he downplays it as a "very mild affair" and then immediately undercutting this view and impressing upon Aldington what is obviously the dire nature of this "lifelong affliction." Like many compulsive sufferers, Eliot seems to want to be caught out in his miasma of deceit. In *The Confidential Clerk,* none of the characters are obviously disabled by whatever afflicts them: they persevere in their paths as captain of industry, society doyenne, confidential clerk; but Eliot's letter to Aldington suggests that beneath a facade of only mild disability may lie a condition of deceptive danger, of seething urgency. (Note that Eliot, before he has gone to Lausanne, emphasizes that there is "[n]othing wrong with my mind." Lady Elizabeth, too, before she had left for Switzerland, believed she needed only "thought control" but finally discovered that she actually needed the more advanced "mind control." This shift could mirror Eliot's own gradual awareness of the seriousness of his disturbance.)

Eliot wrote to his brother, Henry, from Lausanne, on 13 December:

I have not gone into any details with mother about my health, so do not do so yourself. It is not in fact serious. The great thing I am trying to learn here is how to use all my energy without waste, to be calm when there is nothing to be gained by worry, and to concentrate without effort. I hope that I shall place less strain upon Vivien, who has had to do so much thinking for me. I realise that our family never was taught mental, any more than physical hygiene, and so we are a seedy lot. (493)

Again, we see Eliot understating the seriousness of his case, to a degree hard to find credible in view of the desperation with which, numerous biographical sources confirm, he fled his wife, his home, his job, in 1921. To Sydney Waterlow, on 19 December:

I have been under Vittoz, who is not a psychoanalyst, but more useful for my purpose; I was aware that the principal trouble was that I have been losing power of concentration and attention, as well as becoming a prey to habitual worry and dread of the future: consequently, wasting far more energy than I used, and wearing myself out continuously. (495)

In Eliot's letters to his brother and Waterlow, there are strong parallels to what is indicated in *The Confidential Clerk* by "thought control" and "mind control." He writes of his need to focus and improve his concentration, his thinking, his attention. Eliot's memory lapses first seem innocuous enough, merely requiring a jaunt to the Continent for some mnemonic tricks. But as in his letter to Aldington, Eliot contradicts his own cover story as soon as he presents it to Waterlow, belying the facade (of his illness as a minor attention problem) in the same sentence with the drastic mention of habitual worry and dread. Eliot locates his suffering in the realm of the quotidian, as a harmless mild concern, and, at the same time, in some desperate void. The contrast resembles the effect at the end of "The Love Song of J. Alfred Prufrock," where the denouement of the speaker's agon is presented, tamely, as "I shall wear white flannel trousers, and walk upon the beach," and then, six lines later, apocalyptically, "We have lingered in the chambers of the sea . . . Till human voices wake us, and we drown" (7). Or, again, in "Rhapsody on a Windy Night," the speaker appears to conclude the poem's reveries by brushing his teeth, but this mild scene bizarrely culminates in the image of torture at knifepoint.

In his poetry, as in his letters, Eliot *deceptively* offers an initial mild appraisal of the situation at hand, then contradicts that with a statement of its devastating reality. The effect is to demonstrate the horrific condition of the modern world: Eliot presents an atmosphere in which his poetic personae are compelled to appraise their conditions in dry, understated languor—as if numbed, or shell-shocked, by the enormity of the real manifestations of horror that encroach and overwhelm them. The pedestrian, languid self-appraisals are then shown to be individual deceptions, confirming the vastness of external (community) horror and incoherence: not trousers but drowning; preparing not for bed but for torture; and, in the case of Eliot's letters, not a minor mental tune-up but a crisis. Part of the totality of awful bleakness is precisely that the individual, the victim, deludes himself about the reality at hand, obvious though it is.

ELIOT ON THE COUCH, TAKE 2

Ronald Bush characterizes the early 1920s as a period of dull nightmare in Eliot's life, and "it was difficult for him to dissociate the nightmare within and the nightmare without." When tired or worried, "he found himself under the strain of trying to suppress a vague but intensely acute horror and apprehension" (55). The completed draft of *The Waste Land,* which Eliot brought home with him from Lausanne, represented, as Bush writes, "an attempt to 'reconstitute' a personal world—to give it a meaning, a shape, and an order" (69). Lyndall Gordon, too, sees *The Waste Land* as insightful into the poet's mental condition: "the poem seems to follow the course of his sickness and recovery" (*Early Years,* 111). In *Archives of General Psychiatry,* Harry Trosman, a medical doctor who has studied Eliot's biography, agrees that the poem illuminates Eliot's breakdown and recovery (and vice versa): "We are thus confronted in this instance with a significant link between psychopathology, reintegration, and subsequent creative achievement" (709).

Eliot's breakdown consummately illustrates his sense of individual disharmony, self-deceit. His comments about wasting his energy in needless worry suggest he realizes that he is dysfunctionally consumed by some distress: his energy is wasted because he is reacting to what does not merit his attention, and/or not responding to what does. This situation is an example of what I would characterize as the static of internal self-deceit. And again, his self-diagnosis of lifelong emotional derangement (manifested most prominently in his marriage to a woman whom he considered in every way unsuited to his temperament) points to a character living a lie, living behind a mask that he increasingly perceives to be one of complete deceit, untrue to his feelings, desires, and instincts.

If, as I believe, Bush is correct about what *The Waste Land* represented for Eliot—reconstitution of a personal world, imposition of meaning, shape, and order—then it makes sense to assume that during the time of Eliot's breakdown generally (if not, specifically, Vittoz's treatment), he was focused on accomplishing this sort of a reversal in the dynamics of his personal life and psyche.

Eliot sought to stem the horrific pain of living a lie and attempted to restore order—integrity, stripped of deceit—to his life and his aesthetic. Making conjectures about the circumstances that led to the breakdown, Trosman characterizes Eliot's symptom complex as profoundly antisocial: "His personality was vulnerable to specific injuries that disturbed his narcissistic equilibrium. He was aloof and distant, and he guarded himself against the intrusions of others with an icy urbanity" (712). Successful treatment for his condition, then, would imply the remediation of an anticommunity bias; and again the period of breakdown emerges as a peripeteia in Eliot's life and sensibility, a moment of reversal from solipsism to embrace of community. If Eliot, ill, is antisocial, then one would expect him in health to be more amenable to social instincts, to community.

The endnotes to *The Waste Land* demonstrate that work's aesthetic integrity: the poem does not evaporate at its conclusion but connects—at least nominally, even if some of the citations are more pedantic *blagues* than legitimate scholarly references—to a tradition of intellect and culture. The prebreakdown works, by contrast, do not continue beyond themselves: they are "[t]houghts of a dry brain in a dry season" (31), as at the end of "Gerontion," and do not ultimately proliferate or connect. They end with the desperate clutching of the banal: "I remember a slice of lemon, and a bitten macaroon" (23), in "Mr. Apollinax"; "I concentrated my attention with careful subtlety" on stopping the shaking of a woman's breasts (24) in "Hysteria." In the prebreakdown poems that dissipate at the end, there is no possibility for a community extension or support of the ideas, the aesthetic, therein. *The Waste Land* offers the beginnings of an Eliotic aesthetic—much strengthened in his drama—that embodies an extrapolation beyond, outside of, and after the work itself. I posit, once again, that this aesthetic is the consequence of his reversal of sensibility after the treatment with Vittoz: Eliot feels enabled to imagine such extensions and connections after he has changed his own psyche from one steeped in delusions and masks to one headed toward integrity.

Peter Ackroyd describes Vittoz's regimen: "His method of treatment was an unusual one in which the emphasis was on (in lay speech) taking the patient 'out of himself'. . . . Vittoz also believed in a contemporary version of the 'laying on of hands' in which he would by physical contact and suggestion draw off the weight of nervousness or self-absorption which incapacitated or paralysed those like Eliot who came to see him" (116). Ackroyd's description of Eliot's path to recovery corresponds with my reading of Eliot's rejecting the persona, the self, he saw as deceitful. The "new" Eliot is one who emerges, in Ackroyd's terms, as he is taken out of his "old" (prebreakdown) self. The new self gives the lie to the old one, which is thus exposed as having been self-deceitful.

Cleo McNelly Kearns describes Vittoz's treatment as involving "a set of graded exercises in meditation, beginning with concentration on simple movements or on sensations, proceeding through exercises designed to develop greater *control of the mind*" (154, emphasis added). Control was explicitly a crucial element of Vittoz's treatment; "thought control" and "mind control" in *The Confidential Clerk,* then, must have close links in Eliot's mind to his own lessons in control. Kearns explains that Vittoz thought psychological dysfunction was the result of malfunctioning brain waves, and

> he thought patients could overcome most forms of mental illness by learning to control these waves . . . thus gaining mastery over the experiences and feelings they reflected. "Control," for Vittoz, as for the Eastern sages, meant not repression of suppressed memories and desires but a balanced freedom from them. "When we speak of normal brain equilibrium," Vittoz wrote, "we mean that every idea, impression or sensation is controlled by reason, judgement and will, that is to say, that these can be judged, modified, or set aside as required." (153)

Trosman, too, cites the importance of control in Vittoz's treatment: "He saw his treatment as analogous to tuning a piano, bringing harmony and control to a disordered mind. With control would come freedom from vice and impurity. . . . Vittoz began with very simple tasks, enabling the patient to acquire a sense of mastery over partial functions. When some control had been established, tasks that were more complex were assigned" (713).

ENTER THE SWISS DOCTORS: IN DRAFT

In draft (item D8 in the T. S. Eliot Collection, identified as "UR-CLERK"), the play features Lady Elizabeth's trip to Switzerland more prominently than in its final version because the text begins with a scene in which she is preparing to embark. In the final text, we see only Lady Elizabeth's return. At first, then, Eliot saw the trip as something that lay ahead of Lady Elizabeth, something to be confronted within the drama. The drafts show heavy reworking of this episode, and the final text remains elusive about her trip. The audience does not know why she went to Zurich rather than Lausanne or what the difference is between the two treatments she considers, thought control and mind control; this elusiveness is dramatically viable in the final text, though, because of Lady Elizabeth's flighty character.

It is a wise and significant decision for Eliot to have changed the Swiss journey from something that will happen in the future to something that has happened in the past, for two reasons. First, it allows the playwright to describe with greater certainty what *has* happened, as opposed to what *might* happen; what the significance of this episode *is,* rather than what it could be. (Although the nature of Lady Elizabeth's treatment is ambiguous as it stands in the published text, it nevertheless finally offers crucial, if commonplace, lessons; those will be discussed below.) Second, Eliot finally realized, in shifting the episode from the future to the past, how one should write autobiographically: removing artifice and deceptions and acknowledging (at least to himself) that he is in fact writing about something in *his own* past. He makes the Swiss trip something that has already been experienced by Lady Elizabeth, as it is something that he has already experienced himself. The play is about what happens afterward: how a mentally refreshed person functions in society.

Besides changing the Swiss adventure from the future to the past, there are several other significant differences between the drafts and the final text. The play's specific time of year is only vaguely identifiable in the final text: Eggerson mentions Mrs. Eggerson's request that Colby should come visit them in Joshua Park but tells the new clerk it would be inappropriate to have him all the way out there at *this* time of the year—better to wait until spring. One may surmise, then, that the play is set in late fall or winter. In the draft, however, as Lady Elizabeth announces that she is going to Lausanne, Sir Claude immediately responds that a visit to Lausanne in November seems unusual. November 1921 is when Eliot made his own journey to Lausanne. In what is identified as a "second rough draft" of the play (Eliot Collection, item D9), November is canceled in this passage and October is handwritten over it; perhaps this change is Eliot's token attempt at obfuscating autobiography.

In the draft, Lady Elizabeth goes to Lausanne to see Dr. Leroux and study thought control; in the play, Sir Claude believed his wife was seeing Leroux in Lausanne and learning thought control, but he is surprised to discover, upon her return, that she has actually been to see a Dr. Rebmann in Zurich, where she was taught mind control.

In the play, the entire discussion of Lady Elizabeth's Swiss treatment is a sidebar—a confusing bit of business that Sir Claude tries to comprehend in order to determine exactly why she is home unexpectedly. This entire affair is subordinated to the more important business at hand, the need to prepare Lady Elizabeth for the presence of Colby and Sir Claude's plan to bring the three of them together as a family. In the final version, the episode takes twenty lines (38–39), offers few substantial details about the nature of treatment, and has no obvious impact on any plot elements later in the play. In the draft, though, the initial discussion of the Swiss treatment takes thirty-eight lines; coming at the opening of the play, it has a formal prominence. In the draft, unlike in the play, there *is* a later return to this theme: in act 1, scene 3 of the draft, the audience learns that Lady Elizabeth has in fact gone to Zurich to study mind control with Dr. Rebmann (as in the final version). The incidence and *recurrence* of the Swiss treatment would impress upon an audience a sense of its greater significance in the play.

In the draft, Sir Claude asks Lady Elizabeth if her regular doctor has advised the treatment in Switzerland; she responds that he has not and that there is no reason he should. She makes the distinction between her physical health, for which her physician is responsible, and the health of her mind, for which she is seeing the Swiss doctor. Eliot may be interested in distinguishing between physical and mental health as a way to justify his extravagant flight from England (where there were certainly adequate medical specialists to treat physical conditions) and his three-month leave of absence from Lloyds. The remnants of his middle-American work ethic would likely have occasioned some guilt on this count. Further, by distinguishing between physical and mental affliction, Eliot may have intended to separate his type of distress from Vivien's: throughout their marriage she had been afflicted with a range of serious physical ailments. Since a significant aspect of his flight appears to have been an attempt to get away from Vivien, it makes sense that he should locate his illness in a pointedly different realm from hers. Probably Vivien also suffered psychiatric ailments (and quite possibly her husband was at least partly responsible for them), but Eliot seems not to have acknowledged this possibility in the early 1920s, consumed as he was with his own state of mind. When, years later, he does seem to have recognized his wife's mental illness, his instinct was to distance himself from her completely.

The play tells only that mind control is different from, and more advanced than, thought control. In draft, the nature of Leroux's treatment is discussed in more detail:

First, while Leroux is not concerned with *what* people think, he teaches control over whatever they choose to think.

Second, Mildred Deverell has already been to see him. Before Mildred's treatment she was unable to focus her mind; now, thanks to a regimen of breathing and mental exercises, she can remember a dozen things at once. (This description suggests a provocative précis of *The Waste Land* as a twelve-ring circus, with a dozen planes of action and consciousness that the reader must "remember" simultaneously.) The details of Mildred's treatment replicate the regimen of Vittoz, as Trosman describes: "The first lessons were in concentration on sensations. . . . Gradually the exercises became more complicated. They moved from acquiring the ability to experience sensations without thought to breathing exercises, graduated exercises in attention, and concentration on ideas" (713).

Third, treatment lasts about two weeks, the first time. (Eliot's treatment lasted about a month; perhaps he had a double session?)

Fourth, there is the hint of quackery: Sir Claude worries about what he characterizes as the undesirable influences of the analyst, although Lady Elizabeth corrects him, stating that he is not an analyst. (Remember Eliot's letter to Waterlow in which he makes a point of stating that Vittoz is not a psychoanalyst.) One may sense shades of Reilly, another free-floating, free-lance shrink of indeterminate professional standing; perhaps the "doctor" from *The Cocktail Party* is another type of Vittoz. Like Sir Claude, Eliot seems at least somewhat sensitive to a perception of quackery regarding his own Swiss doctor. In the letter to Aldington quoted earlier, Eliot writes that Vittoz "is said to be the best mental specialist in Europe." It is hard not to hear in this statement an echo of the passage from "The Burial of the Dead" describing the quack prophetess Madame Sosostris as one who "[i]s known to be the wisest woman in Europe" (54). In *Eliot's Early Years* (146), Lyndall Gordon writes that the Madame

Sosostris passage either had already been drafted in November 1921 (when Eliot wrote Aldington) or, what seems to me more likely, was being written at exactly that time. (The fortune-teller, Gordon writes, was suggested by "Sesostris the Sorceress" in Aldous Huxley's *Crome Yellow,* published the same month Eliot wrote to Aldington.) This chronological proximity strengthens the likeliness of an intentional connection in Eliot's mind between the passage from *The Waste Land* and the one from the letter to Aldington and, consequently, the implication of a Sosostristic skepticism in Eliot's perception of Vittoz shortly before he began his treatment.

Fifth, in the draft, Lady Elizabeth is more explicit about her condition than in the play: her mind is disorderly. Sir Claude mildly challenges the nature, or even existence, of this disorder; but, she responds, he has been in business his whole life, which has kept his mind orderly; those with imagination are more prone to mental suffering and to forgetting things. (Eliot, of course, would see himself as one of those whose imaginative life would make him prone to mental suffering. He had, like Sir Claude, his work at Lloyds, which might have provided a counterbalancing order, but he would come to reject his business life in the City of London—"Unreal City"—as a self-deceptive, orderly facade. From his ground-level window, the young clerk had watched the feet of the dead flowing over London Bridge, as he described it in *The Waste Land.*)

SWISS DOCTORS: FINAL TEXT

In the play's final version, November, which had become October in a later draft, became extremely vague. The city, the doctor, the treatment, changed. Details are diminished, as is the episode's dramatic prominence. Frankly, I must admit that Eliot's treatment of the entire topic suggests more questions than answers; but, I think, the questions are provocative ones and worth raising, even if I cannot wholly or definitively resolve them. Was Eliot trying to cover his tracks when he downplayed and obfuscated aspects of Lady Elizabeth's mind control, trying to live up to his admonition in "Tradition and the Individual Talent" that "the more perfect the artist the more completely separate in him will be the man who suffers and the mind which creates" (7–8)? When the mental treatment set in the future was moved to the past, was Eliot casting the scene in a haze of nostalgic control, or historical affirmation, rather than future uncertainty?

What is the entire sketchy passage doing in the play at all—is it just a roman à clef tribute to Eliot's own endurance and escape from breakdown, or is there more that the audience is supposed to perceive? Lady Elizabeth's flouncy, airy character seems a strange one for Eliot's authorial self-inscription. Is the fact that *she,* of all his dramatic personae, attends the Swiss doctor a sign of Eliot's looking back humbly, self-critically, admitting that what had once been momentously traumatic now seems just a bit of fluff, an adventure for a socialite with more money than intellectual acumen?

Is there any meaningful difference between thought control and mind control? At first they seem to the audience, as Sir Claude skeptically appraises them, apparently identical—psychological mumbo-jumbo. As Lady Elizabeth tosses these terms around, they may appear as trite as Nutrisystem weight-loss or hair-care clubs are seen today: part of commodified, popular "medical culture." At the same time, though, stripping away the bias of a seemingly pedestrian context, the terminology can, indeed, connote the essence of a stable human intellect and psyche: sanity, organization, *humanitas.* Lady Elizabeth considers both thought control and mind control treatments, before choosing the one she finds more appropriate to her needs. In choosing mind over thought, is she attempting to transcend the apparently empty thoughtlessness of a stereotypical society life? Is she eschewing the triteness of a watery aristocratic existence—in which she finds nothing worth thinking about—and opting instead for a new process (which would inhere in the mind, as yet untapped,) to appraise and mediate the world around her? The play's comic genealogical confusions may be interpreted as a symbolic attempt to establish a community; the details are confusing, sometimes nearly impenetrable. Perhaps, although the audience is not meant to think about these literal details, but should instead try to process the larger picture: Lady Elizabeth is trying to reassociate what had been sundered, long-lost. She may do it sloppily, and she may seem culpable for having forgotten the name of the town where her son lived, but she redeems this vagueness by training her mind to appreciate and demonstrate the value of reassociating the community she had once had and lost.

Trying to determine what exactly his wife has been doing in Switzerland, Sir Claude attempts to pin down the details of her treatment:

SIR CLAUDE

So you went on to Zurich.
But I thought that the doctor in Lausanne taught mind control?

LADY ELIZABETH

No, Claude, he only teaches *thought* control.
Mind control is a different matter:
It's more advanced. But I wrote you all about it. (39)

Mind control is a different matter indeed from the sensibility that had typified Eliot's earlier work and his earlier life. His dramatic communities are, by contrast, increasingly controlled and orderly. Lady Elizabeth's indication of that contrast here is (like all her dialogue) casual and unmomentous, but it is nonetheless significant as a touchstone in the development of Eliot's sensibility. Achieving mind control is a different matter, too, from Eliot's search for where the words are valid, although it is a step, a more advanced step, in the same direction. The mind forms words; the development of a sane, community-oriented mind precedes the formation of the language that emanates from it. Eliot is reaching back even deeper into the individual who is being prepared in his drama to be a member of a community. He attempts to depict what might be termed a "valid mind"—functional amid community rather than solipsistically interiorized—that would then automatically produce valid words. In a way, it is as if Eliot were integrating the Guardians' function from *The Cocktail Party*—oversight, guidance, imposition of community discipline—into the individual herself here.

What are the consequences of mastering mind control? In the larger scheme of life, its importance would be vast: such mastery would result in a vision of coherent ability to participate in the world around one, as opposed to the psychotic deranged stupor of isolation. To be able to get out of bed every morning and advance through life, one needs to be able to remember things, process things, keep things in the mind in perspective and in workable relation to each other. If this effort seems gratuitous—if it seems that such a sentiment is facile, unworthy of Eliot's poetic energy—consider the contrast with those personae and tableaux that profusely inhabited Eliot's early poetry. They are enveloped in painful despair, a despair that Eliot struggled to surmount (finally doing so in his drama). This earlier poetry lacked even the basic vestiges of control: it is peopled by those who wander through the world only to find that "Midnight shakes the memory / As a madman shakes a dead geranium" (16); who are aware, seemingly as a physical reality, of such deranged hallucinations as "the damp souls of housemaids / Sprouting despondently at area gates" (19); who "can connect / Nothing with nothing" (64).

I take Eliot's "moral" in *The Confidential Clerk* not as facile but certainly as quite simple: in the vein of the simplicity that pervades Eliot's drama, and that, late in his life, he seems to have embraced as the only antidote to the desperate pain and uncertainty of his earlier aesthetic. Indeed, at his emotional depths in 1921, Eliot had been taught the virtues of simplicity by the same person who taught him control. Vittoz's remedy for psychiatric disharmony "was simplification. 'Simplifiez-vous,' he would say repeatedly to his patients, troubled by doubts about his methods as well as by the distractions of their obsessions and fears. Vittoz abjured what he called 'words too scientific for profane ears, the long discourse of the learned' in favor of 'quelques paroles, nettes et lumineuses,' which he hoped would heal by their very clarity" (Kearns, 154). It is precisely this sensibility that impels Eliot's turn away from the sort of obscurantist discourse that pervades his early poems and toward where the words are valid.

Complementing the simplicity of sensibility, and the simple quest for control that pervades *The Confidential Clerk,* is a simplicity of diction. Robert A. Colby explains how this diction infuses the play, even in contrast with *The Cocktail Party,* which had a similar tenor. "In both plays the base of diction is colloquial speech, as is Eliot's intention. In *The Cocktail Party* however, Eliot utilized various formalized structures of words—ranging from the banal to the sublime—to enhance rhyme and rhythm, such as epigrams, argumentation, jingles, songs, and prayers. On the other hand, the language of *The Confidential Clerk,* like its action, seems more of a piece, nothing besides conversation, with a deceptive simplicity concealing his intense utilization of the inherent musicality of our 'everyday' language" (800). R. T. Davies, too, confirms a sense of the play's intentional simplicity: "There is no character in this new play who is more than he seems. . . . This is the straight sort of play which was crystalizing out of *The Cocktail Party . . .* Mr. Eliot has come to terms with us, and is no longer, I felt, putting one over on us, or, perhaps, leaving so much unsaid . . . it is pretty clear what *The Confidential Clerk* is about, and the terms it uses appeal immediately. . . . Here is no mystery, and equally no echoing resonances, no footfalls in the mind's less travelled country. Mr. Eliot would appear to have his latest pack of cards well and truly on the table" (411–12).

How then, finally, does one appraise Eliot's simple and simply stated moral? All one can say with certainty about Lady Elizabeth's achievement in her Swiss trip concerns her surprising return from it. Her first entrance in the play is met with astonishment by her husband and Eggerson, because she made her own plans and came home on her own. After all the loose ends raised in the drafts, and all the possible autobiographical suggestions and resonances, this exertion of self-control is the point of the Swiss trip as it finally stands in the finished play: a simplified point, as Vittoz would have had it. The two men have been planning every detail of Lady Elizabeth's homecoming, which she throws into disarray by arriving unexpectedly and in her own charge. Her history is not one of self-sufficiency: Eggerson's career has been "[g]etting Lady Elizabeth out of her difficulties" (32). Her independent return, thus, occasions surprise.

SIR CLAUDE

Good heavens, Eggerson, what *can* have happened?

EGGERSON

It's perfectly amazing. Let *me* go down to meet her.

SIR CLAUDE

Where ought we to be? What ought we to be doing? (33–34)

Sir Claude's last questions literally refer to the need to revise their plans, to manipulate her introduction to the new confidential clerk with consequent plot intrigues; but I like the tenor of existential uncertainty that the line carries out of context.[4] It is as if Lady Elizabeth's new-found independence threatens to shatter the foundations of the old order (represented by her husband and Eggerson and their plot to insinuate Colby into the household), sundering its regularized smoothness and its own dynamics of control (which is antithetical to Lady Elizabeth's newly acquired control).

Lady Elizabeth's literal accomplishment, embodying the apparent fruits of mind control, is that she gets back home on her own. She has, symbolically, seized control of her own destiny, her own itinerary, her own journey, her own way. Because of her new talent of mental control, she has returned to a home that is no longer stacked against her, arranged by Eggerson, "confidentially" conspiratorial. Perhaps arriving home on one's own does not seem like a major accomplishment: but it certainly was for Eliot himself in the 1920s, as he managed to resume his life and edit and publish what would become the most important poem of his century. Like Eliot in 1921, Lady Elizabeth can be lauded for recognizing the need for control, deciding between thought and mind, resolving the differences, getting treatment, and returning back home. She does not have to be picked up at the airport, signifying her self-sufficiency, but perhaps most important is the fact that she comes home a different way from the one she was supposed to. (In the same vein, *Four Quartets* is full of meditations on getting back to the same place by different ways.)

> SIR CLAUDE
>
> What on earth has happened?
>
> EGGERSON
>
> Lady Elizabeth! This is most surprising.
>
> LADY ELIZABETH
>
> What's surprising, Eggerson? I've arrived, that's all.
>
> EGGERSON
>
> I was just starting for Northolt to meet you.
>
> LADY ELIZABETH
>
> That was very thoughtful of you, Eggerson,
> But quite unnecessary. And besides,
> I didn't come by air. I arrived at Victoria.
>
> SIR CLAUDE
>
> Do you mean to say that you changed your ticket?
>
> EGGERSON
>
> Yes, how did you manage to change your ticket?
>
> LADY ELIZABETH
>
> I went to the agency and got them to change it.
> I can't understand why you're both so surprised.
> You know I'm a very experienced traveller.
>
> SIR CLAUDE
>
> Oh yes, of course we know that, Elizabeth. (34–35)

A woman who, like Eliot, had been virtually paralyzed functionally, is able to find a different way of doing things—and this difference represents survival, for the status quo would have consigned her to eventual loss of personality and control at the hands of an endless procession of confidential clerks. She not only makes her way home but makes a splashy entrance to boot. (The completed draft of *The Waste Land* that Eliot brought home is his equivalent to Lady Elizabeth's grand homecoming.) Coming home is the consummate achievement, in terms of laying the foundation for an Eliotic community of drama. Harry Monchensey could barely bring himself to do it once in eight years—his brothers could not do it at all—and then he had to flee almost immediately; but each of Eliot's plays advances farther than the previous one in terms of the maturity of its community sensibility. So we have here Lady Elizabeth's resoundingly confident *nostos* that represents an advance over Harry's much more pallid variant.

As in *The Family Reunion* and *The Cocktail Party,* family and home here represent the microcommunity that betokens the eventual initiation of a larger sense of community: one must first figure out where one's home is, what it means. Lady Elizabeth is poised to do this upon her return from Switzerland. She enters the play, simultaneously (re)entering a home that is renewed. She spends the duration of the play energetically attempting to ascertain exactly who comprises her community, how they are all linked, where they came from, and how they got to be where they are. As she is doing this, the forces of community deception that have endured throughout her married life crumble away. To replace the deceptive void she is uncovering, she implements the fruits of a sane, controlled mind: decorating Colby's flat and taking him under her wing; trying to straighten out her convoluted past and work toward a sounder future; coming to terms with a community that includes everyone who belongs there, although she had wrongly scorned some of them (Lucasta, B. Kaghan) in the past.

In performance, Lady Elizabeth upstages what might have seemed to be the centrality of the title character. Reviewing the play in the *New York World-Telegram and Sun,* William Hawkins writes that Ina Claire, playing Lady Elizabeth, is the dominant star, and her performance is one "of pure brilliance. Nobody in this country, and probably anywhere, has so understood the double plane on which Eliot writes. . . . She has such *control* of her role and her audience, that you feel yourself being spiritually garroted when she does not choose for you to laugh" (emphasis added). My analysis may seem excessively centered on her character, to the exclusion of a considerable amount of the remainder of the play's character and plot development. Yet although I have examined her case most exhaustively, Lady Elizabeth is doing essentially the same thing as everyone else in the play. This must be so, in order for a community to proliferate: everyone must be marching to the same beat. I believe that Helen Gardner, calling the play an unqualified advance in Eliot's oeuvre, is reacting to what I characterize as this community coherence, or coordination, when she writes that the play "has a unity which Mr. Eliot has not achieved before in a play. No single one of the characters has a monopoly of wisdom or virtue. . . . Each in his own way has glimpses of the truth and each is capable of suffering because capable of love" (373).

All the characters, in their own ways, are working to learn control over the entropy, chaos, and deception that surround their lives. Sir Claude must come to terms with his vocation, with the success of his public accomplishments as contrasted with the uncertainty about his private role as father, with the nature of his marriage. Lucasta and Kaghan are both trying to find and fix their roles in their families and in society, to discover and develop their talents, to control the flux in which they find themselves. Colby is tormented by doubt, resulting from having been raised in an atmosphere of subterfuge in which he lacked control of his own destiny. All the play's characters seek control in their lives with the absolute conviction that it will lead toward a beneficent future community. Such a condition, of ideal community, can exist only after they get themselves in order and sort out their minds. They must get rid of whatever static, grudges, and other dysfunctions they have been harboring; they must realize that they have been nurturing various individual deceits, thus contributing to the proliferation of community confusions and deceit. They must learn to control themselves. Colby and Lucasta are both prone to emotional outbursts and rash assumptions about other people. These characteristics disappear, though, by the end of the play, as the two of them fit themselves into the incipient community. Kaghan has a chip on his shoulder about his condition in life, his relation to the aristocracy; by the end of the play, he has resolved and dispensed with this attitude.

Everyone who has been plagued with individual deceit must exercise a kind of control that involves not only the cessation of that behavior in the present but a kind of closure, or burying, of the confusions and manipulations of the past. The process is, for some of the characters, evocative of atonement: Sir Claude, certainly, must atone for his youthful profligacy. Lady Elizabeth's attitude toward her youthful mistakes, and Colby's and Lucasta's youthful thoughts about their parentage, however, do not exactly call for penance. Rather, they demand a kind of covering in forgetful snow, to appropriate an image from *The Waste Land.* There should be not necessarily an admission of guilt for past behavior but an acknowledgment that such attitudes from the past are no longer operable; that those old words are no longer valid, and a new discourse, a new communicative sensibility, is warranted.

DAMYATA

In *The Confidential Clerk,* Eliot sublimates, but does not obscure, the tracks that lead back to his nervous breakdown and recovery. References to what had happened to him in 1921 surface because the 1953 play is a delayed manifestation of Vittoz's success, which was the gradual reestablishment of Eliot's ability to participate in community.

Eliot's appraisal of that success was quite tentative in 1922: when he writes of it then, he embeds the idea of control in a word as arcane as Lady Elizabeth's language is obvious. He chooses a language for this word, Sanskrit, that is about as etymologically distant as possible from his native tongue. He toys with his audience before giving the word: he first offers only "DA"—a baby sound? gibberish? an onomatopoetic evocation of "what the thunder said"? It is almost insultingly basic, not calculated to satisfy his readers' curiosity or desire very fully. Calvin Bedient calls Eliot's "DA" "the most conventional of deific emblems, the thunder, and the seemingly dullest of sounds" (207). Given the context of intensely worked discourse in *The Waste Land,* one suspects a cheap throwaway, a red herring obfuscating the true key to the poem's conundrums. "DA" enlarges into what seems a tryptich, a triad—*Datta, Dayadhvam, Damyata:* "give," "sympathize," "control"—but I suggest that this enlargement is intentionally misleading, a reader-response type of trap to deceive the gullible, erroneous reader. If it were valid, the triad—mirroring the Trinity—would affirm the connection between the Upanishads' wisdom of the East and Western Christian culture, but I do not believe Eliot in 1922 was ready to affirm that degree of intellectual intercultural coherence. He *does* believe in such a link, I think, by the time he writes of "the lotos rose" (176) in "Burnt Norton," punningly unifying the Eastern and Western floral symbols of perfect beauty (as "rose" first appears to be a verb but then subtly melds with the lotos as a kind of compound or hybrid flower). This moment in *Four Quartets,* though, seems to me a *reconsideration* of the link between East and West that he approaches—hoping that his Eastern studies would reward him with a vision that could explain, or redeem, what he saw as the incomprehensible devolution of his Western world—but rejects, in the failed triad of *The Waste Land.*

I take *"Datta, Dayadhvam, Damyata"* not as a triad but, rather, as an avatar of Monty Hall's "Let's Make a Deal." One door offers the big payoff, and the other two only booby prizes. I do not think that Eliot makes a case for the viability (in terms of the poetic that *The Waste Land* establishes) of giving or sympathy. Although he pays lip service to them as ideally desirable in the poem, they actually elude him in 1922. Eliot follows *"Datta"* with the question, "what have we given?" (68). It is a simple question, and the pedantic ratiocination that follows is an evasion, not an answer. The implicit answer, I think, is that we have given nothing. An earlier generation read the poem as profuse, lavish with its heartfelt insights and cultural criticism; today, by contrast, we are much more prone to read the poem as guarded, covert, stinting, and giving little—constrained by the same kinds of individual deceptions that must be surmounted in *The Confidential Clerk.* Eliot himself withholds, represses, much more than he gives in this poem: "The awful daring of a moment's surrender" (68) is an unfulfilled fantasy, or delusion—not something the poem validates. Grover Smith similarly finds the Sanskrit admonition to give disingenuous. He ironizes the image of the awful daring surrender and takes it as a negative answer, the wrong denial, a refusal to submit to the voice of the thunder. It "surely concerns the sexual blunder to which Tiresias has already confessed. The surrender has involved no acceptance of love, of the demands of life, but a yielding to lust. . . . [a] craven surrender to a tyranny of the blood. . . . Joined with him in disgrace is someone else, the conjunct partner in a lust now become bondage" (96).

Sympathy, similarly, is as elusive in the poem as it was in Eliot's life. The vignette Eliot offers to illustrate *Dayadhvam* concerns a prisoner's meditations, and Bedient challenges this image: "how can the protagonist sympathize with others if he is locked in the prison of his own body?" (198). Eliot himself never expressed sympathy for those who were closest to him until his late marriage to Valerie Eliot. Lyndall Gordon amply documents the disappointments, the absolute want of sympathy, suffered by Vivien Eliot, John Hayward, Emily Hale, Mary Trevelyan. *The Waste Land,* too, dissuades and distances immensely more sympathy than it affirms. The poem is a catalogue of possible, but ultimately failed, sympathies: between the Thames maiden and her humble people; between men and women in all three tableaux in "A Game of Chess"; between the typist and her young man carbuncular, or Mr. Eugenides and his would-be lunch mate; between the members of the crowd flowing over London Bridge, undone—a crowd that, had it any sympathy, could have formed a community but certainly does not in this poem.

Control, though, is present—even triumphant—in *The Waste Land.* In 1922, Eliot gives his reader only a one-in-three chance of picking the right door; by 1953, he has made it the only option, the donnée of *The Confidential Clerk*— Lady Elizabeth has already passed this challenge, has correctly chosen the quest for control, when she first enters the play. (Bedient writes that *"damyata"* is technically a reflexive verb, thus specifically an admonition to "control *yourself"* [196]—all the more applicable to Lady Elizabeth's quest of mind control and self-control, and the onus I have identified of rectifying individual deceit in *The Confidential Clerk.*) In 1922, Eliot had attained at least a glimmer of control in his own life, through his visit to Vittoz. This control is not as obvious amid the neurotic spectacle of *The Waste Land* as it will become later in the orderly, rhythmic, melodious *Four Quartets* and in the subsequent plays or as obvious as it will become in later years in Eliot's personal life, when he converts to Anglo-Catholicism and takes English citizenship, leaving Vivien, and fashioning the personality for himself that he carried into his theatrical career.

But control, at least the potent germ thereof, is definitely extant for Eliot in 1922. The poem itself, though it lacks giving or sympathy, does manifest and embody a degree of tight control—indeed, a rather impressive degree (thanks considerably to Pound's augmentation of it) given the minimally comprehensible modern nightmare that it confronts. In terms of language, structure, imagery, poesis, the control that the poem possesses is proven by the extent to which we, its later readers and scholars, are able to educe paradigms of control and consequently exert our own control over it. The poem holds together; it exists as a unified record of a unified quest—the traversing of modern culture and Eliot's analogous confrontation of his darkest demons. The early twentieth-century sense of pervasive chaos and devastation, epitomized by the Great War, "motivated one of the great searches of the modern age," write John Rohrkemper and Karen L. Gutmann, "the search for control." In Eliot's triad, *Damyata* "is the final and most important element of the thunder's command. It is final in the sense that it must emanate from giving and sympathy; it is important in that it is proactive, allowing us to manifest the new-found power we assume when we can give and sympathize. It is not the control of brute power, of the will to dominate; rather it is a power that seeks harmony with the world, a control which Eliot beautifully represents with a seafaring image" (62).

The Waste Land betokens Eliot's emergence from his own personal quest. In the last words of his expansion on *Damyata* in *The Waste Land*—also the end of the entire section presenting the voice of the East—Eliot writes of a calm sea and a gay heart "beating obedient / To controlling hands" (69). (Remember Ackroyd's description of Vittoz's "laying on of hands.") Of giving, sympathy, and control—all attitudes that would certainly help a community rise above the torpid conditions Eliot described in his 1922 masterwork—it is only the last of these with which he has had personal experience, which he has "touched" as he reenacts Vittoz's touch at the end of the poem. This sense of control, so elusive in his earlier poetry, comes to be a stronger and stronger presence in each of his plays.

Genetic examination of the play shows that its drafts began with Lady Elizabeth's discussion of thought and mind control. Control is the point from which Eliot commences in *The Confidential Clerk,* and it offers one of the strongest thematic unifying forces between his poetic and dramatic sensibility. So often, erroneously, critics have split these two facets of Eliot's career apart from each other; here, we see compelling grounds for affirming continuity in the work of the post–World War I–era high modernist poet and the mid-century West End playwright. Whether unconsciously or consciously, *The Confidential Clerk* contains definite echoes of everything in Eliot's career that has come before and that has been necessary for him to arrive at the point he does in this play. It is a kind of analogue of the biological theory that ontogeny recapitulates phylogeny—that an organism, in gestation, reenacts the stages of its evolutionary development. Lucasta, in her first appearance on stage, strongly evokes Dusty and Doris, the women from Eliot's first dramatic experiment. She is sharp, quick, jazzy, and forced into an opportunistic and marginalized existence; she seems, at first, a bit of a tart. Trying to cadge a free meal from Kaghan and Colby, she tells the new clerk,

> I don't mind being seen with you in public.
> You may take me out to dinner. A working girl like me
> Is often very hungry—living on a pittance—
> Cooking a sausage on a gas ring . . . (24; ellipses in text)

Later, Lucasta describes herself in bleak, dehumanized, urban, polluted imagery as if she inhabited *The Waste Land:*

> I hardly feel that I'm even a person:
> Nothing but a bit of living matter
> Floating on the surface of the Regent's Canal. (63)

A few moments after this statement, Colby modifies the atmosphere by drawing upon the trope of Eliot's later spiritually tinged vision from *Four Quartets:* tranquil, measured, ethereally abstracted. Speaking of people who would join him in an idealized religious community, he tells Lucasta that they

> would just have to come. And I should not see them coming.
> I should not hear the opening of the gate.
> They would simply . . . be there suddenly,
> Unexpectedly. Walking down an alley
> I should become aware of someone walking with me. (65; ellipses in text)

The gate opens into a metaphorical garden, suggesting links to various images of gardens and gates from *Four Quartets;* the apparition of a companion suggests the "familiar compound ghost" from "Little Gidding." And just after this scene, when Colby explains to Lucasta his sense of how people can and must function communally, his terms and language replicate the Guardians' sensibility from *The Cocktail Party*—pragmatic acceptance of human nature, mixed with an inspirational impetus to make the best of our foibles:

> there's no end to understanding a person.
> All one can do is to understand them better,
> To keep up with them; so that as the other changes
> You can understand the change as soon as it happens,
> Though you couldn't have predicted it. (67)

This speech recalls the advice Reilly offers the Chamberlaynes as they prepare for their reconciliation.

In each of Eliot's plays, this study has identified prominent echoes of his preceding work. Sometimes these are reenactments and amplifications of a given trope, image, or sensibility, and sometimes refutations; but even when Eliot reacts against something he has written earlier, the effect is still to bolster the integrity and interconnectedness of his canon as a whole, as a unified attempt to address a point in some consistent way, with a determination not to rest until he has done so absolutely. One sees the insistent coherence of the vision embedded in Eliot's oeuvre in the way he chooses, presents, and arranges fragments from his past among each present work, showing readers and audiences how he has arrived at the point he has and how the lessons and mistakes of the past affect time present and time future. Like a real community itself, Eliot's sensibility regarding community does not appear ex nihilo on the stage of a West End theater. Rather, Eliot must build up each of these—the community and the aesthetic of community that he has undertaken to manifest. Each must accrete upon a foundation that becomes increasingly advanced yet retains, somewhere, the underlying and inherent patterns of its origins. As archaeologists discover the patterns of Roman roads, Saxon fields, and medieval marketplaces "underneath" England's urban centers, so this study has attempted to do with the literary fragments, the intellectual sensibilities, the aesthetic and style, of Eliot's canon at its chronological endpoint, his communities of drama.

The Elder Statesman: "The Words Mean What They Say"

Reviewing *The Elder Statesman,* Bonamy Dobrée writes that it

has been called, and is now advertised on the posters as being, "Mr. Eliot's most human play." This may be because of the delicacy with which he treats the young lovers, but one ventures to think that it is to be judged such because of its greater clarity. . . . the phrasing is absolutely sure throughout. There is never a word wasted. . . . The structure of the play too is beautifully balanced, dramatic structure being the way in which the emotions are induced in the spectator to produce a final result. There is no dominant crisis, either in the action or emotionally; there is a kind of inexorable movement from the beginning. . . . *The Elder Statesman* is Mr. Eliot's best play of the peculiar individual kind he has set himself to fashion, enduring [sic] a popular form with a deeper meaning. (114)

Despite the admittedly extravagant New Critical flattery from an acolyte of the master's, Dobrée nevertheless shows an appreciation of some important dramatic goals Eliot had been working toward determinedly. Dobrée indicates Eliot's achievement of clear dramatic discourse—valid words—and proficient technical and structural control; his ability to produce a "final result"—closure, resolution, dramatic completion—which, importantly, the audience perceives and experiences; and his avoidance of the traumatic crisis (which often proved to be an unfortunate and unfitting throwback to his poetry), in favor of a dramatic sensibility with a smoother flow, an even keel.

Many critics view the play condescendingly, as sentimental pap that Eliot wrote for his new wife in a public demonstration of romantic bliss that should have remained private. It is probably the easiest of Eliot's West End comedies to mock; Alan Brien does so enthusiastically, calling *The Elder Statesman* "a zombie play for the living dead. Occasionally across the pallid mortuary scene flits an ironic joke or a haunting phrase but the smell of formaldehyde hangs heavy in the air. It is a play in which Mr. Eliot mistakes snobbery for ethics, melodrama for tragedy, vulgarity for wit, obscurity for poetry and sermonising for philosophy" (305). But the play takes on a richer resonance in the context of Eliot's dramatic enterprise: his attempt to create, perpetuate, and voice communities of drama. Uniquely in his entire canon, *The Elder Statesman* is about love, pure and simple. Elsewhere in his plays, love is diminished and halting: ironic, desperate, clinical. Even in the later plays, as Eliot moves closer to intellectually accepting the centrality of love in his community vision, there remains a detached and stinted coldness to the depiction of love between Celia and Edward, Edward and Lavinia, Sir Claude and Lady Elizabeth, or B. Kaghan and Lucasta Angel. In *The Elder Statesman,* a rich, credible love comprises the *quidditas* of the work, whereas in the earlier plays love is more a dramatic construct. This prolific love, appropriately, brings Eliot's creation of dramatic community to its culmination.

A VOCABULARY FOR LOVE

In the middle of *The Elder Statesman,* Monica Claverton-Ferry is beset by her family's turmoil. Near death, her father, Lord Claverton, ruefully appraises his life's accomplishments; harassment from his old acquaintances exacerbates the anticlimactic culmination of waiting for death in a retirement home. Monica's brother, Michael, in his usual trouble involving hedonism and financial improprieties, aggravates the family's situation by fighting rancorously with Lord Claverton. Monica tries to mend relations, attempting to bring her family closer together through the power of love:

> Father! You know that I would give my life for you.
> Oh, how silly that phrase sounds! But there's no vocabulary
> For love within a family, love that's lived in
> But not looked at, love within the light of which
> All else is seen, the love within which
> All other love finds speech.
> This love is silent. (88)

As often before in his dramatic canon, Eliot here sounds the call for a discourse that can establish and unify a community: a language in which people can imagine, express, and strengthen their bonds to each other. "The prevailing linguistic tone of *The Elder Statesman* is . . . simply the tone of cultivated upper-class English so hateful to the ears of angry young men," writes Rudd Fleming, but "if one listens willingly, this tone has a quality of being suspended within a kind of unheard music which becomes audible at moments heightened by love" (59). What Fleming characterizes as a kind of "music" infusing the play's language—a music that drowns out the mannerly facade of cultivated upper-class English—signifies that these words are empowered, validated, somehow transcendent. They are so empowered because they are the medium of meaningful interchange in what by the end of the play Eliot will have shown to be a vital community endeavor.

Family represents a microcommunity as in Eliot's three previous plays, so Monica's call for "love within a family" hearkens toward a larger sense of community love, beneficence, symbiosis. "[T]here's no vocabulary," as Monica laments, amid a community that, in act 2, remains inchoate; but this play, like the others, is moving toward a place where the words are valid. There, love will possess a vocabulary—it will be verbalized and thus actualized. And although Monica bemoans the ineffability of such love and language of love, her own eloquent loving words show how close she is to voicing what will be the final step in Eliot's enterprise of establishing a community vision and voice. Even if the words are not quite in place by act 2, Fleming explains how the play revels in the imminence of such a language: "The play begins with commonplace banter between the young lovers . . . and then as the word 'love' appears in their conversation, the tone changes. . . . Eliot's effect is achieved not by the words themselves but by his dramatic *timing* of the words. . . . This suspension of ordinary language within a field of emotional music is accomplished by modulations of tone and rhythm and event" (59–60). In an apotheosis evocative of Dante's *Paradiso, The Elder Statesman* brings Eliot's oeuvre to a close with the simple, transcendent vision of love as a force effacing everything that preceded its attainment, whether Eliot's anguished earlier poetry or Dante's miserable voyage through Hell.

As in all Eliot's previous plays, and especially the immediate predecessor, this vocabulary of love must begin with an honest disavowal of dishonest poses and facades. In *The Cocktail Party* and *The Confidential Clerk,* such personal dishonesty, at its extreme, erupted into in psychiatric illness and affliction: strains of schizophrenia, breakdown, and suicide infuse *The Cocktail Party;* lack of mental control would have sundered Lady Elizabeth but for her Swiss treatment. Here, Lord Claverton is fairly obviously suffering from a severe case of depression because of his sense of exclusion from meaningful communal interaction and support. He has nothing remaining to look forward to, nothing that promises to be rewarding or fulfilling in the public world where he once had control of his destiny. (In his private world, it is becoming apparent, he now absolutely lacks this control.) He displays evidence of paranoia in his conviction that his life is certain to be miserable henceforward because of the vengeful actions of others. Claverton embodies antipathy to community affirmation, honesty, and love; as in the other plays, this attitude takes its toll on the solipsist in the form of psychological dissonance, manifested as emotional or mental disturbance.

The Monchenseys, the Chamberlaynes, the Mulhammers, and now the Claverton-Ferrys must be restored to mental health as individuals, a transformation which symbolizes the restoration to health of the communities they will inhabit. They must be purged of the undesirable and counterproductive social behavior which they harbor and which is inimical to community. In *The Elder Statesman,* Eliot works out the vocabulary of love as the characters render themselves fit (or, at least, *fitter*) for community by reforming their behavior: sundering the deceptions, false names, and false accounts from the past. It will be for the next generation, Charles and Monica, to consecrate and validate this language with their love—as Eliot wrote in "Little Gidding," "Next year's words await another voice" (204). In *The Elder Statesman,* "next year's words," valid words, are Eliot's new and improved language of community and love; "another voice" is the voice of the generation that survives Claverton (and Eliot).

A language does not appear in complete form ex nihilo; rather, it develops. In Monica's speech quoted at the beginning of this section, linguistic expression is developing toward her words of total serene understanding that end *The Elder Statesman:* she tells her fiancé at the close of the play that she is "[f]ixed in the certainty of love unchanging. I feel utterly secure / In you; I am a part of you" (132). Such language of community succor and certainty in this play is a development that has been building throughout Eliot's drama. His language has developed from one thing to another, a very different thing at the end from what it was at the beginning but with every developmental step along the way evident, from the stylized symbolist poesis of his youth, through the angst and despair of high modernism in *The Waste Land,* to the Christian faith of *Ash-Wednesday,* the return to solid traditional foundations in *Four Quartets,* and finally the social movement of drama. Throughout Eliot's plays, as he works toward a realm where the words are valid, "next year's words" are more often a theoretical ideal, an only tentatively broached tongue; Monica and Charles, though, promise to make this language a living language, by using it.

INDIVIDUAL DECEPTION

Those who will speak in the valid language must admit and confront their self-deceit (exactly as in *The Confidential Clerk*) and work to recover from it, not with a trendy Swiss therapist but in front of the audience's eyes, messily, on stage. The crucial but subtle focus of individual deception from the previous play is blatant in *The Elder Statesman.* It is exactly this self-deceit that Gomez punctures when he confronts Lord Claverton about the skeletons in his closet. His old school friend is a failure, Gomez charges, despite having hidden whatever mysteries lie in Claverton's past and despite his public pose as elder statesman.

> The worst kind of failure, in my opinion,
> Is the man who has to keep pretending to himself
> That he's a success—the man who in the morning
> Has to make up his face before he looks in the mirror. (43)

In *The Confidential Clerk,* the audience must educe the intricate aspects of this personality trait, self-deceit, that Eliot saw as antithetical to community. But in *The Elder Statesman,* because of such starkly diagnostic accusations as the one Gomez offers here, the condition is completely manifest. As often before, Eliot uses such lessons—solutions that he has identified in one play—as building blocks in his subsequent drama.

The condition of self-deceit is easier to identify in this play because it sticks out so notably. In *The Confidential Clerk,* every character except Eggerson was afflicted with self-deceit. In this play, though, Lord Claverton stands alone as a self-deceiver, and he is therefore all the more obvious about it. (Others, of course, are less than stellar characters, but they are forthright to others and to themselves about their behavior; they have already come to terms with who they are, and they offer no false poses.) This significant diminution in the number of self-deceivers—from almost everyone to one lone holdout—represents an advance in community sensibility from Eliot's previous play. The anticommunity threat is close to being eradicated here. It is, therefore, especially evident how incompatible Lord Claverton's demeanor is with harmonious community values, and it is obvious that his days of self-deceit are numbered. In fact, he reveals all, uncovering his own deceit, in the middle of the play: he confesses to Monica and Charles the lies from his past that Mrs. Carghill and Gomez represent, the falsity in his marriage, and his habit of attempting to disguise the realities of his life. At the play's end Lord Claverton himself explicitly confirms Gomez's earlier accusation of self-deceit. As Michael goes off with Gomez, spurning everything his father represents, Claverton says,

> I love him, even for rejecting me,
> For the *me* he rejected, I reject also.
> I've been freed from the self that pretends to be someone;
> And in becoming no one, I begin to live. (129)

This speech describes the challenge posed for all the characters in *The Confidential Clerk:* reversal and amelioration of the individual deceit that is antithetical to community. The insight could be expressed in classical dramatic terms as anagnorisis, leading to catharsis and the potential for restoration.

RECYCLED MOTIFS 1: THE EMPTY TERMINUS

For most of *The Elder Statesman,* Lord Claverton is wracked with self-deceit, as he had been his entire life. It should follow, then, according to Eliot's criteria, that he is thereby unfit to participate in community; and the play shows us, indeed, how that is true. In *The Elder Statesman,* as in Eliot's first dramatic work, *Sweeney Agonistes,* the protagonist's relation to the community experience is primarily one of negative example: the audience should realize that it would not want to live in a world as hostile to community as Sweeney or Claverton make it. Eliot ironizes both titular characters, by the context of their plays, as the nominal but flawed "leaders" of the communities encompassed by their dramas. Bookends to Eliot's dramatic oeuvre, these two men stand as the most distasteful, wrong-headed protagonists (although another negative exemplar from the middle of Eliot's dramatic career, Harry, Lord Monchensey, runs a close third). For both Sweeney and Claverton, death's KNOCK KNOCK KNOCK at the door signifies that their anticommunity determination is destined to leave them as spectral presences of failure when the curtain falls. Devoid of community sensibility, nothing of themselves can endure.

Early in *The Elder Statesman,* as Claverton appraises his life, he does so in terms that fascinatingly link the alpha and omega of Eliot's dramatic career, his first and last title characters. A connection between *The Elder Statesman* and the unpublished addendum to *Sweeney Agonistes* is Eliot's way of signifying, in 1958, that he has established a point already, about the worst-case community torpor of a hostile, jackknifing lout, and is now using it as an established referent. Of course, the vast majority of Eliot's audience could not be expected to make this connection, but the playwright, like the coy poet of a half century earlier, does not begrudge the occasional obscure reference. In his own mind he evokes a sensibility from the earlier work by recycling images associated with *Sweeney Agonistes,* even though the passage containing these images was never published in any version of the script. Claverton's stasis impels him to look bleakly, nihilistically, toward death in a sort of vacuum now that his public life—itself now seen as empty—is over.

> It's just like sitting in an empty waiting room
> In a railway station on a branch line,
> After the last train, after all the other passengers
> Have left, and the booking office is closed
> And the porters have gone. What am I waiting for
> In a cold and empty room before an empty grate?
> For no one. For nothing. (24)

The comparable passage in *Sweeney Agonistes* is a final fragmentary conclusion to that play, thus a fitting refrain for Eliot's final play about the end of life. For the 1933 performance debut, Eliot sent director Hallie Flanagan an additional twenty-five lines, which Carol H. Smith reprints: An old gentleman, formally dressed, comes from a vacant lot in front of a train station late in the evening. "Nobody knows why I am there. Nobody knows anything. I wait for the lost trains that bring in the last souls after midnight." (*Dramatic Theory,* 62–63). In response to Sweeney's interrogation, he speaks a few lines that seem perhaps profound or prophetic, though they are indecipherable; then he seems to expire, symbolically.

The old gentleman of the *Sweeney* fragment has become Lord Claverton; the ending to Eliot's first play, which he never saw fit to publish as part of that, has become written into the last play. At the beginning and end of his dramatic career Eliot confronts his audience with the image of empty waiting, the point-less search for meaning. In the passages from both plays, the railway station represents the networks of mechanical-technological-industrial bustle that per-vade society. Waiting at the station late at night, when the trains stop running, signifies the futility of modern community life: neither Claverton nor the old gentleman from *Sweeney Agonistes* envisions actually meeting a comrade at the station, or connecting with another person, amid the impersonally regimented train schedules. Trains come and go, run and stop running, with the precision of clockwork; people, however, cannot fulfill their functions in society with such assured regularity or success. Despite the thousands of souls who may pass through during the day, a station is itself not a locus of community but rather its opposite: it is a vacuum, embodying the complete absence of commu-nity, as is revealed at night when it stands in its large, hollow emptiness. Eliot thus conveys the anonymous and desperate role of a wanderer in the over-whelming (yet also vacant, lonely, isolating) modern world. Claverton's Sweeneyesque speech occurs at his first entrance into Eliot's last play. "In my beginning is my end" (182), Eliot wrote in "East Coker," and "In my end is my beginning" (190). In his drama, he implements this view precisely as the sensibility of Sweeney returns for an encore in *The Elder Statesman* to impress upon the audience the threats and dangers posed by anticommunity, existential skepticism, and unfocused self-pity.

RECYCLED MOTIFS 2: INTRUDERS

Other details in Eliot's final play recycle aspects of his earlier dramatic work, indicating the integrity of his theatrical career. In the first rough draft of *The Elder Statesman,* titled "The Rest Cure" (T. S. Eliot Collection, item D15), the scenario refers to Gomez as "First Intruder." This same character designation appears in "The Superior Landlord" (Eliot Collection, item V7), the scenario/draft that evolved into *Sweeney Agonistes.* There, just as Sweeney and his en-tourage have sat down to a dinner party, a knock on the door heralds the en-trance of the First Intruder, who is described as someone such as a Boy Scout or postman in search of contributions. (He is dispatched and is followed by a Second Intruder, Pereira.)

More than just an interesting or coincidental repetition, the recurrence of the "First Intruder" more than three decades later illustrates how Eliot thought of his dramatic settings, especially as he began to compose and formulate them in his drafts. The plays begin by positing a space and a set of conditions, which are then subject to these "intruders"—outside influences that threaten somehow to disturb the initial setting. It is these intruders who set the play's action in motion; without such intrusions, the plays would simply remain in an anticipa-tory stasis. An intruder, then, is the catalyst for those who have been intruded upon to define themselves as a community and react as such a unit to counteract the intruder. A biological analogy would be the intrusion of a virus into an organism, which then springs into action to create resistance, bolstering itself against the viral incursion and doing whatever is necessary to restore itself to a condition of healthy strength. Intruders pose a serious threat to a community, forcing it to rebuff them or integrate them or deal with them in some other way; but the result is a community that is strengthened because it has shown that it can indeed deal with intruders. Such a community thus becomes increasingly attractive to its members because it can now offer a demonstrable record of defense, resistance, against the threat of future intrusions.

This pattern and dynamic recur throughout Eliot's drama. Other incarnations of the Intruder include the Agitator with his unwelcome and inappropriate atheistic harangue of genteel churchgoers in *The Rock;* the Knights, who burst in to assassinate Becket in his cathedral in *Murder in the Cathedral* (especially, for symmetry's sake, the First Knight—the last to speak before the assault upon Becket, his words incite his fellow intruders to their deadly action); and Reilly butting uninvited into Edward's home and his personal upheaval in *The Cocktail Party.* In *The Confidential Clerk,* Lady Elizabeth is figuratively an intruder at her first entrance. Technically, of course, she cannot "intrude" into her own residence, but the sharp character who returns home unexpectedly on her own, having learned mind control in Switzerland, is, indeed, an intrusive presence into the carefully worked plot involving Colby, Eggerson, and Sir Claude; they react to her entrance in the same mode as characters do to the intruders in Eliot's other plays.

RECYCLED MOTIFS 3: MOTOR CARS

Another recurrent and recycled motif, important to various degrees in the different plays, is the automobile; especially, when it betokens discord, the danger of the automobile. In *Sweeney Agonistes,* Sweeney's fantasy of an idyllic crocodile isle excludes motor cars: "No two-seaters, no six-seaters, / No Citroën, no Rolls-Royce" (118). Apparently anticipating what happens with cars in the later plays, this ban is calculated to eliminate from Sweeney's tropical domain the catastrophes Eliot associates with driving. In *The Rock,* the Chorus laments the contemporary profusion of roads and cars: people live "dispersed on ribbon roads," and "all dash to and fro in motor cars, / Familiar with the roads and settled nowhere" (21). Eliot imbues roads and driving with an understated existential confusion, a mild sense of lurking danger; again, this antipathy anticipates the traffic wrecks that will infiltrate three subsequent plays.

One of these wrecks appears only in draft: In early notes for *The Confidential Clerk* (item D8 in the Eliot Collection), the clerk's father was supposed to have been killed in Brighton when he was run over by an omnibus. In *The Family Reunion,* both of Harry's brothers, Arthur and John, meet with auto accidents; the consequence is that they are unable to attend the family reunion and are thus unable to enter into the play or into the community. Sergeant Winchell tells Harry that John was driving "in the fog, coming along / At a pretty smart pace" and "ran into a lorry / Drawn up round the bend" (81)—as if John were dashing to and fro on one of the ribbon roads depicted in *The Rock*. John's accident causes the family to speculate about Arthur's whereabouts: they discuss his reckless driving, and Violet tells of how she remembers driving with him being "so undignified: you're blown about so . . . And the pace he went at was simply terrifying" (87); moments later, they read a story in the evening paper that confirms Arthur's fate. Headlined *"Peer's Brother in Motor Smash,"* the story tells of how Arthur "demolished a roundsman's cart," and "While trying to extricate his car from the collision, . . . reversed into a shop-window" (92).

Finally, in *The Elder Statesman,* an auto accident is at the root of Claverton's haunting ghosts from the past and, further, symbolically links the sins of the father with those of the son. Gomez's secret hold over Claverton derives from a late night when the two were motoring near Oxford and Claverton kept driving after running over an old man lying in the road. Though Claverton later learned that the man was already dead when he ran over him, his shame was that he refused to stop. Behind the wheel of the car, Claverton had become impervious to the common decency of community standards. As in *The Family Reunion,* this car crash is "doubled"—Michael, who has a record of driving accidents, walks up to Badgley Court in act 2 because his car is out of commission: he ran into a tree. Claverton responds, "I've lived in terror of his running over somebody" (74), which represents, he realizes, a reenactment of his own past shame.[1]

The cars that careen out of control throughout Eliot's plays are a metaphorical force of danger: they stand for unbridled and reckless speed, sloppiness, chaos, entropy. A car crash is an assault upon the community in which it occurs (and certainly, to connect it with another of Eliot's recycled motifs, a crash is also an intrusion). A crash keeps people from partaking in the community's rhythms and functions, as in *The Family Reunion;* it supplants these functions with its own dynamic of undignified terror, as Violet relates. A crash (and the driver's dishonorable subsequent behavior) brands people as morally unsuitable to participate in the community, as befalls Lord Claverton in *The Elder Statesman.*

In a good, cohesive community, people would obey traffic signs and drive carefully, so car crashes reflect a community's flaws. Beyond this analysis, I cannot precisely explain the profusion of car crashes in Eliot's plays; perhaps Eliot himself had once experienced some trauma associated with a motor accident. But these driving episodes clearly illustrate the cyclical-recyclical impetus of Eliot's drama. The point is that Eliot deals with the same issue over and over, just as a community must. One can never "solve" the problem of traffic accidents or the community danger it symbolizes. People simply have to drive carefully throughout their lives, if they (and other drivers and pedestrians—other members of the community) are to survive and prosper. Similarly, one has to keep one's community behavior in top form, continually, if the community is to endure; as the Boy Scouts remind us, one must do a good deed *every day*. The repetition of the motif of motor car crashes points to the repetitive nature of what is needed to keep a community functioning smoothly.

TOWARD A BETTER COMMUNITY

Despite the numerous echoes in *The Elder Statesman* (terminals, intruders, cars) of community failures from earlier plays, Claverton is not as socially intractable as Sweeney or Harry; he does not need to do a girl in or push one overboard. Although dramatic motifs and themes repeat in Eliot's dramatic canon, they do so with a difference and an advancement.

Claverton is saved from Sweeney's absolute vacuum of dehumanity because his daughter seems, somehow (the play does not explain how, which is a dramatic flaw), to have learned from his mistakes; after his death, her generation will facilitate a more harmonious community than Claverton and his peers have done. Monica has prospered by negative example—exactly as the audience must do—appreciating and rejecting Claverton's self-deceit. This enlightenment is an essential difference between Eliot's first and last plays: *Sweeney Agonistes* sucks its viewers up into its jazzy, dithyrambic frenzy of song, dance, and primordial rhythm, thus tempting an engaged and seduced audience to founder along with its drunken characters. *The Elder Statesman,* by contrast, includes within its cast a vicarious representative for the right-thinking, community-minded audience member. Throughout the play, and most important at the end, Monica leads the audience absolutely *away* from her father's personal and community failures. Her final words, "Now take me to my father" (132), might seem to contradict this view, except that they occur *after* her father has died. They in no way signify her movement toward him or any sense of her following in his footsteps; Michael, who *is* reenacting his father's career, seems destined to repeat his errors. Monica asks to be taken to her father after his death to make her peace with him, to forgive him, to empathize with his life in a way that cannot harm her; she is thus all the more clearly acting as her father never could have, and so, without hostility or pride, she is moving farther away from him.

Throughout the play, Lord Claverton is confronted with numerous chances to join in a community, but they are uniformly false communities that promise affliction rather than succor. The dubious terms upon which a community threatens to be established around Claverton—the passive syntax is intentional—reflect the profoundly dubious histories of all involved. When Gomez first approaches Claverton, he claims to be attempting to restore a community rapport with his old acquaintance. Asked why he has returned to England, Go-

mez replies, "To see you, Dick, a natural desire! / For you're the only old
friend I can trust" (33). As the scene unfolds, Gomez amplifies on what he
seeks and what he feels Claverton can offer him: he speaks of trust and companionship and of Claverton's obligation to accept responsibility for his impact
upon another person's life. He aspires to confront the reality of his past and
present and to affirm a bond that has always connected them.

> I've been trying to make clear that I only want your friendship!
> Just as it used to be in the old days . . .
> I'm a lonely man, Dick, with a craving for affection.
> All I want is as much of your company,
> So long as I stay here, as I can get.
> And the more I get, the longer I may stay. (47)

The terminology and sensibilities of community that Gomez presents are all
nominally correct and real. Although his background obviously ironizes it, Gomez invokes an ideal version of community. His overtures ring false, though,
because he is trying to force, fabricate, and contrive a community that has no
natural foundation. Both Gomez's and Claverton's past experiences, laden with
deception, forestall the foundation of community. As the Mulhammers learned
in *The Confidential Clerk,* communities cannot be manipulated; they have a
natural dynamic of their own, and they bring people together in ways that are
not necessarily comprehensible or logical on the surface. But one cannot contrive, as Sir Claude tried, to ensure that a certain person will be one's son or,
as Gomez attempts, to determine that a certain person will be one's friend,
one's community companion.

Mrs. Carghill reenacts Gomez's assault on Claverton, recalling an incident
from his past that she tries to parley into a present intimacy, or communion.
Charles suspects that Claverton's two old associates are blackmailing him; he is
partly right, partly wrong in his suspicion. Legalistic standards are not precisely
applicable to the issue at hand, which is the affirmation of a community (and
which must be freely willed). But his suggestion of extortion attunes the audience to the fact that Gomez and Mrs. Carghill are trying to connive at something underhandedly, which is, once again, antithetical to community.

It is in Badgley Court, the rest home to which the elder statesman has retired,
that Mrs. Carghill approaches her old beau and Gomez renews and presses the
claims he first raised in Lord Claverton's drawing room. Badgley Court is a
physical incarnation of the false community that Gomez and Mrs. Carghill connote. It appears, at first, that people are living together here, interacting, being
cared for amid the frailty of old age, at a time when they need assistance,
support, reassurance. It becomes apparent, though, that Badgley Court's resi-
dents are mainly concerned with avoiding one another, certainly not a community-minded sensibility. Monica tells her father, for instance, how to escape
other people's approaches:

> If you spy any guest who seems to be stalking you
> Put your newspaper over your face
> And pretend you're pretending to be asleep.
> If they think you *are* asleep they'll do something to wake you,
> But if they see you're shamming they'll have to take the hint. (60)

The skills of cunning and exponential dynamics of deceit—"pretend you're pretending"—signify the utter absence of any hope for establishing an effective community at the rest home. Its members have all paid handsomely for its services, but a real community cannot be created or sustained on a financial basis. Mrs. Piggott embodies the facades that pervade Badgley Court. Upon first meeting her, Monica says, "We don't know how we ought to address you. / Do we call you 'Matron'?" (56). As with several other characters, Mrs. Piggott's name and identity fluctuate—an obvious sign of deception that is not conducive to a community (in which people should know exactly who they are, who everyone else is, and what role they all play). In response to Monica's question, Mrs. Piggott blathers:

> Oh no, not "Matron"!
> Of course, I *am* a matron in a sense—
> No, I don't simply mean that I'm a married woman—
> A widow in fact. But I was a Trained Nurse,
> And of course I've always lived in what you might call
> A medical milieu. . . .
>   But you mustn't call me "Matron"
> At Badgley Court. You see, we've studied to avoid
> Anything like a nursing-home atmosphere.
> We don't want our guests to think of themselves as ill,
> Though we never have guests who are perfectly well. (56)

Is she a matron or isn't she? Married or not? Exactly what sort of medical care does the home provide? Why does a nursing home attempt to avoid seeming like what it is? Are the guests actually well or ill? Mrs. Piggott is a tour de force of equivocation, contradiction, uncertainty. Badgley Court is obsessed with the facade of smooth, mannerly propriety, and anything that challenges that image is repressed. This is not the way a community should operate. Mrs. Piggott's sham for-profit community, like Mrs. Carghill's and Gomez's false personal attempts to create a community with Claverton, merely shows by contradiction what sort of a community would be valuable and desirable. Such a community, though, does not exist here.

By the play's end, Lord Claverton realizes that his public life has been an empty charade, meaningless to him now amid the depressing reality of the community he has earned for himself; Badgley Court is exactly what he deserves. He has confessed to his children his lapses of judgment and painfully exposed his defects of character, debunking his public facade of statesmanship and his private image of fatherly leadership and deserved respect. And yet even having been brought to this point—forced to abase himself and acknowledge Gomez's and Mrs. Carghill's humiliating power over him—comfort and content still elude him: the confession is not cathartic. Although he finally admits his lapses, he seems nevertheless fated to endure the ghosts represented by the two intruders from his past (and one suspects there must be others as well).

Claverton does realize there should have been more of a community in his life. He knows he should have treated his son, daughter, wife, friends, and colleagues with higher respect, with the compassion and consideration that people deserve of one another when they participate in a community. *The Elder Statesman* is an act of contrition, for both Claverton and Eliot; and it is especially striking in that there is no pot of gold at the end, just an intellectual moment of resigned acceptance. In his closing appearance he states, "This may surprise you: I feel at peace now" (127). It *is* surprising, because dramatically it is unlikely, if not wholly gratuitous for the tormented and shamed protagonist. The moment reenacts another moment of unexpected peace in Eliot's canon: "Shantih shantih shantih" (69)—a similarly abrupt termination to an extensive display of internal suffering, a closure that the audience has to find indeterminate: sincere, or contrived?

Claverton's sense of peace comes moments before his death. His achievement carries no other concrete rewards, certainly no attainment of community succor for himself, at least not in this life. (As in all Eliot's plays, there is a trace element of Christian redemption underlying the secular drama, although it is dramatically faint, little more than a habitual nod on Eliot's part.) Several critics have remarked that this play lacks Eliot's habitual transcendence of the quotidian world, his usual deus ex machina redemption of mortal suffering and emotional anguish. Anthony S. Abbott characterizes this change in orientation as a setting of sights on average daily life, a "movement away from an elitist view. . . . a world without saints. There are no Beckets, Harrys or Celias, not even any Colbys or Eggersons. There is only everyman, Dick Ferry" (111). Gerald Weales writes that the play "has no saint or martyr, no Celia or Harry, no special case to throw ordinary life into the shadow. More likely, Eliot is now willing to say that there is a possible human relationship which, in itself, gives meaning to life. . . . there is, for the first time, the suggestion that there is another genuine possibility, another kind of salvation, this side of the saints and martyrs" (477). Joyce M. Holland concurs, noting the striking absence of the "more sympathetic divine hero" in the play, which "turns away from the elect entirely to concentrate on the problems of the human community" (158).

ELIOT ON ELIOT

Claverton's brief moment of peace is the reward for his extensive mea culpa, which is essentially what the play offers; and Claverton fairly explicitly tenders Eliot's own apologies as well. Lyndall Gordon calls *The Elder Statesman* "a clearly autobiographical play about a great public figure who has become hollow at heart, and is 'saved,' at the very end of his life, by the steadfast love of his daughter" (*New Life,* 241). The play's daughter, she suggests, is an emblem of Eliot's second wife: "Composed as Eliot fell in love with Valerie Fletcher"—the thirty-year-old, young enough to be his daughter, married Eliot, sixty-eight, in 1957—the play "looks toward their union" (246).

"Eliot had said [in *The Three Voices of Poetry*] that a character might speak 'in unison' with the author," Gordon writes, "even call out his latent potentialities, and through Claverton, he returned to the most intractable material in his life" (246). In *The Elder Statesman,* as in all his plays to some degree, Eliot's determination to work out a community ethos is concommitant with his intention to locate himself, and to confront what Gordon calls this "most intractable material," with respect to his burgeoning community values. Confessionally and cathartically, Eliot examines his social and private history and inscribes it in the play. In his earlier poetry he was chary of self-exposition, self-revelation, but autobiography flows freely in his drama and increasingly with each successive play. He seems to feel that the medium of drama dignifies and justifies the writer's total personal commitment, rewarding this commitment, as it does, with the communities of drama he has been producing.

The title, obviously, has a strong autobiographical resonance: Eliot was precisely the elder statesman in the world of poetry, publishing, and letters, from his perch at Faber & Faber. In the 1950s he was looking back on his life— appraising what he had done, what it had been worth, wary of the heaps of public platitudes that promised to conclude his career. (Sometimes overwhelmed by the public life that surrounded him, Eliot escaped for rests to the London Clinic, as Claverton had retired to Badgley Court, Gordon writes.)

Eliot explicitly presents *The Elder Statesman* as his final literary work, modeled as it is on Sophocles' final play, *Oedipus at Colonus,* with Monica as a modern Antigone supporting her aged father as he prepares for his departure. Eliot's identification with Sophocles reflects "his uncannily precise talent for finding and firmly occupying his own most tenable position within the literary cosmos," writes Rudd Fleming. "Eliot focused upon Sophocles' last and most self-reflective play . . . in which the aged and blind Oedipus undergoes at Athens his mysterious apotheosis. . . . Even in antiquity this play was felt to be a mystical self-projection of the poet himself as he stood, an extremely old man, upon the very outposts of human wisdom" (61).

At the end of the play, Charles sees Lord Claverton as we see Eliot at the close of his public career: "as if he had passed through some door unseen by us / And had turned and was looking back at us / With a glance of farewell" (130). Eliot offers a final farewell and withdraws through some unseen door— symbolically exiting the stage, leaving the theater in a way that forestalls his audience from following. But before this exit, he displays a profoundly probing and ruthless self-examination. In front of an audience, in his public dramatic community for the last time, he works through his autobiographical quandaries in search of insights that will ultimately strip away his self-deceit and repressions, making him worthy to enter into a community himself on honest terms and fit to interact with others.

First of all, Eliot uses Claverton to puncture absolutely the fragile facade of propriety that he had so carefully nurtured for decades, during the time when the reality very close beneath the facade was one of personal emotional failure, coldness, isolation, and brooding refusal to make a sincere commitment to any community. Claverton states,

> Perhaps I've never really enjoyed living
> As much as most people. At least, as they seem to do.
> Without knowing that they enjoy it. Whereas I've often known
> That I didn't enjoy it. Some dissatisfaction
> With myself, I suspect, very deep within myself
> Has impelled me all my life to find justification
> Not so much to the world—first of all to myself.
> What is this self inside us, this silent observer,
> Severe and speechless critic, who can terrorise us
> And urge us on to futile activity,
> And in the end, judge us still more severely
> For the errors into which his own reproaches drove us? (54)

The introverted, constrained, reserved, usually dour persona of Eliot's younger days clearly justifies an autobiographical reading of this speech. Gordon concurs that this darkly self-reproachful strain of Claverton's finds a strong parallel in Eliot's personality: "Like Eliot himself," she writes, "Lord Claverton is a man of 'morbid conscience' " (245; her quote is from act 3, where Claverton tells his daughter, "I know what you think. / You think that I suffer from a morbid conscience, / From brooding over faults I might well have forgotten" [110].) The insecurity Claverton conveys—the dissatisfaction with himself that has, dysfunctionally, driven him—evokes Eliot's youthful fears. His family disapproved of his path, and his father, who died before his son had become a success, contributed especially to his feelings of inadequacy and a craving for approval that was unrequited despite the world's acclaim. The sense of Eliot as his own harshest critic, disdainful of the world's ignorant judgments, befits the tenor of his writing, especially his lofty, self-centered criticism.

The "self inside us, this silent observer," is the younger Eliot. In Lausanne in 1921, Dr. Roger Vittoz's task was to bring Eliot out of himself—to bring a new, healthier Eliot out of the depraved younger one. Here, an older Eliot offers the final response to the younger Eliot and his anticommunity poetic. This younger self is severe and speechless, evoking the severity of the modern wasteland, and the pervasive ineffability that indicated that Eliot's earlier poetry had not yet come to where the words are valid.

The terror is of stark modernity, interior breakdown, vacancy: in *The Waste Land* it is alternately as striking as London's fetid and rat-infested landscape and as subdued as the wind under the door. The futile activity that one is urged on to symbolizes Eliot's early verse: the poetic of solipsism, of arcane noncommunication, that does not foster community. Eliot here rejects that poetic as pointless. The severe judgment of errors at the end is exactly what is happening, for Eliot, as Claverton intones this passage. Eliot's earlier work had been haunted by legions of ghosts—literal ones in *The Family Reunion* and figurative phantoms of history, literature, and culture throughout his poetry of the 1910s and 1920s. *The Elder Statesman* confirms that our ghosts *do,* in fact, come back to haunt us, and our worst fears do in fact come true; but still, through self-acceptance, self-awareness, painful contrition, we can transcend the realm in which the ghosts wreak their harm. We cannot fight this wasteland on its own terms; we must ascend to a higher plane, rising above its angry and isolated poses of solipsism, which is what Eliot's drama embodies for him. The closure that Eliot ultimately imposes on the fraught sufferings of earlier youth is concurrent with the closure he imposes on his entire canon.

Besides excoriating his individual self-deceptions in *The Elder Statesman,* Eliot atones for his treatment of others, specific people who had been close to him. Mrs. Carghill confronts Lord Claverton with the wrecks of his past emotional life:

> A man may prefer to forget all the women
> He has loved. But a woman doesn't want to forget
> A single one of her admirers. Why, even a faithless lover
> Is still, in her memory, a kind of testimonial.
> Men live by forgetting—women live on memories.
> Besides a woman has nothing to be ashamed of:
> A man is always trying to forget
> His own shabby behaviour. (66)

Certainly this speech is Eliot's apology for his shabby behavior toward Emily Hale and Mary Trevelyan; perhaps, even, also toward his first wife, Vivien: all women who had "nothing to be ashamed of" yet suffered at his hands as he found himself incapable of reciprocating reasonable emotional bonds. Condemning himself as the faithless lover, acknowledging his own shortcomings, Eliot further indicts himself by confessing to the passion he knows these women retained for him, a passion he nevertheless dismissed in dropping each of them. Eliot brands his own behavior as casually, heartlessly, self-serving: "A man may prefer to forget."

But along with inscribing his own past failures, the times when he betrayed, or otherwise conveniently dispatched, those who loved him, Eliot also inscribes his surmounting of this fault, his personal peripeteia. He does it manifestly in the poem to his wife that serves as the play's dedicatory epigraph. This poem is certainly the most unabashedly sentimental, personal testament he had ever written; he included a revision of it in the final edition of *Collected Poems* published during his lifetime (as if, perhaps, to counterbalance all his earlier poetry of solipsistic, anticommunity despair). He also writes his new, late love into the script. In happy relief that his daughter has successfully found love with Charles, Claverton tells Monica,

> If a man has one person, just one in his life,
> To whom he is willing to confess everything—
> And that includes, mind you, not only things criminal,
> Not only turpitude, meanness, and cowardice,
> But also situations which are simply ridiculous,
> When he has played the fool (as who has not?)—
> Then he loves that person, and his love will save him. (102)

Love has saved Eliot. The sentiments of love, trust, interdependence, that Claverton expresses to his daughter are simple, obvious, irrefutable, comprehensible. An ominous mystery had enveloped Eliot's idea of love at the end of his poetic career: in "Little Gidding," "Love is the unfamiliar Name" (207). Now, Eliot's play of love is perfectly clear: in the love poem to his wife that stands at the opening of this love play, Eliot announces the achievement of his dramatic enterprise in a fittingly simple victory cry: "The words mean what they say" (7). He had theoretically envisioned such a condition in his earliest dramatic works. He knew of the centrality of language in any enterprise involving a union of people: they would have to communicate—as Sweeney puts it, "I gotta use words when I talk to you" (123). And in his next dramatic work, Eliot showed at least a theoretical, ideal appreciation of what was possible with language, what this language would have to do: in *The Rock,* he writes, "Out of the slimy mud of words, out of the sleet and hail of verbal imprecisions, / Approximate thoughts and feelings, words that have taken the place of thoughts and feelings, / There spring the perfect order of speech, and the beauty of incantation" (75). Eliot believed in the 1930s that this perfect order, this beauty, could exist. His mission in the theater is to approach it, to actualize it, to grasp it. He signifies his achievement of this task at the end of his public life in the proclamation of elemental linguistic, poetic, dramatic, and community simplicity: "The words mean what they say." Dedicating this play to his wife, the person who offered him the rewards and support of human interaction more than anyone else in his life, Eliot has arrived along with his drama at where the words are valid.

Notes

INTRODUCTION

1. "Fragment of a Prologue," actually, had appeared in the October 1926 issue of *Criterion*; the play's publication was completed with the next installment, "Fragment of an Agon," in the subsequent issue of January 1927.

2. Linda Wyman has also recognized a potent resonance in this phrase, which she used titularly in her dissertation and again in an article, " 'Where the Words Are Valid': The Language of Eliot's Drama." *Yeats Eliot Review* 11, no. 2 (fall 1991): 44–45.

CHAPTER 1

1. This ending has never been published in any editions of Eliot's writing, but it is reprinted in Hallie Flanagan's *Dynamo* (New York: Duell, Sloan, & Pearce, 1943), 82–84; and in Carol H. Smith's *T. S. Eliot's Dramatic Theory and Practice,* 62–63. It begins with the entrance of an old man resembling Father Christmas, carrying an alarm clock and an empty champagne bottle. He speaks of time and of waiting nihilistically at the depot—by a heroic statue of the Paraguayan General Cierra, the presence of which is a mystery—for lost trains carrying the last souls. Sweeney banters briefly with him, posing questions that are partly evocative of Zen philosophy and partly rambling nonsense. The old gentleman answers in similar vein, evoking the omnipotence of the forces of time and possible biblical archetypes of quest, fruition, and the cycles of life. He departs as the alarm clock goes off.

2. In its engagements at the Group Theatre Rooms, the play was an avant-garde spectacle of nervous stychomythic patter, shadowy jabs of action and emotion, and a dithyrambic continuum of sensory (especially jazzy musical) dance, sparring, and collapse. Michael Sidnell describes the effect: "Eliot's fragments were utterly contemporary

in feeling and their very fragmentariness—which [director Rupert] Doone emphasized by a series of blackouts—gave the effect of a preconceived Expressionist montage" (103). As fringe theater, the play was intimate and personally interactive: at the beginning, "the playing space is set as a seedy bedsitter with no definite boundary between it and the audience. The furniture is rudimentary" (104). At the end of "Fragment of a Prologue," "there are drinks all round, a clinking of glasses, a little sexual groping and dancing to the gramaphone. The first fragment ends with Wauchope and Dusty collapsing, in drunken laughter, on the floor. Blackout. In the dark the gramophone plays on and somebody groans" (105). Sidnell quotes Desmond MacCarthy's review in the *Listener,* discussing the scene where Sweeney tells Doris about a man who has killed a woman: "If you want to suggest in terms of actuality retribution for some sordid crime, could it be done better than this? Sweeney is speaking. You must imagine a man under a lamp sitting at a table . . . speaking the lines . . . with unemphatic horror, speaking out of himself, but he is also addressing us: it is half a sinister soliloquy, half a confession—or perhaps a threat to her" (106). For further information about production aspects of *Sweeney Agonistes,* see Sidnell's *Dances of Death: The Group Theatre of London in the Thirties,* and my own chapter on the play in *T. S. Eliot's Drama: A Research and Production Sourcebook.*

3. William V. Spanos writes in "God and the Detective: The Christian Tradition and the Drama of the Absurd," that "Sweeney's audience, like the manager in *Six Characters in Search of an Author* who hates Pirandello's 'authorless' drama, want quite clearly to make a well made play out of the dreadful experience Sweeney has confronted them with" (19).

4. John Dankworth showed a stellar appreciation of the play's jazziness in the score he wrote and conducted for Peter Wood's production of *Sweeney Agonistes* in 1965. That performance, part of a memorial program for Eliot, has been preserved in the recording by His Master's Voice called *The Memorial Record of Homage to T. S. Eliot at the Globe Theatre,* Record CLP 1924.

5. My chapter on Eliot in *The Language of Modernism* discusses at greater length the cohering attributes and principles of his language.

6. A *New York Times* article from 16 July 1922, "Flapping Not Repented Of" (reprinted in Mowry, *The Twenties,* 173–75), gives a sense of the term's contemporary connotations: "A flapper is proud of her nerve—she is not even afraid of calling it by its right name. She is shameless, selfish and honest, but at the same time she considers these three attributes virtues. Why not? She takes a man's point of view as her mother never could. . . . She can take a man—the man of the hour—at face value, with no foolish promises that will need a disturbing and disagreeable breaking" (174).

In England in the 1920s, the word gained currency in the term "flapper vote," which referred to the women who remained disenfranchised by the Reform Bill of 1918 (granting "household suffrage," that is, giving the franchise to men over twenty-one and women over thirty). The vote for women was known as the "matron's vote," and it was not until the 1928 Representation of the People Equal Franchise Bill that women were allowed to vote on the same terms as men. During the 1920s, the issue of whether women in their twenties were qualified to vote—presumably, a questionable proposition because of their dubious demeanor, or personality, or sexuality—was known as the question of the flapper vote. "The 'flapper vote' came to symbolise instability," writes Billie Melman. "It was regarded as a reflection of the disaster of the war and a catalyst to imminent catastrophes" (2).

7. *The Great Gatsby* gives a sharp sense of the popular images of danger associated with the jazz age. Eliot read that novel three times; Grover Smith writes that its style and atmosphere influenced *Sweeney Agonistes* (114).

8. In the King's College draft, the eighteen knocks at the end of the play appear typed in two different ways: The first nine are typed in upper- and lower-case letters ("Knock"), while the last nine are more prominently typed all in upper-case, as in the published texts.

9. Another indication of the parallel between Sweeney and Orestes appears in producer Rupert Doone's note to the program of the 1935 Westminster Theatre production of *Sweeney Agonistes:* "I see Sweeney himself as a modern Orestes (the only three-dimensional character in the play)."

10. No discussion of the variety of levels in Eliot's plays can match the treatment of this subject in Carol H. Smith's enduring 1963 work, *T. S. Eliot's Dramatic Theory and Practice.* "The dramatic theme of all his plays," she writes, "has been the plight of the individual who perceives the order of God but who, forced to exist in the natural world, must somehow come to terms with both realms. In order to express this theme, Eliot developed a multi-level drama intended to lead the audience from the ordinary perception of reality to an awareness of a reality transcendent to but immanent in the natural world" (viii–ix). Smith's study examines Eliot's creation and presentation of these parallel dramatic levels throughout his plays.

11. I do not believe that the closing passage Eliot added for the Vassar production substantially adds a sense of closure to the play or obviates the need to go beyond its ending. David Galef, though, does trace some transcendent elements in the Vassar ending that I see in my own extrapolated interpretation. This ending, which Galef sees as explicitly Christian, "shifts the thematic structure toward spiritual rebirth" (497). The entrance of an old gentleman "brings a slowing of the pace. The jazz rhythm is gone and the religious tenor is finally out in the open" (505). Further, he writes, the name "Cierra," Spanish for "he/she/it closes or shuts down," thus "represents something greater than Pereira. In the context, *cierra* is the spiritual end of things, the end of the body's reign as the soul departs" (506).

12. E. Martin Browne writes that Eliot's proficiency in writing the dialect of Cockney workmen in his next play, *The Rock,* shows his quick ear and sure dramatic sense for capturing the tenor of a social milieu alien to him; and that this talent had manifested itself similarly, though in a different milieu, in *Sweeney Agonistes.* Of Eliot's effort on *The Rock*—committing himself, as in his first play, to attaining accurately the language of a community—Browne writes, "This was the job to be done: and by doing it, even the drudgery of it, he was learning something about the theatre from the inside. He wanted to write for the stage; well then, he would do what the stage asked of him, and do it as well as he could" (16).

CHAPTER 2

1. Parts of the work, though, have been excised and performed, such as Martin Shaw's 1934 choral arrangement of *The Builders: Song from 'The Rock'* (London: J. B. Cramer) and his 1966 score for tenor solo, double choir, and organ from part of Chorus X called *The Greater Light Anthem* (London: J. Curwen).

2. David Perkins, for example, in his generally excellent and authoritative two-vol-

ume overview, *A History of Modern Poetry,* completely ignores *The Rock* in his chapter "Eliot's Later Career," where he discusses Eliot's other poetry of the 1930s. Perkins dismisses Eliot's poetic drama offhandedly in one sentence: "In general, they wasted his creative energy, and as he moved [from play to play], each was less interesting than its predecessors" (vol. 2, p. 24). Ronald Bush cites Eliot's "groping use of the chorus" in *The Rock* as merely a stepping stone in his explorations of "the possibilities of a twentieth-century meditative lyric" (189).

3. Toby A. Olshin insists that *The Rock* is fully a part of Eliot's canon despite its unusual conditions of authorship. "Eliot allowed the work to be published with his name alone on the title page, albeit as part of a curious phrase: 'Book of Words by T. S. Eliot.' . . . what this expression means is that while the actual words were his own, the form which they covered was not. The fact to be remembered, however, is that Eliot created 'the words' and those words appeared in publication under his name" (311). The text "cannot be ignored as a part of Eliot's writing, all impressionistic evaluations notwithstanding. . . . in a collaboration of this nature [chiefly with Browne], the final work does not deserve dismissal because it is based on an idea originating with someone other than the author. Rather, it should be closely examined because an author's acceptance of a given form may be as revealing as his own writing. . . . In considering Shakespeare's use of Holinshed or the classical dramatists' use of religious myth, we normally study the elements in the given plot which appealed to them or focus our attention on their treatment of that plot. Let us use this same system for Eliot and realize that the nature of the given scenario touched something within him with sufficient strength to lift him from what might be called 'poetic depression' "(312).

4. Browne writes that this scene "proves how acute his dramatic sense already was. It makes use of the methods of the German Expressionists of the twenties, reminding one of some of the earlier plays of W. H. Auden and Christopher Isherwood who were influenced by them" (10).

5. *Collected Poems* contains nearly all of the passages from *The Rock* that are explicitly choral (in a section called "Choruses from 'The Rock,' " 145–71, divided into ten passages), though a few choruses are not included, such as the ones on pp. 78–79 and 80–81 of *The Rock.* Some of the pageant's other verse passages are reprinted as well— the Workmen's Chant and some of The Rock's speeches are, but not The Rock's striking speech that ends part 1, or the Builders' Songs. The alternating verse passages by Redshirts, Blackshirts, Plutocrats, and Chorus are not included in *Collected Poems,* nor is any of the "lowbrow" verse such as music-hall types of ballads. All the prose passages are excluded in *Collected Poems,* so the Cockneys are completely absent there. Editions of *The Rock* are fairly rare, so most people are familiar with the work only through what is included in *Collected Poems,* but those excerpts distort its true nature. There are some good passages from *The Rock* that are not included, although, by and large, *Collected Poems* does present most of the best poetry from the pageant. Nevertheless, the excerpts in *Collected Poems* fail to convey the sense that the pageant covers a wide social spectrum—from masses, workers, and commoners, to priests, prophets, and intellectual luminaries—giving a sense mainly of the "higher" end of this spectrum.

6. For contrast, consider Virginia Woolf's reaction to Eliot's dazzling, elaborate syntactical construction in his earlier poetry. In her 1924 essay "Character in Fiction," she describes the process of reading it: "As I sun myself upon the intense and ravishing beauty of one of his lines, and reflect that I must make a dizzy and dangerous leap to the next, and so on from line to line, like an acrobat flying precariously from bar to bar,

I cry out, I confess, for the old decorums, and envy the indolence of my ancestors who, instead of spinning madly through mid-air, dreamt quietly in the shade with a book" (3: 435).

7. The sensibility evokes such characters as H. G. Wells's single-minded capitalist moguls—for example, George Ponderevo in *Tono-Bungay*—who are somehow, despite themselves, palatably engaging.

8. Of the term, Bergonzi writes, "The supplement to the *Oxford English Dictionary* cites the first occurrence of 'Audenesque' in a quotation from *Scrutiny* in 1940. This is far too late: the word occurs much earlier, in the title of Gavin Ewart's 'Audenesque for an Initiation' published in *New Verse* in December 1933" (40).

9. Further extending his discussion of community in this tract, Eliot identifies a more elite segment of society, "the Church within the Church," which he terms the "Community of Christians," who "will be the consciously and thoughtfully practising Christians, especially those of intellectual and spiritual superiority" (28). Despite the similarity of this term to "the Christian Community," the "Community of Christians" is a more intricate concept—more advanced, in Eliot's mind—and does not infiltrate his drama until *The Cocktail Party,* where the Guardians are meant to be representative of this group.

CHAPTER 3

1. R. P. Blackmur's judgment on this is typical: "Contrary to custom in English drama, it is the objective, the witnessing, the only indirectly participating, passages in these plays [i.e., the Choruses] that are the finest poetry and that do the most work" (211).

2. Carol H. Smith's seminal study of Eliot's plays, *T. S. Eliot's Dramatic Theory and Practice,* for example, covers the two plays in a single chapter (unlike every other play, which is covered in its own separate chapter), which begins, "When T. S. Eliot returned to dramatic writing in 1934, it was as a writer of occasional drama, for both *The Rock* (1934) and *Murder in the Cathedral* (1935) were 'made-to-order' works intended for church occasions" (76). In E. Martin Browne's study of genesis and development, *The Making of T. S. Eliot's Plays,* the chapter on *Murder in the Cathedral* begins by explicitly detailing how it grew out of the previous play: "Among the audience attending *The Rock* during the second week was George Bell. He had come to see what had evolved from the contacts made at that weekend in 1930 [where Bell, then Bishop of Chichester and a proponent of religious drama, brought Eliot and Browne together in an attempt to recruit the poet to his cause], and to judge for himself whether he had been right in urging Eliot, when they met then and subsequently, to write for the stage. Clearly the performance convinced him that he had been a good prophet; and soon afterwards he approached Eliot about writing a play for the Canterbury Festival of the following year, 1935" (34). And in his essay from *The Double Agent* entitled "T. S. Eliot: From *Ash Wednesday* to *Murder in the Cathedral*," R. P. Blackmur links Eliot's second and third plays on the grounds that "the Christian discipline is dominant and elemental" in them (187).

3. Contrast Eliot's depiction of medieval community with the community of partygoers in *Sweeney Agonistes:* sharp and dazzling but with a sense of enduring coherent meaning so negligible as to approach irrelevance. Eliot must have meant to convey this retrospective sense of his first play's ephemerality, in terms of social meaning, when he

spoke to an Irish radio reporter in 1936 on the occasion of a visit to Dublin for a University College production of *Murder in the Cathedral.* "He revealed that . . . *Sweeney Agonistes* was written in two nights between ten o'clock and five in the morning," writes A. Walton Litz, " 'with the aid of youthful enthusiasm and a bottle of gin' " (875).

4. In earlier drafts of the play, Harry's period of exile from his family was actually seven years—perhaps indicating a typological parallel to Becket's exile, but more likely, I believe, for personal reasons of Eliot's, which will be discussed in the next chapter.

5. Again, as in *Murder in the Cathedral* and at least in drafts of *The Family Reunion* (see note 4 above), Eliot uses the seemingly significantly repeated number of seven years in *The Cocktail Party*—five past and two present—to connote the experimental or tentative time that preceeds the all-important time future. The sources for typological resonances in this number may be Jacob's seven years of labor for Rachel's hand, repeated because of Laban's deceitful substitution of Leah, or the seven years of plenty that anticipate seven years of famine in Joseph's dream prophecy (perhaps, both of these). In both cases (as in the repeated seven-year periods in Eliot's plays), the chunk of time embodies a period that must be carefully and dutifully endured in the present to ensure a community's prosperity in time future: the generation of a chosen people by the patriarchs and matriarchs, in the case of Jacob's labor, and the empowerment of the Hebrews (amid the Egyptians, bolstered by Egypt's agricultural resources and their debt to their Hebrew advisers), in the case of Joseph's prophecy. Both seven-year cycles (of Jacob's labor and of Joseph's dream) are doubled to ensure that the subjects understand their significance and appreciate the symmetry of undergoing trials in time present to reap a corollary reward subsequently. Such emphasis via repeating may be intended in the recurring seven-year cycles of community regeneration that Eliot's plays present.

6. A legion of scholars have examined the function of Becket's martyrdom as the foundation of a Christian community. A few examples: Rasma Virsis discusses the Chorus's struggle "to witness, to accept, and to consent to the suffering and insecurity the martyrdom of Thomas will bring. . . . the chorus . . . is at the center of the tragedy in the second part" (405–6). Kurt Tetzeli von Rosador writes about what he calls "the exemplariness of *Murder in the Cathedral*": "To be fully and correctly understood, Becket's decision, taken out of time, and *Murder in the Cathedral* itself, need an audience of saints. . . . the dramatization of the Christian theory of history is not complete with Becket's true martyrdom. Nor is the imitation of an action restricted to part 1, even if Becket's conflict ends there. Another conflict, another development, takes the place of Becket's in part 2, that of the 'type of common man,' of Priests, Chorus, and audience" (525–26). Scott Samuelson argues that Becket's martyrdom is intended "to transform reciprocal physical violence into a sort of verbal awakening—or reawakening—of interpretive activity" (73). He concludes that "Becket's words help us achieve salvation insofar as we heed their invitation to reintegrate" (80).

7. E. Martin Browne writes that Eliot definitely intended the tabloid titillation inherent in the play's title: "He had always wanted the ritual aspect of the play to be balanced by the homicidal; he was a devotee of Sherlock Holmes; and this title, with its sardonic implications, had a contemporary quality which would induce in an audience an attitude favourable to the acceptance of the ironies . . . as a natural part of the play" (56–57).

8. Numerous critics have remarked upon Eliot's significant biographical identification with Becket and a sense in which Eliot inscribes himself in the personality of Becket. Peter Ackroyd, for instance, writes that the play "is concerned with a figure, not

unconnected with the author himself, who has some special awareness of which others are deprived, and yet whose great strengths are allied with serious weaknesses" (237). Lyndall Gordon writes that "In Becket [Eliot] found a model who was not so different from himself. Here was a man to all appearances not born for sainthood, a man of the world . . . who moved from worldly success into spiritual danger" (*New Life,* 28). Alethea Hayter offers a direct link between the missions of the two Thomases and an ultimate resolution through poetry: "Poets have to surrender their wills to the truth of what they feel, as martyrs surrender theirs to the Will of God. Poets, too, have their temptations, assaults on their single-mindedness. It is possible to see the temptations offered to Becket . . . as, among other things, the temptations offered to a poet's integrity in writing his poetry" (95).

9. I remember pointedly my reaction to the opening line of *The Waste Land* when I first read it, and I still find that reaction instructive in elucidating the response Eliot means to evoke in his troubling early poetic: I found the sentiment patently ridiculous. A month, impersonally abstracted, cannot be cruel; months do not conspire to afflict us, and if this poem is based upon the premise that they *do,* then we are in for a difficult trip ahead, under the guidance of a paranoid soul in the throes of a conspiracy theory about the outside world. Eliot, I thought, has a big, and possibly implacable, chip on his shoulder.

10. Sandwiched between the highly worked, modernistically stylized language at the end of part 1 and the beginning of part 2 is Thomas's interlude, his Christmas sermon. The Christian language of the interlude is the traditional realm of "valid words." To paraphrase Eliot in "Little Gidding," we are here to listen (though only briefly) where language has been valid. The interlude is a microcosm of the play as a whole: just as the interlude represents the Archbishop's exegesis, in the terms of his own time, of an earlier authoritative text, the Bible, so *Murder in the Cathedral* represents an exegesis, in the terms of the modernist era, of the historical "text" of Becket's martyrdom.

11. The *Oxford English Dictionary* entry for "Humankind" explains that it is "properly two words, *human kind;* now commonly written as one, after *mankind.*" Usage examples present the substantive as two words for the 1645 and 1709 sources but then as a single word in sources from 1728 and 1860.

CHAPTER 4

1. Eliot seems to have retracted some of the play's chauvinism during its composition. The Cambridge draft D5 has Gerald following his statement, "I am used to tangible danger" (which remains in the final text, 67), by stating that he is not, however, used to silly women who panic. This gratuitous hostility toward his sisters, and toward women in general, was cut from the subsequent draft, D4; perhaps Eliot found such misogynistic bravado too obvious. His original text connotes the panic of silly women as some sort of intangible danger outside the realm of rationality that is bravely traversed by sensible men: this connotation echoes his sensibility from the 1909 poem "Conversation Galante," which portrays woman as "[t]he eternal enemy of the absolute" (25).

2. In *Poetry and Drama* (1951), Eliot enumerated the considerable shortcomings he found in the play. Among his self-criticisms: he was too concerned with versification at the expense of plot; the use of actors to portray both individual characters and members of the Chorus was unsuccessful; certain passages, meant to be trance-like incantations,

inappropriately suspend the play's action; the audience's attention wanders during part 2, and the conclusion is too abrupt; the play's Greek origin and latter-day situation were not smoothly melded; and the Furies seem to be unperformable. The play's focus is not clearly defined, Eliot concludes, and so the audience finally does not know if the play is about Amy's tragedy or Harry's salvation.

3. See the section headed "Time and the Archbishop" in chapter 3 which examines how Eliot grapples with the meaning of time in his drama and the necessity of its being properly understood if a community is to endure. The section headed "The Dialect of the Tribe" in that chapter explains how Eliot's consciousness of seasons manifests itself in *Murder in the Cathedral;* there, as in Amy's speech at the opening of *The Family Reunion,* the Chorus announces its macrocosmic instability by its fear of seasonality, its inability to inscribe itself successfully in sync with nature.

4. It is difficult to diagnose with precise etiology the fatal flaw of an unsuccessful drama. But I suggest that it is, to a considerable extent, the dramatic unworkability of Harry's character that leads to such critical appraisals as Carol H. Smith's: "*The Family Reunion* was not a theatrical success, and the public and the critics alike were disturbed by the fact that the play did not fit existing classifications" (*Dramatic Theory,* 112). She elaborates by quoting Raymond Williams, who writes in *Drama from Ibsen to Eliot* that he "saw the transitions from the superficial to the profound as 'dislocations' and commented that 'this kind of failure is what might be expected of Eliot's attempt to come to apparent terms with the methods of the naturalist theatre' " (112). Smith's sense of misfitting and Williams's of dislocation, I believe, derive from an inherently and insurmountably unfeasible characterization of the protagonist. Eliot may have been thinking of this problem (and perhaps, in addition, the problems he cited in *Poetry and Drama,* summarized in note 2 above), when he stated in a 1959 *Paris Review* interview that the play was not well constructed.

5. Sena concurs with my sense of Eliot's seemingly reckless perseverance in this work. Though he is discussing a different aspect of the play (the specific technical issue of awkward choral declamation), he concludes: "The Chorus of *The Family Reunion,* in its unwarranted attempts at multiple 'jumps'—to say nothing of its resistance to all attempts at thematic integration—becomes an image of the whole play, reflecting its author's determination to go ahead with a chosen scheme regardless of incompatibility or the recalcitrance of the material on which it is imposed" (921).

6. Other details from Eliot's Cambridge typescripts show him inscribing himself in the play: for example, from the earlier draft of the play (D5) to the later draft (D4) he effaces lingering Americanisms from the text, as he had long been doing in his own life. Amy instructs the family to act as if Harry's absence had been only a long vacation in D5; the phrase is revised to English usage—a long holiday—in D4. (Neither phrase appears in the final text: Amy tells her family to "behave only / As if nothing had happened in the last eight years" [21].) And again, in Downing's speech explaining his feeling that a married couple should not see too much of each other, "Quite the contrary of the usual opinion" (40), Eliot makes a point of stressing the middle syllable (with a penciled stress mark over the "a" in D5, that becomes a typed apostrophe superimposed over the letter in D4), indicating a pronunciation stress—English rather than American pronunciation—that Eliot apparently wanted the actor to note; perhaps, too, he meant to remind himself as well that he was English now and had to guard against revealing any telltale details of his American past.

7. Agatha explains that Harry will return to Wishwood to meet the boy who left; that boy will be lurking

> down the corridor
> That led to the nursery, round the corner
> Of the new wing, he will have to face him—
> And it will not be a very *jolly* corner. (18; Eliot's emphasis)

This allusion was even more obvious in drafts: A draft (D5) shows Eliot striking lines he had written in which Agatha adds an apology to Charles for alluding to a writer with whom he was unfamiliar; I presume that Eliot's original intent was to make sure that the audience realized a literary allusion was being made but that he later decided that the allusion was clear enough on its own without Agatha's clumsy heavy-handedness. Agatha refers again to "the world around the corner" (21) to which we must attend despite the overwhelming demands of the world at hand. Gerald has been "in tight corners" most of his life (27); and Downing describes seeing Harry on board the ocean liner, just before his wife's drowning, on "the corner of the upper deck" (40). The whole family, it seems, haunts a world of not-very-jolly corners.

8. A letter Eliot wrote to John Hayward (31 March 1938, in item D4 of the T. S. Eliot Collection) shows that Eliot, in discussions with producer Ashley Dukes during the play's composition, saw a dramatic connection between Harry's brothers and uncles, and their absence or presence. Dukes, Eliot writes, first wanted Eliot to remove Gerald and Charles from the play, substituting Arthur and John, and later wanted Harry's two uncles to remain but the brothers removed from the play altogether. (Dukes felt characters should not be mentioned if they are never seen.) In a letter to Browne, Eliot stated that Harry's brothers are meant to be seen as weaker images of his uncles (reprinted in *The Making of T. S. Eliot's Plays,* 106).

9. The partial anaesthesia, the detached suffering, and the feeling of automatism evoke the urban trance atmospheres of "Prufrock" and "Preludes," as well as the typist who smooths her hair with automatic hand in *The Waste Land.* Harry's characterization of himself as an old house evokes "Gerontion." His depiction of waking to a nightmare evokes the Sweeney nightmares. The stained, tainted flesh, the discolored bone, and the landscape of noxious smells connote the fetid nature of *The Waste Land.* Harry's discussion of the infusion of the past into the present, and of an unredeemable degradation, is cast in the language of "Burnt Norton."

CHAPTER 5

1. I am especially reluctant to slog through the criticism since I have already done so once; those determined to advance where I now prefer not to are referred to my companion volume to this work: *T. S. Eliot's Drama: A Research and Production Sourcebook* 111–36 and 229–40.

2. Schizophrenia should not be confused (as it often is in popular imagery) with multiple-personality disorder; that condition is characterized by a person's manifesting various personalities that are wholly developed, clearly delineated, and enduring, alternating from one to another. Within each personality, a victim of multiple-personality disorder perceives ego boundaries and grasps external reality; this is not the situation that Eliot means to convey with his dramatic schizophrenia. Aspects of the psychiatric

dysfunctionality Eliot depicts do indeed evoke multiple-personality disorder; this probably reflects the fact that symptoms and effects of many types of personality and mood disorders anticipate, or overlap with, more profound schizophrenic illnesses.

3. In a further (though tentative) resonance, this aunt may be a device Eliot uses to deconstruct whatever lingering remnants of familial connection endure from *The Family Reunion,* with its copiously absent family members. Additionally, there is another slight connection between the two plays: like *The Family Reunion, The Cocktail Party* begins with the furor caused by an absent wife; but Eliot is more charitable here and has a more beneficent sense of community vision, so he does eventually allow Lavinia to appear.

4. On a more literal and mundane level, E. Martin Browne notes another criterion for grouping the final four plays together: Eliot's choice of a title for *The Cocktail Party* "set the mould for subsequent titles; *The Family Reunion* had begun what *The Cocktail Party* now carried on, a pattern of three words beginning with the definite article" (*Making,* 174). One might also include in this series *The Waste Land,* which, as I have suggested throughout this study, has myriad subtle but provocative links to Eliot's drama.

5. Barbara Ehrenreich and Deirdre English's examination of the predominantly cultural and political (as opposed to medical) constructs of such illness in *Complaints and Disorders: The Sexual Politics of Sickness* sheds light on Eliot's tropes of illness in his late plays.

6. Simonds raises the qualification, though, that while self-help literature *claims* to rectify individual inadequacies, in many ways it may only palliate them or, at best, may challenge them more tepidly than it pretends.

7. In an appendix, Simonds lists by title and year 112 self-help books that appeared on the best-seller list of the *New York Times* from 1963 to 1991—beginning with Betty Friedan's *The Feminine Mystique* but clustered mainly from the mid- and late-1970s through the 1980s. Many of these books appeared on the list for a year or longer.

8. In *T. S. Eliot's Drama: A Research and Production Sourcebook* (167–87), I list and synopsize sixty-one critical essays Eliot wrote and interviews with him, from 1919 to 1961, that detail his theoretical and practical opinions on this and numerous other dramatic concerns.

CHAPTER 6

1. *The Elder Statesman* begins with a similar implicit affirmation of community. Charles explains to Monica the importance of eating at a restaurant where he is well known, where the waiters seem to be his friends and serve him well rather than treating him as stranger. Though some might regard a restaurant's most obvious attraction as good food, Charles indicates that the community atmosphere is more important to him, just as, for Lucasta, a specific program has nothing to do with the appeal of going to the opera.

2. Anthony Hartley identifies the play's main theme as follows: "The farce of misunderstanding and recognition is used with great skill to symbolise what is the real subject of the play: self-knowledge. . . . Colby Simpkins's search for a father and the resulting farcical revelations symbolise this coming to terms with one's permanent self" (364–65). Self-knowledge, or anagnorisis, implies recognition of one's *true* identity. To get

to what Hartley sees as the center of *The Confidential Clerk,* I believe, one must first distinguish between true and false identity and must therefore be able to identify the presence of individual deceit (which is antithetical to true self-knowledge). Illuminating the fact of self-deceit and grappling with it are what I consider to be the core of Eliot's play and a prerequisite for what Hartley calls "this coming to terms with one's permanent self," which, I would agree with Hartley, is the eventual desirable result. Having modeled four of his plays on Greek dramas, Eliot would certainly affirm the Hellenic belief that all knowledge begins with self-knowledge.

3. My article "Frankenstein's Monster: The Gothic Voice in *The Waste Land*" examines how this line from the poem functions as its most pointedly autobiographical exposition. Eliot, describing the nadir of his mental collapse, inscribes himself in the character of Mary Shelley's monster and uses allusions to the monster's condition and to a Gothic landscape as a metaphorical model for his own breakdown and recovery.

4. Davis D. McElroy calls *The Confidential Clerk* Eliot's most mature confrontation of existentialism, a "treatment of the interesting problem of establishing the identity of the self"; Colby is "preoccupied throughout the work with the question Who am I? and What kind of a person am I supposed to be?" (44–45). The confidential clerk is made to confront this theme, McElroy writes, "when he feels that he is being accused by the ghost of his true self, the disappointed musician," and "is forced to realize that he is not living an authentic existence—in other words that he is really, and not merely conventionally, illegitimate" (46). By the end of the play, "Colby recognizes his inauthentic existence as Sir Claude's natural son" (47).

CHAPTER 7

1. In the scenario accompanying the first draft, Michael's automobile accident involves another person rather than a tree and thus parallels his father's accident even more closely; the son had injured a man in a speeding accident and would have to ask his father for money to settle out of court.

Bibliography

PRIMARY MATERIAL

The following editions of each play are most easily accessible in the United States; page numbers throughout this book refer to these editions.

Sweeney Agonistes. In *Collected Poems: 1909–1962.* New York: Harcourt Brace, 1970, 111–24.
The Rock. New York: Harcourt, 1934.
Murder in the Cathedral. 1935. New York: Harcourt, 1963.
The Family Reunion. New York: Harcourt, 1939.
The Cocktail Party. 1950. New York: Harcourt, 1978.
The Confidential Clerk. New York: Harcourt, 1954.
The Elder Statesman. New York: Farrar, 1959.

Unless otherwise identified, all discussions of Eliot's dramatic manuscripts, typescripts, drafts, and acting editions refer to the archival holdings of the T. S. Eliot Collection bequeathed to King's College, Cambridge University, by John Davy Hayward. Holdings consulted (as catalogued in the library's handlist of literary manuscripts) include items D1, D3, D4, D5, D6, D8, D9, D10, D11, D12, D14, D15, and V7.

SECONDARY MATERIAL

Abbott, Anthony S. *The Vital Lie: Reality and Illusion in Modern Drama.* Tuscaloosa: Univ. of Alabama Press, 1989.
Ackroyd, Peter. *T. S. Eliot: A Life.* New York: Simon & Schuster, 1984.
Aeschylus. *Oresteia.* Trans. Richmond Lattimore. Chicago: Univ. of Chicago Press, 1953.

Aiken, Conrad. "After 'Ash-Wednesday.' " *Poetry* 45 (December 1934): 161–65.

Ames, Christopher. *The Life of the Party: Festive Vision in Modern Fiction.* Athens: Univ. of Georgia Press, 1991.

Arundell, Dennis. *The Story of Sadler's Wells: 1683–1964.* London: Hamish Hamilton, 1965.

Auden, W. H. *Selected Poems: New Edition.* Ed. Edward Mendelson. New York: Vintage, 1979.

Barrett, William. "Dry Land, Dry Martini." *Partisan Review* 17 (April 1950): 354–59.

Bedient, Calvin. *He Do the Police in Different Voices: The Waste Land and Its Protagonist.* Chicago: Univ. of Chicago Press, 1986.

Beehler, Michael T. "Troping the Topic: Dis-closing the Circle of *The Family Reunion.*" *Boundary 2* 8, no. 3 (1980): 19–42.

Bergonzi, Bernard. *Reading the Thirties: Texts and Contexts.* Pittsburgh: Univ. of Pittsburgh Press, 1978.

————. *T. S. Eliot.* New York: Macmillan, 1972.

Billman, Carol. "History Versus Mystery: The Test of Time in *Murder in the Cathedral.*" *Clio* 10, no. 1 (fall 1980): 47–56.

Blackmur, R. P. *The Double Agent: Essays in Craft and Elucidation.* Gloucester, MA: Peter Smith, 1962.

Blamires, Harry. *Twentieth-Century English Literature.* New York: Schocken Books, 1982.

Brien, Alan. Review of *The Elder Statesman. Spectator,* 5 September 1958, 305–6.

Browne, E. Martin. *The Making of T. S. Eliot's Plays.* Cambridge: Cambridge Univ. Press, 1969.

————. "T. S. Eliot as Dramatist." *Drama* 76 (spring 1965): 41–43.

Bush, Ronald. *T. S. Eliot: A Study in Character and Style.* New York: Oxford Univ. Press, 1983.

Carpenter, Humphrey. *A Serious Character: The Life of Ezra Pound.* New York: Delta, 1988.

Cheshire, D. F. *Music Hall in Britain.* Rutherford, NJ: Fairleigh Dickinson Univ. Press, 1974.

Coghill, Nevill, ed. *The Family Reunion.* London: Faber & Faber, 1969.

Colby, Robert A. "Orpheus in the Counting House: *The Confidential Clerk.*" *PMLA* 72, no. 4 (September 1957): 791–802.

Cunningham, Valentine. *British Writers of the Thirties.* Oxford: Oxford Univ. Press, 1988.

Davies, R. T. "Mr. T. S. Eliot's *The Confidential Clerk.*" *Theology* 56, no. 400 (October 1953): 411–14.

Day Lewis, C. *Collected Poems of C. Day Lewis.* London: Jonathan Cape, 1954.

Dobrée, Bonamy. "The London Stage [review of *The Elder Statesman*]." *Sewanee Review* 67, no. 1 (winter 1959): 109–15.

Ehrenreich, Barbara, and Deirdre English. *Complaints and Disorders: The Sexual Politics of Sickness.* Old Westbury, NY: Feminist Press, 1973.

Eliot, T. S. "The Art of Poetry, I: T. S. Eliot." Interview by Donald Hall. *Paris Review* 21 (spring/summer 1959): 47–70.

————. *Collected Poems: 1909–1962.* New York: Harcourt, 1970.

————. "Five Points on Dramatic Writing." *Townsman* 1, no. 3 (July 1938): 10.

————. *The Idea of a Christian Society.* In *Christianity and Culture.* New York: Harcourt, 1968.

————. "In Memoriam." In *Selected Essays.* New York: Harcourt, 1964, 286–95.

————. *The Letters of T. S. Eliot: Volume I, 1898–1922.* Ed. Valerie Eliot. New York: Harcourt, 1988.

————. "Marie Lloyd." In *Selected Essays.* New York: Harcourt, 1964, 405–8.

————. *Old Possum's Book of Practical Cats.* New York: Harvest, 1967.

————. *Poetry and Drama.* In *On Poetry and Poets.* New York: Noonday, 1957, 75–95.

————. *Religious Drama: Mediaeval and Modern.* New York: House of Books, 1954.

————. *The Sacred Wood.* London: Methuen, 1928.

————. *The Three Voices of Poetry.* In *On Poetry and Poets.* New York: Noonday, 1957, 96–112.

————. "Tradition and the Individual Talent." In *Selected Essays.* New York: Harcourt, 1964, 3–11.

————. *The Use of Poetry and the Use of Criticism.* London: Faber & Faber, 1933.

Ellis, Steve. *The English Eliot: Design, Language, and Landscape in Four Quartets.* London: Routledge, 1991.

Evans, Gareth Lloyd. *The Language of Modern Drama.* London: J. M. Dent, 1977.

Everett, Barbara. "The New Style of *Sweeney Agonistes.*" *Yearbook of English Studies* 14 (1984): 243–63.

Fish, Stanley. *Is There a Text in This Class?* Cambridge: Harvard Univ. Press, 1980.

————. *Surprised by Sin.* Berkeley: Univ. of California Press, 1967.

Fleming, Rudd. "*The Elder Statesman* and Eliot's 'Programme for the Métier of Poetry.' " *Wisconsin Studies in Contemporary Literature* 2, no. 1 (winter 1961): 54–64.

Freedman, Morris. "Jazz Rhythms and T. S. Eliot." *South Atlantic Quarterly* 51, no. 3 (July 1952): 419–35.

Fussell, Paul. *Abroad: British Literary Traveling Between the Wars.* Oxford: Oxford Univ. Press, 1980.

Galef, David. "Fragments of a Journey: The Drama in T. S. Eliot's *Sweeney Agonistes.*" *English Studies* 69, no. 6 (December 1988): 481–96.

Gardner, Helen. Review of *The Confidential Clerk. New Statesman,* 20 March 1954, 373–74.

Geraldine, M. "The Rhetoric of Repetition in *Murder in the Cathedral.*" *Renascence* 19, no. 3 (spring 1967): 132–41.

Gilbert, Sandra, and Susan Gubar. *No Man's Land: The Place of the Woman Writer in the Twentieth Century.* Vol. 1, *The War of the Words.* New Haven: Yale Univ. Press, 1988.

Gordon, Lyndall. *Eliot's Early Years.* Oxford: Oxford Univ. Press, 1977.

————. *Eliot's New Life.* Oxford: Oxford Univ. Press, 1988.

Harben, Niloufer. *Twentieth-Century English History Plays.* London: Macmillan, 1988.

Hartley, Anthony. "The Drama and Mr. Eliot." *Spectator,* 26 March 1954, 364–65.

Hastings, Michael. *Tom and Viv.* London: Penguin Books, 1985.

Hawkins, William. "Comedy, Pathos Mix in *Confidential Clerk.*" *New York World-Telegram and Sun,* 12 February 1954.

Hayter, Alethea. "Thomas à Becket and the Dramatists." *Essays by Divers Hands* n.s. 34 (1966): 90–105.

Holland, Joyce M. "Human Relations in Eliot's Drama." *Renascence* 22 (1970): 151–61.

Isaacs, J. *An Assessment of Twentieth-Century Literature.* London: Secker and Warburg, 1951.

James, Henry. "The Beast in the Jungle." In *The Novels and Tales of Henry James,* vol. 17. New York: Charles Scribner, 1909, 59–127.

Jayne, Sears. "Mr. Eliot's Agon." *Philological Quarterly* 34 (October 1955): 395–414.

Jones, David E. *The Plays of T. S. Eliot.* Toronto: Univ. of Toronto Press, 1960.

Kearns, Cleo McNelly. *T. S. Eliot and Indic Traditions: A Study in Poetry and Belief.* Cambridge: Cambridge Univ. Press, 1987.

Kennedy, Andrew J. *Six Dramatists in Search of a Language.* Cambridge: Cambridge Univ. Press, 1975.

Kenner, Hugh. *A Sinking Island: The Modern English Writers.* Baltimore: Johns Hopkins Univ. Press, 1987.

Litz, A. Walton. Introduction to "Tradition and the Practice of Poetry" (by T. S. Eliot). *The Southern Review* 21, no. 4 (October 1985): 873–75.

MacCarthy, Desmond. "Some Notes on Mr. Eliot's New Play." *New Statesman,* 25 March 1939, 455–56.

McClain, John. "Rewarding Drama." *New York Journal American,* 12 February 1954.

McElroy, Davis D. *Existentialism and Modern Literature.* New York: Philosophical Library, 1963.

Malamud, Randy. "Frankenstein's Monster: The Gothic Voice in *The Waste Land.*" *English Language Notes* 26, no. 1 (September 1988): 41–45.

———. *The Language of Modernism.* Ann Arbor: UMI Research Press, 1989.

———. *T. S. Eliot's Drama: A Research and Production Sourcebook.* Westport, CT: Greenwood Press, 1992.

Mander, Raymond, and Joe Mitchenson. *British Music Hall.* London: Gentry Books, 1974.

Melman, Billie. *Women and the Popular Imagination in the Twenties.* London: Macmillan, 1988.

Mitchell, John D. "Applied Psychoanalysis in the Drama." *American Imago* 14, no. 3 (fall 1957): 263–80.

Mowry, George E., ed. *The Twenties: Fords, Flappers & Fanatics.* Englewood Cliffs, NJ: Prentice-Hall, 1963.

Olshin, Toby A. "A Consideration of *The Rock.*" *University of Toronto Quarterly* 39, no. 4 (July 1970): 310–23.

Palmer, Richard E. "Existentialism in T. S. Eliot's *The Family Reunion.*" *Modern Drama* 5, no. 2 (September 1962): 174–86.

Perkins, David. *A History of Modern Poetry: Modernism and After.* Cambridge: Harvard Univ. Press, 1987.

Review of *The Rock. Blackfriars* 15, no. 172 (July 1934): 499–500.

Review of *The Rock. Everyman,* 17 August 1934, 189.

Review of *The Rock. Tablet,* 4 August 1934, 138.

Roby, Kinley E. "Introduction," to *Critical Essays on T. S. Eliot: The Sweeney Motif.* Boston: G. K. Hall, 1985, 1–29.

Rohrkemper, John, and Karen L. Gutmann. "The Search for Control: Eliot, Hemingway, and *In Our Time.*" *Midamerica* 15 (1988): 59–71.

Rosador, Kurt Tetzeli von. "Christian Historical Drama: The Exemplariness of *Murder in the Cathedral.*" *Modern Drama* 29, no. 4 (December 1986): 516–31.

Samuelson, Scott. "The Word as Sword: Power and Paradox in *Murder in the Cathedral.*" *Literature and Belief* 7 (1987): 73–81.

Sass, Louis A. *Madness and Modernism: Insanity in the Light of Modern Art, Literature, and Thought.* New York: Basic Books, 1992.

Sayers, Michael. "Mr. T. S. Eliot's *The Rock.*" *New English Weekly,* 21 June 1934, 230–31.

Schneider, Elisabeth. *T. S. Eliot: The Pattern in the Carpet.* Berkeley: Univ. of California Press, 1975.

Sena, Vinod. "Eliot's *The Family Reunion:* A Study in Disintegration." *Southern Review* 3 (autumn 1967): 895–921.

Sewell, J. E. "Satire in Church Pageant-Play." *London Daily Telegraph,* 29 May 1933, 4.

Sidnell, Michael J. *Dances of Death: The Group Theatre of London in the Thirties.* London: Faber & Faber, 1984.

Simonds, Wendy. *Women and Self-Help Culture: Reading Between the Lines.* New Brunswick, NJ: Rutgers Univ. Press, 1992.

Smith, Carol H. "Sweeney and the Jazz Age." In *Critical Essays on T. S. Eliot: The Sweeney Motif.* Ed. Kinley E. Roby. Boston: G. K. Hall, 1985, 87–99.

———. *T. S. Eliot's Dramatic Theory and Practice.* Princeton: Princeton Univ. Press, 1963.

Smith, Grover. *T. S. Eliot's Poetry and Plays: A Study in Sources and Meaning.* Chicago: Univ. of Chicago Press, 1960.

Spanos, William V. "God and the Detective: The Christian Tradition and the Drama of the Absurd." *Newsletter of the Conference on Christianity and Literature* 20, no. 1 (1971): 16–22.

———. " 'Wanna Go Home, Baby?': *Sweeney Agonistes* as Drama of the Absurd." *PMLA* 85, no. 1 (October 1970): 8–20.

Staunton, Stephen, ed. *Camille and Other Plays.* New York: Hill & Wang, 1960.

Styan, J. L. *The Elements of Drama.* Cambridge: Cambridge Univ. Press, 1960.

Taylor, John Russell. *The Rise and Fall of the Well-Made Play.* London: Methuen, 1967.

Thurber, James. "What Cocktail Party?" *New Yorker,* 1 April 1950, 26–29.

Trosman, Harry. "T. S. Eliot and *The Waste Land:* Psychopathological Antecedents and Transformations." *Archives of General Psychiatry* 30, no. 5 (May 1974): 709–17.

Virsis, Rasma. "The Christian Concept in *Murder in the Cathedral.*" *Modern Drama* 14, no. 4 (February 1972): 405–7.

Ward, David. *T. S. Eliot Between Two Worlds.* London: Routledge & Kegan Paul, 1973.

Watts, Richard, Jr. "T. S. Eliot's *Confidential Clerk.*" *New York Post,* 12 February 1954.

Weales, Gerald. "The Latest Eliot." *Kenyon Review* 21, no. 3 (summer 1959): 473–78.

Williams, Raymond. *The Long Revolution.* New York: Columbia Univ. Press, 1961.

Woolf, Virginia. "Character in Fiction." In *The Essays of Virginia Woolf,* vol. 3. New York: Harcourt, 1988.

Wyman, Linda. "*Murder in the Cathedral:* The Plot of Diction." *Modern Drama* 19, no. 2 (June 1976): 133–45.

Index

About the Author

RANDY MALAMUD is Assistant Professor of English at Georgia State University, where he teaches Modern Literature. He is the author of *The Language of Modernism* (1989), *T. S. Eliot's Drama: A Research and Production Sourcebook* (Greenwood, 1992), and articles on Virginia Woolf, James Joyce, and other modern figures. He is currently working on an interdisciplinary study of modernism in literature and the other arts, as well as a cultural studies project about literary images of zoos.

ISBN 0-313-27818-0

HARDCOVER BAR CODE